LEARNING TO LEAD IN HIGHER EDUCATION

Higher education is going through a revolution. There are more students, much less public money, and steadily greater pressures from employers and students for universities to be more account-able. At the same time, lecturers face job insecurity and confront bigger workloads, while universities are forced to become more efficient and business-like.

The future success of our universities depends on academics' capacity to respond energetically to change. To help academics face new and uncertain demands, we need an entirely different approach to their management and leadership. This book shows academic leaders how to increase research productivity and enhance teaching quality. It also demonstrates how leaders can help their staff through momentous change without compromising professional standards.

Drawing on ideas from the world of business leadership as well as research into what makes academics committed and productive, *Learning to Lead in Higher Education* provides heads of departments and course leaders with practical tools they can use to improve their management and leadership skills. It shows academic and university leaders at all levels how they can turn adversity into prosperity.

Paul Ramsden is Director of the Griffith Institute for Higher Education and Professor of Higher Education at Griffith Univer-sity, Brisbane, Australia.

LEARNING TO LEAD IN HIGHER EDUCATION

Paul Ramsden

London and New York

First published 1998
by Routledge
11 New Fetter Lane, London EC4P 4EE

Simultaneously published in the USA and Canada
by Routledge
29 West 35th Street, New York, NY 10001

© 1998 Paul Ramsden

Typeset in Garamond by
J&L Composition Ltd, Filey, North Yorkshire
Printed and bound in Great Britain by
Creative Print and Design (Wales), Ebbw Vale

British Library Cataloguing in Publication Data
A catalogue record for this book is available
from the British Library

Library of Congress Cataloging in Publication Data
Ramsden, Paul.
Learning to lead in higher education/Paul Ramsden.
p.   cm.
Includes bibliographical references (p.).
1. Education, Higher–Administration.   2. Educational leadership.
I. Title.
LB2341.R32   1998   97–24258
378.1'01–DC21   CIP

ISBN 0–415–15199–6 (hbk)
ISBN 0–415–15200–3 (pbk)

TO MY FATHER

CONTENTS

CONTENTS

FIGURES AND TABLES

Figures

Tables

PREFACE

Possibly the best known book about leadership is *The Prince*, published in the early sixteenth century. Anthony Jay has pointed out how significant it is that Machiavelli did not call his book something like *The Art of Government*. The idea behind *The Prince* is embodied in its title. Leadership matters. The qualities of the leader are the keys to a state's success.

Machiavelli was nothing if not pragmatic. Instead of trying to establish what was right and wrong about power and leadership, as so many others have done before and since, he looked at what worked. He examined practical problems facing leaders and offered advice based on the analysis of empirical data. He believed that leaders could learn how to lead if they studied the experiences of others before them.

In these respects, if in few others, the present book is similar to his. This book is addressed to anyone who exercises academic leadership in a university, although its special audience is the 'middle management' level of department head. It assumes that academic outcomes matter more than management competencies; it is focused on processes and skills only as a way of getting practical results. The general argument I have tried to make is that academic leadership, particularly at the level of the head of department, can improve academic outcomes and staff commitment in an exceptionally rigorous, highly competitive, and rapidly altering climate for higher education. Simply put, research activity and productivity, and the quality of teaching and learning, are influenced for better or worse by the way in which a department is managed and led. Moreover, the capacity of staff to respond positively to new and uncertain demands depends on the effectiveness of academic leadership. Energetic leadership can transform both an ailing state and a weak department into a vital force.

This book will probably displease three groups of people. For some conservative academics, it will seem like a manifesto for managerialism, a call for even greater inroads to be made into collegiality and academic freedom, and an apology for applying irrelevant business practices to the necessarily different world of higher learning. For some contemporary university leaders, it will seem altogether too easy on academics in its stress on providing a fertile and collaborative environment for professional work. And for heads of departments who see themselves as caretakers and temporary administrators of their colleagues' work, its advice to lead dynamically and innovatively will appear bossy – even, perhaps, Machiavellian.

I have tried to offer advice based on the actual experiences of lecturers and on empirical research linking academic leadership, departmental environments, and academic outcomes. I hope to convince you that closely studying the experiences of academic staff, and creatively applying these ideas to our own circumstances, can help us to learn how to lead. I want also to show that the effort is worthwhile – for our own development, and for the survival and growth of our universities and the people who work in them.

Brisbane
April 1997

ACKNOWLEDGEMENTS

I am pleased to acknowledge the many people who provided material that made it possible to compile this book. These include the staff who were interviewed at various times to collect academics' perceptions of effective leadership and the academics on whose experiences the short case studies in chapters 7, 8 and 9 are based. These stories are composites based more or less loosely on actual transcripts and notes. They have all been amended in various ways to ensure that no person, department or university can be identified. Changes have also been to the interview material in chapter 5 when I judged that it might be possible to distinguish departments and individuals. Any remaining similarities to real cases are wholly coincidental.

I am grateful to colleagues in several countries, including the UK and Australia, who answered my request to participate in the survey of challenges to heads of departments, and experiences of outstanding academic leadership, which was conducted by electronic mail in 1996–7. Participants in academic leadership seminars and programmes in Australia kindly provided data for the tables in chapter 2 comparing their perceptions of university 'cultures', now and in the future, with McNay's results (McNay, 1995).

Chapter 10 was written jointly with Alf Lizzio and much of it is based on a developmental planning guide prepared for academic leadership programmes conducted by the Griffith Institute for Higher Education (GIHE), Griffith University. The section in chapter 7 on resource management was written in collaboration with Eva Lietzow. The *Leadership for Academic Work* questionnaire (Appendix) is a product of GIHE. It was developed by Alf Lizzio and me with support from John Swinton.

Chapter 4 contains results from research projects funded by the Australian Research Council, whose support I am pleased to acknowledge. The results from the project on the effects of academic leadership on teaching processes and student learning outcomes include data from preliminary analyses which will no doubt be subject to amendment when the complete set of data is examined. I should like to thank my colleagues in this project (Elaine Martin, Mike Prosser and Keith Trigwell) for their permission to use the material at this early stage.

I must particularly thank the following people for their special support, advice and patience while I was writing this book: Linda Conrad, Mark Drew, Fiona Grant, Faith Howell, Royce Sadler, Tracey Sleigh, John Swinton, and Lynne Watts.

Part I

LEADERSHIP IN HIGHER EDUCATION

1

INTRODUCTION

Leadership and learning are indispensable to each other.
                                        John F. Kennedy

Leadership and change in higher education

I have prepared this book against a background of momentous change in higher education. Everyone who works in a university knows just how troublesome these days are. There is no prospect of them becoming any easier in our lifetimes. It is idle to pretend that the growing pressures placed on universities in the last few decades by governments, employers and students will abate. We face an almost certain future of relentless variation in a more austere environment. There will be more competition for resources, stronger opposition from new providers of higher education, even more drastically reduced public funding. There will be even greater pressure to perform and be accountable combined with the challenges of new forms of learning, new technologies for teaching, and new requirements for graduate competence. Underlying all this is deep uncertainty about the proper role and functions of different universities in systems of mass higher education. And to complete the picture, these changes and uncertainties must be managed through the medium of an academic workforce whose confidence and spirit have been severely degraded.

This is a book that aims to help academic people address this seemingly depressing future with vigour, energy and optimism. These are sharp and stimulating times. These are the times when leadership comes into its own. It is the task of academic leaders to revitalise and energise their colleagues to meet the challenge of tough times with eagerness and with passion. We have seriously underestimated the power of leadership in higher education. It is perhaps the most practical and cost-effective strategy known to organisations that are struggling to survive and to make progress through troubled waters. As I hope to show through reporting the experiences of academic staff, it can transform the commonplace and average into the remarkable and excellent. The most substantial advantage a university in a competitive and resource-hungry higher education system can possess is effective academic leadership.

Yet these are not the only reasons why learning to lead in higher education is a course deserving our attention. The process of learning to lead is itself an intensely satisfying experience for those who undertake it; it is a process of developing expertise and growing as a person. People move from a search for 'right answers' to a realisation that they possess a store of tacit knowledge that they can use to make better judgements about people and resources. Moreover good leadership, as we shall see, can make academic work a more enjoyable and more productive experience for everyone – including the leader. My aim is to convince readers that it is worthwhile learning how to lead.

There are two dangerous myths of academic life related to academic leadership. One is that management is an intrusive and unnecessary activity which confines academic freedom and wastes the talents of a leader such as a head of department in trivial administrative tasks. The other is that academics are a fundamentally unproductive group who need the exercise of some managerial power and control to get them out of bed earlier in the morning. There is still far too much unprofessional academic leadership, of both these kinds – excessively lax and responsive, or dumbly aggressive and assertive – at all levels of universities. Staff are rightly critical of both types. They will never give their best to people who appear not to understand them and their needs. Too much of academic management in the past has been reactive, leisurely, cloistered, and amateur. Too much of academic leadership in the present is focused on short-term goals and betrays a lack of trust in people. There are ditches on both sides of the leadership road, and I will try to show how to plot a course to avoid them, through listening to the experiences of our colleagues, and learning from them.

Academic leadership: process and people

When I refer to leadership in this book, I mean nothing mysterious or obscure. Nor do I mean only the people who retain titles such as head of department or vice chancellor, although it will often be these people who carry the greatest leadership responsibilities. I imply instead a practical and everyday *process* of supporting, managing, developing and inspiring academic colleagues. In this second sense, leadership in universities can and should be exercised by everyone, from the vice chancellor to the casual car parking attendant. Leadership is to do with how people relate to each other.

4

However, while I hope that everyone who works or studies in higher education will benefit from reading it, the book is addressed primarily to a certain group of staff. These are people who are, or have recently been, researchers and teachers; those who occupy academic positions and work in universities as 'middle managers' of academics and support staff. Typically these people are called heads of academic departments.

In many British and Australian universities, this traditional role has gained new importance and new duties as institutions have struggled to respond to unfamiliar demands. As long ago as 1988 a standard text on academic leadership in the USA could assert that the 'quality of the core academic success of the institution depends upon the quality of the chairpersons – their dependability, their resourcefulness, their appreciation of academic values, and their insight into the abilities and weaknesses of their colleagues' (Bennett, 1988). Now more than ever in the UK, Australasia and much of Asia, the position is a key one. Now more than ever heads of departments stand at the three-way crossroads between the world external to the university, the people who constitute its senior management, and its academic and support staff. Heads must look to the future and survive the present. They must maintain standards of teaching and research output with fewer inputs. They must somehow motivate a group of workers whose status, prospects and job security relative to similar professionals, and their own profession a generation ago, have plummeted. They must be superb planners and competent business people who are not averse to risk-taking and enjoy entrepreneurial activity. That most of these staff require new skills, and more knowledge, development and support is not in question. Leadership is about learning.

Oscar Wilde defined 'experience' as the name we give to our mistakes. The memory of my experience of the first few months of being the director of an academic work unit remains vivid. I could not have been more naive, despite my twenty-odd years in higher education and fair reputation in my special field. I had no conception of the processes of budgeting, strategic planning, managing staff, or even how I should work with a secretary. I had hazy ideas about running staff meetings and allocating workloads. I had vague notions of inspiring staff and celebrating their attainment culled from airport books on leadership. No-one asked me to compile a set of goals for my performance and to discuss what indicators of achievement I would like to use. I had thought I had worked reasonably diligently as an academic, but the workload of being an academic leader and the constant oscillation between different types of problem during a normal day took my breath away.

5

In these experiences I was certainly not unique. I shall try to demonstrate that universities have a long road to travel before they have fully mastered the process of developing their leaders. Their achievement of this objective will determine their future prosperity in the no-holds-barred adverse market of contemporary higher education. No book can be a substitute for making mistakes and learning from them, but I hope that this one will help both new and experienced heads to master some of the principles of effective academic leadership. Since the process of reflection is the engine that drives performance improvement among professionals, I hope it will also help them reflect profitably on their experiences as part of a lifetime programme of improving their leadership ability.

A central idea of this book is that we can enhance our leadership performance through studying the experiences of academic staff. Running through it is the idea of listening to them about the challenges they encounter and the kind of academic work environment which enables them to achieve success. 'Leadership develops', said an experienced school principal, 'Not through either responding or asserting. Rather it develops through establishing a foundation of productive responses to people' (Donaldson, 1991).

With this in mind, an appropriate starting point is an examination of the views of a sample of heads of departments about the leadership issues they face in today's higher education environment. In the next chapter I will look, among other things, at how heads foresee the future organisational structures of their universities.

Academic leaders' views of leadership challenges

During 1996 I used electronic mail to survey a hundred university staff from the UK, Hong Kong, Singapore, New Zealand and Australia who occupied positions as heads of department. The institutions surveyed included ancient foundations and 'new' universities. I asked them to nominate up to three key challenges facing academic leaders such as themselves in the years 1997–2005.

The most nominated area concerned *maintaining quality with diminished resources, or 'doing more with less'*. Three quarters of the respondents mentioned this type of challenge. The issues mentioned included better financial management, survival in a leaner environment, strategies for establishing new student markets, balancing teaching and research funds, income generation, gaining more research support, and achieving high quality research with reduced funding.

The second most mentioned area was the *management and leadership of academic people at a time of rapid change*, named by sixty per cent of heads. This included selection and recruitment, helping staff through change, developing new skills, setting clear goals, mentoring younger staff, helping staff to cope with increased workloads, maintaining motivation and morale at a time of declining public respect for the profession, and rewarding performance.

Next in the frequency order came *issues associated with turbulence and alteration in the environment* of higher education, mentioned by over a third of heads. These consisted of the need for vision and innovation in teaching and research, problems of technological change, information overload, and the globalisation of higher education markets.

A similar proportion of heads mentioned *student numbers and standards* – attracting more students, teaching students who were less academically motivated and less well-prepared, and responding to the need to develop students' lifelong learning skills.

The only other area mentioned by more than ten per cent of heads was the personal dilemma of *balancing their own academic work (especially continuing to produce research output) with the demands of leadership and administration.*

Table 1.1 summarises these responses. Less frequently nominated topics included the need to reduce bureaucracy and improve administrative processes; the need for more regional and international collaboration; the need for more cooperation between universities; and the need to maintain a strong defence against government attacks on higher education. Perhaps surprisingly, only one respondent mentioned the challenge of 'getting rid of managerialism' and returning to more traditional forms of collegial university administration.

Table 1.1 Main challenges 100 university leaders say they face

Challenge	Frequency of mention
Maintaining quality with fewer resources; doing more with less; stretching and managing budgets	76
Managing and leading academic people at a time of rapid change	60
Turbulence and alteration in the higher education environment	35
Student numbers and responding to new types of students	33
Balancing own academic work with the demands of being an academic leader	15

Challenges and models

Most of the challenges recognised by academic leaders at head of department level can be understood in terms of the simple 'systems model' at Figure 1.1. The core academic leadership responsibility represented by the middle block is twofold. We will find ourselves returning again and again to this dual accountability as we move through the following chapters.

First and foremost, academic leadership must provide the means, assistance and resources which enable academic and support staff to perform well. Leadership is about producing excellence. Second, it must focus on change and innovation, and the harnessing of traditional academic values and strengths to meet new and sometimes strange requirements. Leadership is about change. Higher quality outcomes, and people geared to change, combine to influence the internal and external presage factors in the system by means of the feedback loop shown, and thus generate more favourable conditions for effective academic leadership processes.

In addressing this agenda, a recurrent theme of the book is the problem of managing conflicting priorities. Leadership is about tensions and balances. The concept is embodied in an old German proverb: 'Those who would rule must hear and be deaf, see and be blind'. We must trust people; but not everyone can be trusted. We must focus on traditional academic values; but we must also respond to new demands from employers, companies, governments, and students. We must look outwards to the strategic advantage of our work unit; but we should never neglect internal processes and

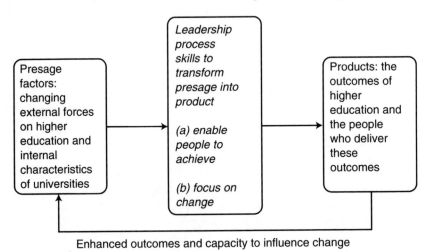

Enhanced outcomes and capacity to influence change

Figure 1.1 A simple 'model' of academic leadership

relationships. We must listen and consult; but we must have the wisdom to know when the advice we receive is correct. We must walk ahead; we must also serve. We must be risk-takers; we must also be reliable risk assessors. We must manage efficiently and firmly for today; we must lead people sensitively so they can independently address the new problems of tomorrow. We must mentor our staff; we must also assess their performance. We must enhance the quality of student learning; we must ensure the scholarly productivity of our colleagues. And we need to decide the degree to which our careers as academics are to be traded against our careers as academic managers.

Reconciling these differences means that academic leaders need to combine several qualities in order to survive. They must be thinkers and visionaries, and people of action too. They must develop their personal and human skills as well as their objective and analytical abilities. They must acquire resolution, for the daily reality of academic leadership is usually chaotic and often bewildering. There will always be plenty of people around to tell them that they could have done it better.

The structure of the book

Unlike other books on the subject that I have seen, this one tells a story about leadership. It is neither a report of empirical research on university leadership, nor a manual for how to run an academic department. Instead it builds on the experiences of academic staff to provide research-based evidence and models of academic leadership which inform recommended practical strategies.

The present book does not by any means cover the vast territory of academic management and leadership. The emphasis leans towards establishing principles rather than to detailed 'how to do it' techniques. Many of the latter, and the knowledge which informs them, are local phenomena which are best introduced in specialist orientation and induction programmes, or made available in electronic form for leaders to access when they need them. And much of the less local advice would be too rapidly out of date. In this respect it is eerily fascinating to read manuals on departmental headship published only a decade ago: they conjure up a world of elite higher education, unhurried change, small classes, dazzlingly brilliant academics, vice chancellors who tremble beneath the lash of collegial committees, and heads of departments as elected paperpushers who would rather be doing something else. This is not the world of higher education in which most of us now live; advice on how to manage it is merely quaint. We need instead a manual for the future, and a manual for the future must needs provide a convincing map of the whole territory rather than signposts at every corner.

I have tried to point the way to more detailed treatments of subjects which I have introduced fairly superficially, such as the management of conflict and the organisation of staff meetings. Nevertheless, I am aware that some parts of the text may appear a little daunting in the amount of content they present. Partly, of course, this reflects my subject matter: managing today's academic work unit is a monumental task. There are numerous ways of reading the book, and Parts II and III in particular I have tried to provide summaries of practical advice, and anecdotes from the experiences of academic leaders, which can be read independently of the main text. While Part I presents the theoretical and empirical background on which the practical advice is based, it is possible to move straight to Part II without having studied all of it.

Part I of the book introduces the context of leadership in today's universities. In addition to reviewing some of the contemporary pressures on universities arising from both internal and external sources, it covers some of the main ideas that have grown out of studies of how both academic leaders and academics perceive the processes of leadership. Underlying this approach is a belief that leadership should be judged on its capacity to deliver high performance in the core business of an organisation. In universities there is no doubt that this business is the advancement of learning in its broadest sense. The focus of this part of the book is on the qualities of academic environments and their leadership which motivate staff to achieve higher levels of scholarly productivity and better teaching. In this respect it attempts to answer questions of *why* we should bother about improving our capacity to lead. It shows that leadership, the academic work environment, and academic productivity are linked, using research results and less formal material from staff experiences.

I would not assert that detailed knowledge of these connections is an indispensable part of every head of department's toolkit; but a complete understanding of the area and a full complement of practical skills cannot be gained without some acquaintance with them. Part I concludes with an examination of similarities and differences between some ideas in the massive general literature on leadership and management and the processes of academic leadership. From this discussion I identify a series of six core principles and four main responsibilities to guide the programme embodied in Parts II and III.

Part II of the book shows how the foundations previously established can be used to build a leadership improvement plan for a head of department. I explore the process of creating a vision for a department, and securing staff commitment to it; and I examine the tasks and skills of resource management and project planning. Chapter 8 is divided into two sections. The first considers questions of motivation, equity and teamwork in relation to different organisational paradigms for academic departments; the second deals with the primary accountabilities of leadership for research and leadership for teaching. I conclude Part II with an extended discussion of performance management and ways of properly developing and recognising staff achievement – an area in which universities and their leaders have a great deal to learn from the processes of effective university teaching and student assessment.

Part III is about our own development as academic leaders, and about the ways in which universities can create a fertile environment for leadership to grow. Such an environment will embody the principles of effective academic leadership in the way it is managed. It will enhance the capacity of a university to survive and expand in the next twenty years, no matter what new threats assail it, through simultaneously increasing the ability of its academic leaders to learn. Leadership is about the future. 'It is the business of the future to be dangerous,' said Alfred North Whitehead; the greatest challenge for universities is to ensure that their academic leaders can step confidently into that future.

2

THE LEADERSHIP CHALLENGE IN THE CONTEMPORARY CONTEXT OF HIGHER EDUCATION

I felt as if I were walking with destiny, and that all my past life had been but a preparation for this hour and for this trial.

Winston Churchill on taking up the Prime Ministership, 1940

Outstanding leaders base their hopes for the future on what they have learned through assessing their past experiences. Through personifying change they inspire others to master its terrors. In higher education, implacable external forces combine with the nature of the academic culture – the fundamental values and beliefs of academic and other university staff – to produce a potent mixture. This mixture makes up the unique challenge which each person who undertakes a leadership role in a university must address.

In this chapter I want to review some key aspects of this dynamic environment, in the hope that we can better understand the extent of the challenge. The problem of sustaining academic productivity in teaching and research, and maintaining confidence during trying times, is not one that can be solved by individual academic staff alone; it must be addressed through organisational changes in human resource policy, reward and performance management systems, and staff training and development. Academic leaders such as heads of departments are placed at a critical point of influence in relation to this problem. They are able not only to exert pressure for change on the organisation and its policies as a whole, but also to influence the culture of the work unit for which they are responsible. We shall see later how the environment of universities influences staff motivation, teaching effectiveness and successful research outcomes, and how critical the leader's role in moulding this environment is.

12

Contemporary management theory stresses the 'situational' nature of leadership. Rather than considering leadership as a set of attributes of an individual, modern theories conceptualise it as an active process that contains elements of followers' desires, leaders' hopes, and the context in which they each operate. It involves an interaction between leaders, followers, and situations. Another way of putting this is to say that leadership is always the leadership of someone and of something. Effective leaders are adroit conductors of the elements in this orchestra, realising that their influence on others is balanced by the influence of others on them. To be a competent academic leader requires close and constant study of the outside world (the rest of your university, and the economic and political context in which it sits) as well as the inner world (the resources you control and staff with whom you work).

These inner and outer worlds form the first component of the simple three-stage 'model' previously introduced (Figure 1.1): the presage or background for academic leadership. My aim is to expose the texture of these worlds, and the tensions they generate which provide the uncertainty and excitement of academic leadership. Putting the presage components together with an examination of academics' experiences of university environments, and linking them to some of the mainstream ideas about leadership in successful organisations, we shall arrive at a point where we can start the journey of developing the leadership tools – the processes – that will help transform presage factors into practical outcomes.

In many ways these leadership skills mirror those of good university teaching; in many ways the processes of effective academic work reflect those of effective student learning processes. These are ideas to which we shall return more than once in the book. It is possible to derive most of the principles of effective academic leadership from a study of academics' experiences. Deep at the heart of effective teaching is an understanding of how students learn; deep at the heart of effective academic leadership is an understanding of how academics work.

Presage factor one: mass higher education and the growth of knowledge

'Higher education and great numbers. That's a contradiction in terms' said Nietzsche. Time has proved him wrong. The first problem that today's academic leaders must face is the fundamental change from an elite system of higher education, largely confined within national boundaries, to a mass higher education system in a global business. Numbers, finances, structure, purposes, students, governance, confines, technologies, the amount of available knowledge and its diversity have all changed. These largely external movements have had and will continue to have revolutionary consequences for how universities are run, what university staff do, and how academic leaders work.

But we all know about the shift to mass higher education in the UK, Australasia and many parts of Asia – or do we? University education has become the biggest of big business. The number of universities doubled in England from 1991 to 1996. Already the UK system has passed the target of 1.5 million students and 100 universities, including one of the largest universities (the Open University) in the world. Even in a country as small in population as Australia (with around 18 million inhabitants), there are perhaps two million people directly connected to a university, either as students or employees themselves, or as parents and other relatives of someone at university as a student or an employee (Sarros, Gmelch and Tanewski, 1997). In 1946, there were 8 universities in Australia teaching about 26,000 students; now there are 36 universities and 610,000 students; there are now more lecturers than there were students in 1946. The faculty of which I am member – one of 14 in the university – has as many students as the entire University of Lancaster had when I worked and studied there in the 1970s.

The changes wrought by mass higher education go far beyond larger class sizes, more diverse groups of students, and different student attitudes. They have altered management patterns, public perceptions of higher education, and the whole apparatus of professional standards and accountability. The massive expansion in numbers has been accompanied by an extension of the range of occupations which are seen to require a university education. And increasingly, higher education is expected to earn its funds, based on performance, rather than receive government support. Indeed the entire relationship between governments and universities has changed; they are no longer conceptualised as partners, but as 'two parties with different interests and priorities that sometimes converge and sometimes sharply conflict' (Clark, 1996, p. 417). There is an international movement towards connecting both public and private funding with performance; a shift from an input-run system which funds higher education on the basis of what an institution is – or was – to an output-driven system where achievement in research and teaching determines funding.

Increased complexity and competition, greater differentiation of university functions, global higher education markets, stakeholder pressure, reducing staff numbers, contract employment, performance management, work with new technologies, flexible learning, the possibility of high quality courses being delivered through new media direct from Harvard and Stanford to students in North Yorkshire or Tasmania – all these rub hard against an academic ethos still struggling to emerge from the values and practices of an earlier system. The academic leader has the heavy responsibility of managing this web of differences and providing the means for staff to embrace change with alacrity. Small wonder that the task sometimes appears daunting.

Possibly the most telling effect on academic staff resulting from the move from elite to mass, and the changed university–government relationship, has been the pressure to perform more highly in all aspects of academic work, and to do it with fewer resources. There are more students to teach, and they are no longer a gifted and motivated academic group, capable of surviving the bleakest of bad teaching, but much more like school students in their range of ability and the corresponding demands they place on our time and energy. In Boyer's study of the international academic profession (Boyer, Altbach and Whitelaw, 1994), less than 20 per cent of Australian academics surveyed agreed that undergraduates were adequately prepared in written skills and mathematical skills. Halsey's 1989 survey of UK university staff showed that nearly a third of respondents said that the academic ability of students at entry had declined. It could hardly be otherwise in a mass system.

Coupled with this more exacting population of students has been an increased emphasis on quality and accelerating progress towards stakeholder power. Beginning undergraduate students are now more critical of the lack of enthusiasm for teaching and the poor quality of support for learning they receive from staff (McInnis and James, 1995). The customers are more troublesome and more demanding, and in publicly-funded systems they have governments resolutely on their side. The quality movement in UK and Australasian higher education is now a way of life, even though, as we shall see in a moment, it is widely perceived by lecturers to be a drain on their time and a diversion from 'real' academic work – despite the fact that as many as a third of them in the UK do not believe that higher education can be trusted to exercise control over its own quality (Ince, 1997). HEFCE inspections, Good University Guides, Times league tables, quality audit, systematic student evaluation of lecturing performance, quality monitoring, course experience questionnaires, employer surveys, appraisal and performance management – academic staff are 'under virtually daily monitoring from very public and often critical audiences' (McInnis et al., 1994).

15

They had better get used to it as quickly as possible. It will be the scenario for the foreseeable future. Students will be at once harder to teach and less tolerant of bad teaching. However mass higher education is funded, its massive cost means that those who pay the piper will want to call the tune. As students' contributions to the cost of their own tuition increase, the necessity of delivering high quality university education and be seen to be delivering it will grow even stronger. Universities are less insulated from the cutting winds of national and world marketplaces than they used to be. Shrinking government financial support means finding new sources of funding, creating greater awareness of what they have to offer in the community, and increasing student numbers and quality. If education of acceptable quality at reasonable cost is not provided by the universities within a country, there will be many opportunities offered through new communication technologies for international competitors to undermine their market share. In 1996 the vice chancellor of the Open University warned of the dangers posed by the fact that India could deliver distance education at one fiftieth the cost of the OU. Sometimes there will be a need to remember that high quality does not always have to mean the highest quality.

Differentiation through substantive knowledge growth

All these changes are associated with mass higher education and student demand: but it would be a mistake to think that they are entirely caused by these things. Other forces, often acting in the same direction, are at work. Pressures to increase university research and consultancy have been similarly inflated. Expectations that research will contribute to economic objectives have expanded. In large part this is a consequence of universities' own success in increasing the quantity of knowledge, the degree of differentiation between subjects, and the amount of knowledge that can be applied to 'real' problems. The differentiation of knowledge influences academic and outside labour markets, and creates pressure for increased competitiveness among higher education institutions within and across national lines (Clark, 1996). The perceived need among senior university managers for a more entrepreneurial and innovative approach, coupled with sound business practice in managing operations, can be traced to this substantive growth in knowledge as much as to increase in student numbers.

Substantive growth has had two other effects: pressure towards increased differentiation among and within institutions, which has run counter to the integrating effects of the dissolution of binary systems; and a devaluing of the teaching function. Both these effects are in opposition to traditional models of single ideal university types which propound the advantages of a full range of disciplines and a close relationship between teaching and research. Combined with an increased emphasis on performance-based (output) funding, substantive growth leads institutions to focus on strengths and prune weaknesses in an effort to maximise returns and establish a distinctive market position. Strong existing research areas and historically well-funded institutions have an enormous advantage in this environment, as the results of research assessment exercises so clearly reveal. There is no need to classify institutions for funding purposes or to provide special funding allocations to 'research' universities: differentiation occurs naturally in such a climate. Performance-based funding of research has raised the sheer quantity of output, though whether quality has been maintained is questionable; 67 per cent of the *Times Higher Education Supplement* respondents in the late 1996 survey (Ince, 1997) believed that standards had declined since 1980.

As for undergraduate teaching, substantive growth and performance-based funding place it in an invidious position. Its status is eroded since it is seen as a distraction from research brought about purely by the external forces of mass higher education. In the USA, well over half of Boyer's respondents from research universities thought that the pressure to do research reduced the quality of teaching at their university (Boyer, 1990). Since teaching performance is not tightly linked to funding in the way that research performance is, those staff who are strongly committed to teaching often feel marginalised. Requirements to do more research and to obtain research degrees have pressed especially hard on staff who were appointed to polytechnics and colleges before the demise of binary systems.

Information technology

In its fundamental sense, information technology is another aspect of external environment that impels change. It is not so much the techniques of communication technology and computer-based technology that are critical, but rather the underlying concepts of versatility in time and place of learning, and new ways of thinking about the human aspects of teaching and learning, which these techniques can make more easily realisable. In the early 1950s the idea of automation was similarly misunderstood in terms of machines and contraptions. Naturally the manufacturers of machines and devices had an interest in maintaining the misunderstanding. But it is only after the concepts of stability of systems, feedback and control, and their application to organising work are understood, that the techniques associated with automation can be fruitfully applied (Drucker, 1955).

Information technology (IT) in higher education is really about 'flexible learning': it is a concept which implies a different relationship between institutions, staff and students. Whether we will see the demise of the traditional campus in favour of the virtual university is unclear; what is almost certain is that IT will place new requirements on lecturers in terms of those parts of teaching and learning which involve personal interaction with students. Just as automation contributed to enormous growth in the service sectors of economies (by freeing up people to do things that people can do and automated machines cannot) so IT will lead to a greater focus on the human aspect of teaching and learning – the aspect which IT cannot handle. The implications for academic work are potentially profound. Not only will it mean that most academic staff will need to learn new skills in developing and maintaining course and assessment materials, that their time will be spent differently, and that the products of their teaching will be open to public scrutiny; it will also mean that some lecturers will have to make a radical shift in their orientation from a view of teaching as transmitting information and ideas to one of directly attending to the process of learning in their students. The demand on academic leaders will be to help their staff realise that it is no longer possible to hide behind a lectern.

Presage factor two: the waning status of academic work

When my mother heard I had scraped a place at a college which later became part of a new polytechnic, back in 1967, it was cause for celebration. When I got a job as a lecturer, it was reason to call the neighbours in again. Whether she would do either of these things now is rather doubtful. For it is no longer special to be a student, and not very exceptional to be an academic staff member. They are no longer an elite. Their special status has been eroded by a massive influx of new people. They are part of the mainstream of public life and policy. But many staff entered the system when it *was* special to be an academic; while others who have since joined present, like their students, a wider range of ability. The declining status of academic work is the second big challenge within the presage component of the leadership model.

The phenomena of mass higher education and knowledge differentiation are inextricably linked to changes in internal management and the external relationships of universities with their environment, including greater national and international competition. Traditional self-government and professional determination of standards is rapidly being replaced by stronger central administrative control and a more customer-driven view of quality. Autonomy and academic principle, including commitment to fundamental values such as the right to protect a specialist area of knowledge, and to make decisions related to academic matters within the group, appear to be vanishing.

Moreover, public respect for academics has been eroded. In the Cambridge of the 1930s, to be a don was to be close to the pinnacle of the hierarchy of status, and no one doubted their value: 'For many it was a profound comfort to be one of a society completely sure of itself, completely certain of its values, completely without misgivings about whether it was living a good life' (Snow, 1956, p. 312). Today, people seem to think that lecturers are not productive, do not look after their students well enough, may not be maintaining high standards, and should work harder (Lucas, 1995). In 1989 and again in 1993, an overwhelming majority of academics agreed that public respect for academic staff was declining (Halsey, 1992; Boyer, Altbach and Whitelaw, 1994). I shall explore some of these criticisms in relation to the outcomes of higher education in the next chapter.

Probably the best modern analysis of the trend to a different and inferior conception of academic work has been made by the sociologist A.H. Halsey (1992). For him, 'the British common room today presents a spectacle more interesting than joyful'. We will surely agree. Academics have lost power and advantage in their work and market position. They have changed from being largely autonomous professionals in indulgent organisations to being somewhat more like supervised workers in tightly-managed businesses. Their earnings relative to other occupational groups have declined. While the average salary of a British academic in 1929 was nearly four times that of the average earnings of a worker in manufacturing industry, by 1989 it was only 1.54 times greater (Halsey, 1992, p. 131). In comparison with professionals and managers in both the private and public sectors of the economy, academics are now poorly paid. The former group enjoyed an increase of 33 per cent in real terms between 1975 and 1992, while academic salaries remained stationary. Small wonder that about a third of lecturers in 1989, compared with 20 per cent in 1976, agreed that they would choose a profession other than university teaching if they had the opportunity to start afresh (Halsey, 1992, pp. 137, 289).

A majority of lecturers feel that they are working harder than they used to do. Whether they actually work longer hours in the nineties compared with twenty years ago is questionable. Surveys other than those sponsored by staff associations, such as that reported by McInnis (1996), indicate that the increase has probably been modest, from around 45 hours a week in 1977 to 47 or 48 in 1993. This is a smaller increase than the average for all workers. What is significant is the change in academics' work patterns. They report a decline in the amount of time given to research and an increase in time given to 'other activities'. These include work related to quality assurance, appraisal, staff development, alternative modes of delivery, pursuing consultancies, and marketing courses and services. These activities are seen as peripheral or marginal, as unpleasant distractions from their training and interests as scholars, by many staff. They engender a feeling of reduced control over the organisation of their own work and a sense that its integrity has been compromised through fragmentation.

Academic staff also feel they are working harder because they have larger classes to teach and less time to spend with students; trying to use traditional ways of teaching and assessment with larger groups produces frustration and anger. As we shall see, a critical aspect of academic leadership for good teaching involves addressing this problem through imaginative approaches to helping larger numbers of students to learn. Staff are also reported to be experiencing more stress, to have less time to talk with colleagues, to have less time away from work, to be more isolated from each other than they used to be, and to be more dissatisfied with 'management's' attitude to them (Coorey, 1996; Roche, 1996). As one of them said:

> The feeling that I'll never be good enough, that I'll never be able to achieve enough is quite detrimental to my self esteem. We fill out forms every month to show what community service we've done and to put out every month that I've done no community service, to fill in the blank form every month, is not a building experience. I feel the university has lost track of and sight of people. People are human resources and not just a commodity to use.
>
> (Roche, 1996, p. 4)

At the same time as these changes in work patterns have occurred, security in work has declined, with a growing army of casual or sessional staff in the system. The majority of Australian universities employ between 10 and 20 per cent of their academic staff on a casual basis, and in the last ten years the proportion of tenured academic staff has fallen from 80 per cent to about 50 per cent (Department of Employment, Education and Training (DEET), 1996). In the UK, the proportion of academic staff whose salaries are financed wholly from university funds fell from 84 per cent in 1970 to 63 per cent in 1989; promotion opportunities also worsened (Halsey, 1992, p. 135). 'Dons are no longer set apart so clearly from the professional, administrative classes. Their prestige, salaries, autonomy, and resources have been much humbled' (Halsey, 1992, p. 146).

The trend from professional to proletarian, combined with an increasingly diverse workforce and changing work patterns, is another environmental phenomenon that is unlikely to be arrested. It represents a weighty responsibility for academic leaders. It is clear that the pressure on staff to develop new skills and use their time differently is a management problem of the first order, one which no head of department can escape and which is fully recognised as a significant challenge in their job (see p. 7).

Presage factor three: academic values and culture

This new disease that is sweeping through higher education in this country takes the form of corporate management, a particularly nasty virus which has the potential to slowly but surely cripple and destroy the fabric of the social relationships of our organizations.

(Smyth, 1989, p. 143)

The third significant challenge for academic leadership is caused by a discrepancy between traditional academic culture and the changes brought about by mass higher education and knowledge growth. The problem sketched out in the previous section was deftly outlined by the vice chancellor of a new university:

The problems faced by mass higher education arise from a system which has become mass in its size but remains elite in its values. The recent external changes of numbers, structures, finance and governance have not been matched by appropriate internal changes of values, purpose and activity.

(Wagner, 1995, p. 21)

In other words, there is slippage between the demands of the new environment and the methods of leadership and management we are using to run universities. Around 55 per cent of academics in the UK and Australia in 1991 were dissatisfied with the way their institution was managed (Sheehan and Welch, 1996); the proportion is almost certainly greater now.

There has been necessary progress towards more professional and businesslike operations management. There has been much less movement towards alternative models of leading and managing people. Sometimes it seems that we are running universities that require new levels of enterprise and responsibility among their staff by using routines that ignore the fundamentals of academic work, reward passive receptiveness, and assume that academics are themselves solely responsible for adapting to change. The presenting symptoms on the one hand include belligerent and arbitrary management tactics, complete with admonishing statements about academics' ostrich-like unwillingness to accept 'reality'; and on the other eloquently-expressed acrimony, enmity and nostalgia for a better, freer time when the fatal disease of 'corporate management' had not invaded our universities. A better understanding of the phenomena of collegiality, academic autonomy, and academic bitterness is a essential step towards finding a suitable treatment for these problems.

Collegiality

> It appears, then, that the intrusion of business principles in the universities goes to weaken and retard the pursuit of learning, and therefore to defeat the ends for which a university is maintained. This result follows, primarily, from the substitution of impersonal, mechanical relations, standards and tests, in the place of personal conference, guidance and association between teachers and students; as also from the imposition of a mechanically standardized routine upon the members of the staff, whereby any disinterested preoccupation with scholarly or scientific inquiry is thrown into the background and falls into abeyance.
>
> (Veblen, 1918, p. 165)

A characteristic aspect of traditional academic culture is the concept of collegiality. 'Collegiality' is an idea that has been made to do duty for an extraordinary range of valued academic processes, including the intimacy and flexibility whose loss was felt so deeply by Veblen in the American university of the early twentieth century. It has acquired an iconic meaning related to values of unselfish collaboration among small groups of scholars. It may be better for our purposes to concentrate on its more restricted meaning as a form

22

of shared decision-making. Collegiality is closely related to ideas of individual academic freedom, disciplines as frames of reference, separation from external pressures, conservation of special knowledge, and academic professionalism, of which more in a moment. But it is represented in concrete practice in the form of numerous university committees which arrive at decisions through discussion and debate.

The benefits of collegiality relate to the sense of community and ownership which it gives all academics, senior and junior, over their joint affairs; this feeling has been described as a 'precious aspect of academic life, one of the intangible factors that make up for diminishing financial rewards' (Baldwin, 1996). Collegiality has come under pressure from mass higher education because its weaknesses are more evident in a system where there are more decisions to be made and where quick responses to external changes are at a premium. It is a slow form of decision-making. It is intrinsically inward-looking. Its procedures are unwieldy. It exudes an air of protective self-interest. To succeed, it demands among other things a group of people who are individually committed to excellence and equally capable of realising it. A higher education system whose institutions need to search for new funding sources, plan strategically, and compete with each other in a market with manifold clients no longer possesses the homogeneity and stability which can make collegiality an effective form of getting things done.

Collegiality's problems are not entirely those of recent changes in higher education, however. It is one of those models which is fine in theory but has often not been applied in practice. One only has to look at academic novels such as *The Masters* to see that it has the potential to disempower, marginalise, and injure staff who are not part of the favoured group; and to see that important political decisions in academic contexts are typically arrived at by a small cadre of decision-makers. The committee often provides a veneer alone. And one only has to study the operations of university committees candidly from within to see that manipulation and craftiness frequently dominate over open, consensual decision-making, and that it takes courage and even foolhardiness to question the chair's authority. When Ambrose Bierce in his *Devil's Dictionary* defined 'consult' as 'To seek another's approval of a course already decided on' he may well have had the collegial academic committee process in mind.

Academics tend towards criticism, scepticism, and sometimes destructive negativism. Collegiality allows these attitudes and behaviours free rein. The asserted advantage is that proposals that are vague and empty are easily exposed (Baldwin, 1996). The disadvantages are that decisions are often only arrived at after a long and usually painful interval, or are not arrived at at all; and in the process, several people may be subject to savage maulings in front of their peers. Collegiality can be used by the unscrupulous to block all progress. One determined person can sometimes wear a group out so that nothing changes. Moreover the process allows individuals to evade responsibility, leading to situations where actions agreed upon by a group are not taken and no one is clearly to blame for not taking them. In a traditional university,

> No individual has over-riding power of action, but many have enough power for obstruction, and decision-making is difficult, even in the most minor matters. Change in a university comes about through many tiny increments, no one of which is large enough to rock the boat. These increments are represented as small reasonable remedies in response to great pressures, and take account of personal and territorial interests. The collegiate approach leads to a lack of individual accountability: everyone must agree, but no-one is accountable.
> (Woodhouse, 1994, quoted in Harvey, 1995b, p. 136)

Collegiality has had a rather better press than it deserves because of some lamentable reactions by universities themselves to external changes in higher education. Autocratic decisions by senior managers, lack of consultation over matters such as staff reductions and closure of departments, crisis-making as a form of legitimising centralised power, vice-chancellorial statements such as the fact that Higher Education Funding Council for England (HEFCE) deadlines leave 'no time for democracy' (quoted in McNay, 1995) have created a backwash of resentment and a longing for a better time when academic managers were 'first among equals'. Most of this could and should have been avoided by defter management of people.

The inherent disadvantages of collegial decision-making, added to its poor fit with mass higher education's swift rate of change, the obligations of external accountability, a different and more varied academic workforce, and the need to explore new funding sources, invite us as leaders to consider alternatives. These should aim to retain the benefits of community discussion, devolved power, ownership of process, and rigorous filtering of the quality of new propositions. At the same time they must avoid the hobbling effects of unresponsive and irresolute decision-making processes.

Autonomy, academic freedom and professionalism

These are collegiality's first cousins in the academic culture. Most of us will be familiar with the established idea of academic autonomy, which is a conception that is becoming more and more difficult to describe without parody, despite the fact that nearly all of us will feel some commitment to it. It is that academic power should reside within the community of scholars who profess their disciplines. These disciplines are firmly-demarcated mysteries whose arcane knowledge is revealed slowly and painfully, and whose mastery can only ever be achieved by a few dedicated disciples. In this culture students are typically seen as apprentice academics.

The pursuit of truth within the disciplines is directed inward; it does not necessarily have to address issues in the world beyond the university. Evaluation and standards are determined through peer review and the international community of scholars, never by external agencies. Academic freedom in its strongest form implies the absolute personal right to pursue the truth wherever it may lead, uninfluenced by 'management' and accountable only to a community of scholars. The university as an organisation receives limited commitment from its scholars; corporate loyalty, even loyalty to the department, is low: the traditional academic's reference group is the external 'invisible college', the university providing a convenient and comfortable shell in which to practise. Within this system, individuality and excellence are so highly valued that academics often display extreme levels of competitiveness. The culture's commitment to tradition and internally-determined standards is associated with a characteristic reluctance to adapt to external change. Attachment to the value of autonomy may result in high levels of intellectual arrogance, particularly towards non-academic staff, who are seen as servants rather than partners. Needless to say, mass higher education's drive towards greater vocationalism and the development of generic, employment related skills is viewed with much disfavour from this standpoint.

These views are of course strongest in the older universities, where research and scholarship and focused disciplinary competence are most highly valued. Discovering, interpreting and exchanging knowledge in an intellectually rigorous way are fundamental to all forms of higher education; but the values of tradition, strong adherence to disciplines, and individual liberty to pursue learning and teaching are more powerful in research-orientated universities, at all levels. Opinions critical of the pressures of mass higher education towards a more student-focused view of a university's mission are not confined to rank-and-file academics.

There are two important aspects of academic autonomy to which we need to direct special attention. The first is the curious nature of academic professionalism and its relation to management. The second is the reaction of academics to quality processes.

The academic profession is a peculiar profession in several ways. It shares aspects of expertise, autonomy, commitment, identification, and standards with other professions such as medicine and engineering. But it has no prescribed period of specialised training or set of required standards for one of its most important (perhaps its defining) function – the teaching of students at an advanced level. And, although its practitioners work almost exclusively in organisations rather than in private practice, they are mainly managed not by a separate group of administrators, but by other professionals. The problems of managing academics are therefore in some ways similar to those of managing professionals in general, but in other ways quite different.

Many academics naturally deplore and continue to deplore changes in higher education whose attendant effects have been declining status, lower pay, and fragmented patterns of work. Their lives are not only less comfortable; their very survival in employment is in doubt. At times like this, other organisations have found that they need visionary leadership and excellent management if they are to endure and grow. Ironically, in a phase of higher education's history when there might be advantages in embracing resolute leadership that will help us through quite exceptional changes, the values which many of us uphold as academics are antithetical to the whole idea of 'being managed'.

Managing academic staff has been likened more than once to a process of herding cats. Cats don't need leaders. Experts perform best when left to their own devices. Scientific and artistic productivity depends on freedom to follow serendipitous leads and to be inquisitive without someone breathing down your neck. Leave us alone to get on with the job. We believe in the power of academic democracy and hold the liberal view that good ideas come from the bottom up, not the top down. We will defy authority and disregard organisational procedures that don't suit us: just try and train us, and we'll show you!

Many of these assertions and complaints sound in the cold light of day – especially to salaried professionals such as doctors and airline pilots who accept much more intense scrutiny – like the self-interested calls of a favoured occupational group seeking to protect itself from rational examination. There is no evidence that professional status is eroded by working in an organisation, but there is plenty to suggest that extreme freedom to self-manage leads to underperformance among academics. Although self-assessment of performance and autonomous goal setting is a critical aspect of many professions, self-management alone is probably not enough to ensure productivity. Pelz and Andrews, for example (quoted in Raelin, 1991), found that most of the staff in their study of salaried scientists performed best when they formulated their expectations and goals jointly with supervisors, senior professionals and colleagues, rather than individually. The need for clear expectations of academic work is a theme I will explore in chapter 7.

Ambitions for leadership, success in management and administration, a commitment to more efficient business operations – valued qualities in most organisations other than universities, even among professional employees – tend still to be looked on with disfavour by many academics. The 'two cultures' of management and academic cross swords along the frontier defined roughly by the caricatured problems they have with each other, as shown in Table 2.1. The greatest care is needed to manage academic professionals well; the further away from the daily life of the teacher and

Table 2.1 Two cultures

Academics' problems with management	*Management's problems with academics*
Lack of understanding of academic imperatives; denial of specialist expertise	Self-indulgence; lack of relevance; denial of managerial competence
Interference with the right to work autonomously; excessive supervision	Attempts to challenge proper administrative authority
Rejection of collegiality and the right to open decision-making	Excessive emphasis on discussion and due process; time-wasting, inefficient meetings; unwillingness to take responsibility
Pressure to lessen commitment to an 'invisible college'; rise of corporate culture; individual needs ignored	Poor departmental and institutional cohesion; marginal loyalty to work unit and university; lack of entrepreneurial spirit
Less time to do core tasks owing to increased administrative load; larger classes; less able students; low morale	Unwillingness to share burden imposed by tighter budgets; negativism; culture of complaint and accusation
Softening of key distinction between academic and support staff	Inability to accept blurring of roles in the modern university
Increasingly intrusive quality processes	Lack of accountability
Erosion of core values of commitment to discipline and professional control	'Overprofessionalism': narrow, excessive specialism; slowness to change to accommodate new external demands

27

scholar an academic leader becomes, the more she must regularly remind herself of this apparently obvious point. The way in which an academic leader handles the fundamental dilemma of the need for leadership and management in a professional culture that does not really think it needs leadership and management it is likely to be critical to his or her success.

The negative views of academics towards processes of quality assurance and accountability (including the use of student comments to judge teaching performance and a strong preference for peer review), are well authenticated. Prescriptions for review, performance management, appraisal, and rewards for achievement, together with concepts and techniques such as customer- and stakeholder-driven definitions of quality, team work, quality audit, total quality management, and performance indicators, have proved difficult for universities to implement. Indeed, relatively few academic staff have genuinely embraced such ideas; they sound to many lecturers like the tolling of the bells of increased external control and a muffling of the song of academic freedom.

Boyer, Altbach and Whitelaw (1994) found that 57 per cent of Australian academics felt that there was 'far too much governmental interference in important academic policies'; a similar proportion felt that communication between themselves and administrators was poor. Nearly two-thirds of their UK and Australian samples believed that the university administration was often autocratic, while nearly half felt that top-level administrators were not providing competent leadership.

McInnis and his colleagues (1994) reported that less than one in five staff believed that quality assurance mechanisms would ensure genuine improvement in the higher education system; only 12 per cent thought that appraisal had increased their research productivity. In another recent survey of 1500 academics, respondents were asked to say whether a series of 41 processes designed to improve teaching quality would be effective. Among the items least likely to be endorsed (percentage agreements shown in brackets) were 'Undertaking national quality audits of teaching' (21) and 'Conducting compulsory student ratings of individual teaching performance, linking the results to promotion and/or extra financial rewards' (32). In contrast, 58 per cent endorsed 'Encouraging more collaboration and discussion about teaching among staff in academic departments' and 77 per cent endorsed 'Creating a working environment in which staff can gain intrinsic satisfaction from teaching students' (Ramsden *et al.*, 1995). In a similar international survey of what instructional development experts believed would have the most impact on improving the quality of teaching (Wright and O'Neil,

1995), the authors found that annual reports on teaching, university review of courses, and compulsory student evaluation were ranked towards the bottom of the list.

Lecturers, as we have seen, grudge the diversion of their time and effort from 'core tasks' such as research to the demands of quality processes. Scepticism and cynicism, suspicion of management motives, resentment at interference, and anger at being blamed for the failures of previous senior management decisions, are common concomitants. Partly the resentment is due to a lack of shared discourse about quality: the methods and concepts have been introduced in a way that runs against the tide of academic values and expression; partly it can be attributed to over-enthusiastic, top-down approaches to change which involve too little consultation and debate (Moses, 1995).

But this, the most common view, is far from being the complete picture. Even attempts to introduce quality assessment systems which have involved the most careful efforts to embrace academic values such as peer review and joint goal-setting have been difficult to implement. This is particularly true of teaching quality assessment and associated improvement systems (Clark, 1996; Reeders *et al.*, 1996). The reasons for discontent lie not only in poor communication, unfortunate management styles, and inherent academic conservatism, but also in differences between groups of academic staff in a heterogenous higher education system, the difficulty of demonstrating that the processes are cost-effective in terms of staff time, and the problem of attaching credible rewards (particularly for teaching) to high performance. The leadership challenge in relation to quality and accountability is to address these issues of difference, value, and reward effectively. The desired outcome is a group of academic staff who deploy their powers of intellect and creativity towards continuous improvement and intrinsic satisfaction rather than building negativism and subverting change. Sympathy is not enough; help is essential.

Bitterness and difficult people

The premise, simply stated, is that many faculty members in our colleges and universities are embittered to a quite surprising degree and that the very real losses caused by their feelings of regret, envy, frustration, betrayal, and isolation constitute one of the continuing unresolved problems in higher education.

(Jensen, 1995, p. 8)

In any management training programme for academic staff, one of the topics at the top of participants' agendas is 'How do I deal with difficult colleagues?'. The phenomenon of difficult, resentful colleagues is one which is not peculiar to higher education but it is more common in universities than elsewhere. By no means all academics experience the condition but few readers of this book will not have come across it in one form or another. It presents another critical challenge for leadership. Its symptoms include cynicism, disaffection, self-isolation, and negative attitudes, and in its more malignant forms, mean-spiritedness towards colleagues, contempt for students, minimal performance in research and teaching, refusal to participate in support activities, harassment of administrative staff, and outright condemnation of the organisation which provides their support and salary.

The symptoms may also include denigration of the head of department, subversion of meetings through sarcasm and lack of cooperation, and articulate destructiveness in discussion. Academic qualities of rhetoric and beliefs in the importance of protecting academic freedom allow for a level of criticism and negation that would not be possible or tolerated in other organisations (Jensen, 1995).

In Part II I will look at practical ways of addressing this problem. It has been intensified by recent changes in higher education but its underlying causes are much deeper in the academic culture. These causes lie in a combination of factors: a reward system that very strongly favours publication over teaching performance; infrequent recognition of achievements; a culture which upholds open criticism as a way of making progress; the traditional tolerance for eccentricity and delight in uniqueness in academic institutions; a permissive management climate that discourages early intervention when unacceptable behaviour takes place; heads of department who do not see their role in terms of developing and counselling their staff; laissez faire leadership generally (the view that academics are best left to their own devices); and in some cases the protection of tenure.

The leadership challenge in this case involves a conceptualisation of the head's role as a much more proactive one than it has conventionally been understood to be. A clear knowledge is needed of the reasons why such bitterness arises and how such antecedents can be prevented from taking effect. For it is often a condition which, once entrenched, is almost impossible to cure.

Models of the future university

Are there any ways of making sense of the various changes and dilemmas we have explored in this chapter? Two fairly recent analyses of university change provide some useful apparatus for understanding the implications for leadership of the transition to new forms of higher education in the UK and Australia.

McNay (1995) has described university change using a model based on the degree of 'tightness' or 'looseness' on two dimensions: policy definition and control over implementation (Figure 2.1).

Type A, with loose policy definition and loose control over implementation, is the collegiate university, with a focus on freedom to pursue university and personal goals unaffected by external control. Discipline-based departments are the main organisational unit. Standards are set by the international scholarly community, and evaluation is by peer review. Decision-making is consensual, the management style is permissive, and students are seen as apprentice academics.

Type B is the bureaucratic university, representing 'managerialism' in higher education; its focus is on regulation, consistency, and rules; its management style is formal-rational. A cohort of senior administrators wields considerable power. Standards are related to regulatory bodies and external references; evaluation is based on the

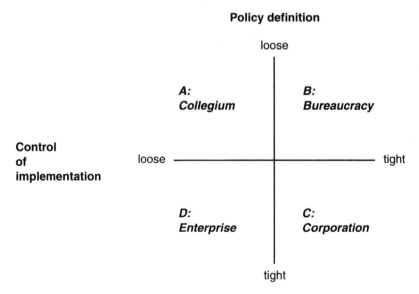

Figure 2.1 Four university models (after McNay, 1995)

31

audit of procedures. Decision-making is rule-based, and students are statistics.

Type C is the corporate university, with tight control over both policy and implementation. Here the focus on loyalty to the organisation and senior management; the management style is commanding and charismatic. There is a crisis-driven, competitive ethos; decision making is political and tactical. Standards are related to organisational plans and goals; evaluation is based on performance indicators and benchmarking. Students are units of resource and customers.

Type D is the enterprise university. Its focus is on competence. It is orientated clearly to the outside world, and it espouses continuous learning in a turbulent environment. Its management style is one of devolved leadership; its decision-making is flexible and emphasises accountable professional expertise; its dominant unit is the small project team. Its standards are related to market strength; and evaluation is based on achievement and repeat business. Students are seen as clients and partners in the search for understanding.

According to McNay, all universities draw on some components of each type. However, the dominant pattern of change for UK and Australian higher education would appear to be from A to B to C to D. This is supported by the views of samples of academic leaders at head of department level. McNay's own survey results, for one post-1991 university, are shown in Figure 2.2. Subsequently I asked two other groups of Australian heads to answer the same question of how they would distribute 100 points among the four cultures to represent their own university – now, five years ago, and five years into the future (Figures 2.3 and 2.4). All three graphs show a decline in the culture of the collegium, an increase in the corporate and enterprise cultures, and a steady or declining bureaucratic culture.

There are interesting similarities between McNay's model and Peter Scott's view of mass higher education (Scott, 1995). For Scott, mass higher education is a phenomenon of 'plural meanings'. It is characterised by heterogeneity and diversity rather than similarity. Differences between types of post-secondary institutions are becoming more permeable and fuzzy, and priorities can no longer be derived from single ideals such as the university as a liberal community of scholars, or the polytechnic as a training ground for the 'real world'. Heterogeneity in terms of ethos and organisation now characterises British and Australian post-school education; each university can no longer be considered to be providing the same experience for its students as every other university. At the

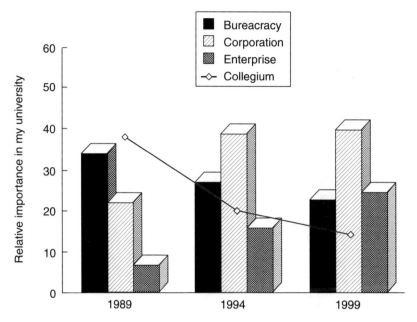

Figure 2.2 Organisational cultural shifts in one 'new' UK university (25 heads)
Source: McNay (1995)

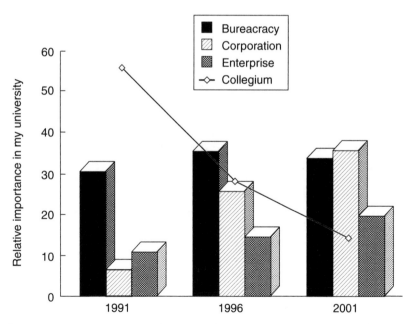

Figure 2.3 Organisational cultural shifts in one Australian university (10 heads)
Source: Data collected from participants in a leadership seminar for heads of departments,
October 1996

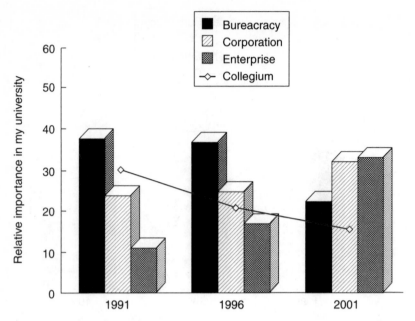

Figure 2.4 Organisational cultural shifts in fifteen Australian universities (21 heads)

Source: Data collected from participants in an Australian Vice Chancellors' Committee national leadership programme for heads of departments, November 1996

same time, the continuities of 'critical rationality', academic freedom, expert knowledge, elite culture and other older academic certainties have diminished; mass higher education is characterised by more open intellectual systems. Although some universities still claim that their usefulness to society is predicated on their autonomy, critical distance from the mainstream of commerce and central government, disciplinary purity, and self-accountability, such appeals no longer carry the conviction that they once did. Mass higher education is expensive and it attracts greater attention from its patrons – especially governments committed to reducing public expenditure. It implies accountability to stakeholders and open economic, technological and intellectual interchange with them, not closure and insularity.

Mass higher education also entails a shift from a conception of the head of department as an amateur administrator, managing by consensus, and occupying the office as a temporary elected chair (the 'first among equals' role) to the role of trained professional leader. This change needs to be understood not as some kind of managerialist conspiracy, but as part of a broader requirement to administer larger institutions in a different social and economic climate. Quite simply, mass higher education and knowledge growth have fundamentally altered the nature of university management structures. Smaller universities catering for academic elites were less complicated organisations to administer than large diverse ones. Management by unanimity and self-government is evidently incompatible with the efficient operation of huge organisations. It is too slow to respond, too unwieldy to direct, too focused on process rather than outcomes, and too short on professional expertise to guarantee quality, financial probity, and on-time delivery to multiple customers. We have seen the development of senior management teams, the reduction in the size of councils, and in some cases a shift of the role of head of department from colleague to line manager. As demands on university staff have changed and larger numbers of staff have been appointed from more diverse backgrounds, heads are also increasingly required to act as mentors to and active supporters of each of their colleagues, helping them to maximise their potential and looking after their development, training and welfare.

As much as many academics regret these contextual changes, they are unlikely to be reversed. Scott (1995) makes a convincing case that collegial management (academic self-government assisted by a reactive rather than proactive administration) may only be appropriate for institutions forming part of an elite system without the many new core functions, such as technology transfer, flexible learning, 'the corporate classroom' and continuing professional development, that have arrived since the 1960s. These elite universities typically had less than 10,000 students. Beyond this number, a new organisational culture can be observed to develop in universities. Professional managers in areas such as finance and personnel work alongside a senior executive cadre including both academic and administrative staff. The growth in the number of pro-vice chancellor positions in UK and Australasian universities is one of the concrete manifestations of this development.

This model seems to fit well with McNay's type B university. Above about 20,000 students, Scott and others have maintained that this 'managerial' form will itself give way to a 'strategic' or 'reflexive' one, characterised by greater flexibility and volatility and flatter hierarchies – a model which has aspects of McNay's Type C and more especially Type D. The centralised managerial model of type B is incapable of solving the administrative problems of really large higher education institutions. A new form of devolved power is needed with a different function for the centre. Departments and faculties in the enterprise university will become part of a federation of business units, and the senior management at the centre will take on the role of synthesising strategic vision and developing a shared culture.

It is perhaps not too fanciful to understand the future role of the academic leader in such a way. It is certainly unlikely that earlier forms of collegial management will return, but it is equally improbable that strong management, bureaucratic regulation, or even the dynamic and charismatic authority of the corporate model will be sufficient to ensure effective leadership of tomorrow's academic department. We will return to these models of higher education when we explore in more detail the skills needed to manage these departments.

Conclusions

Surveys of academic staff show that they are driven mainly by an absorbing interest in what they do. One recent investigation found that eight out of ten of them were motivated almost solely by the intrinsic interests of their work (McInnis, 1996). Affiliation with an academic discipline remains very or fairly important to 93 per cent of UK academics and 94 per cent of Australian ones (Boyer *et al.*, 1994); autonomy and self-determination of priorities continue to be vitally important to all academic staff. They continue to be an essentially 'cosmopolitan' occupational group whose loyalties lie outside the organisation as well as within it.

We have seen how, set against beliefs and values such as these, are the imperatives of mass higher education, knowledge growth and differentiation; of higher education systems that are moving rapidly and irrevocably to be more accountable and public; of reduced government funding, 'doing more with less' and increased competition; of institutions which seemingly can no longer be managed in the old ways if they are to survive; of a more business-like view of resource and operations management; of a series of changes which have greatly reduced the standing of academic work as an occupation; of an altered view of the purposes of undergraduate education; and of variations between institutions in how they are responding to more encroachment from their stakeholders.

The results of the surveys of a small number of academics with head of department responsibilities in both the UK and Australia point to a recognition that the direction of change is towards a more outgoing and vigorous university spirit. If they are right, universities will be more flexible in their planning, clearer about their markets, stronger in their administration, and more committed to learning how to do better. External performance and wider accountability will share the stage more equally with peer review and professional self-regulation. Simple dichotomies of collegial versus managerial governance, of professional management versus leadership of equals, and of reactionary academics versus mercurial administrators are notably unhelpful ways of understanding the complexity of this future (Coaldrake, 1996).

By and large, universities have responded to recent changes more effectively in their financial and resource management processes than in their leadership of people. In subsequent chapters I hope to show how we might do this better by drawing on the experiences of other organisations and of academic people themselves. It is unfortunate, to say the least, that attempts to introduce change with dash and dispatch have often antagonised the very workforce on whose commitment to embracing change all future success depends. One effect has been to make the task of leadership for those who manage academic departments intrinsically more difficult.

Set against this problem of morale are particular characteristics of academic culture and academics which make the leader's task easier rather than harder. These include their high levels of intrinsic motivation and love of academic challenge; the fact that they are self-starting, self-regulating, independent professionals; their willingness to discuss and debate issues openly; their lifelong learning skills and commitment to constant enlargement of their knowledge; their excellent communication skills; and their talent for imaginative thinking. We will look again at these benefits in relation to the functions of leadership and management in chapter 6.

Indifference to the ways in which today's academics are motivated, and ignoring their fears and hopes, will evidently not enable academic leaders to work with them effectively. Nor will simple acceptance of conservative academic values; there is no way back to a honeyed age of academic harmony and fulfilment. Resourceful leadership will activate established aspects of academic life to seek new and better paths to academic effectiveness in a changed and changing environment.

3

ACADEMIC PRODUCTIVITY
AND THE OUTCOMES OF
HIGHER EDUCATION

A productivity measurement is the only yardstick that can actually gauge the competence of management and allow comparison between the managements of different units within the enterprise, and of different enterprises.

Peter Drucker (1955, pp. 92–3)

In the last chapter I looked at some aspects of the contemporary context of higher education which make up the presage or environmental factors that academic leaders need to take into account – the first component of the presage–process–product model introduced in chapter 1. As we have seen, these include external pressures – such as knowledge differentiation, mass higher education, and reduced public funding – as well as the internal properties of academic culture and universities' responses to new demands.

I now want to explore some aspects of the academic outcomes or products which constitute the third part of the model. A leader's job is to increase productivity. How productive is higher education? How do academics think about university outcomes?

Different conceptions of productivity

The outcomes of higher education traditionally embrace a wide field. They include educated students, trained researchers, contributions to public debate and critical thinking, scientific and technological advances, publications, consultancy for public and private organisations, and community service of various kinds. Another important though less tangible outcome is the morale and satisfaction of the people who work in universities, on whom the quality and quantity of research, service and scholarship finally depends. We have already seen that on this measure the efficacy of today's universities leaves something to be desired.

We cannot properly understand the outcomes of higher education unless we realise that there are different interpretations of what academic productivity means. The conventional view of outcomes in all these fields is shaped by the idea of excellence and high standards; many academic staff perceive themselves to be guardians of quality in teaching and research, and most are sceptical of attempts by those outside higher education to assess aspects of quality outcomes in higher education. Moreover, some of them believe that the quantification of academic outputs (student numbers, course completion rates, publications, citation counts, and so on) may actually diminish the quality of outcomes: they see quality becoming traded for quantity; quantity and quality are perceived to pull in opposite directions. And quality is measured by professional, internal standards – the evaluations of one's peers. So authoritative are these views that research assessment exercises (RAEs) in the UK have used an extremely expensive peer review process instead of the relatively cheap but almost as accurate method of counting citations and refereed publications, which of course incorporates peer review at an earlier stage of the process.

The stress on quality over quantity in conceptualising academic productivity can also be seen in a recent study of Australian university staff views about rewards for teaching and research. Whereas nine out of ten respondents felt that the *quality* of research and publication should count a great deal in promotion decisions, only half thought that the *quantity* should count a great deal (Ramsden *et al*, 1995). Academics in other countries share similar views, and they express them in relation to teaching as well as research. A professor of physics in an American research university said, for example:

> There are many gauges of productivity. As far as teaching is concerned, I don't like the word productivity because it sounds like a factory or something like that. Excellence in teaching is a better word. You obviously want to be conveying to these students more than the minimum amount of information, and at the same time instilling a love of physics and an enthusiasm for the subject.
>
> (Massy and Wilger, 1995, p. 11)

There is a tension between certain academics' conceptions of themselves as the exclusive protectors of excellence and the imperatives of mass higher education in systems which are (precariously) publicly-funded. Not only do stakeholders (governments, taxpayers, employers) expect to have a role in determining what quality outcomes should be; they also look to measures of productivity which are broader and more quantifiable. Moreover they are less likely to assume that quantity and quality are in opposition. Measures of student and graduate satisfaction, student ratings of teaching, employment rates of graduates, numbers of students, numbers of publications and the value of research grants, use of internal quality management systems, and value for money in terms of efficient use of resources are all more likely to be seen as legitimate indicators. Resistance by some academics to prevailing business methods of assessing and improving productivity has resulted in negotiations between stakeholders and university interests, and these have often led to the use of compromise measures which incorporate more traditional academic processes, in the area of teaching quality as well as research quality. But the pressure remains.

Academic leaders believe they play a central role in encouraging effective academic outcomes. They also have their own conceptions of productivity and quality. In the international survey of heads of departments (see chapter 1), the most frequently-mentioned challenge these leaders said they faced was the problem of maintaining quality of research and teaching while resources were being reduced. Perhaps it is significant that they did not speak of *increasing* productivity and quality in a climate of reduced resources, nor of reducing costs as a means of increasing productivity. They focused on outcomes – not on costs. For many academic staff and university leaders, there is a direct relation between resources used and outcomes achieved. Hence increasing productivity by reducing costs does not figure in the picture; reduced resources are assumed to cause lower quality.

Massy and Wilger (1995) have persuasively shown that academics' conception of productivity is different from the standard one operating in the world of business and commerce. In the regular non-academic view, productivity is defined as the ratio of outputs to inputs, or benefits to costs. But the typical academic view is that outputs are directly related to inputs. University staff tend to equate quality with resources rather than measures of outputs: 'Faculty view inputs and outputs as being proportional to each other, and they associate deviations from proportionality with changes in quality' (Massy and Wilger, 1995, p. 13).

These phenomena are demonstrated in numerous ways. These include assumptions that increased class sizes or teaching loads must reduce the quality of student learning; in the stress placed in university league tables on *input* indicators such as library provision, equipment levels, and student entry qualifications; and in the emphasis in research performance indicators on the quantity of external grant money received. (The last of these calls to mind Ian Lowe's observation (Lowe, 1994) that research productivity measured by value of grants is equivalent to awarding the Melbourne Cup to the horse that ate the most oats). The distinctive academic emphasis on separate disciplines and compact fields of expertise reinforces the belief that costs in teaching are fixed.

These differences in conceptions help us understand the nature of the problem of enhancing academic output in the context of mass higher education. From the point of view of stakeholders, universities do not appear to be maximising their productivity; but from the academic point of view, productivity is at its upper limit, and reducing costs can only compromise quality (Massy and Wilger, 1995, p. 20). It is not that academics are unconcerned about maximising productivity and achieving high quality: they are very concerned about these things. But the importance they attach to outputs, and their tendency to view themselves as guardians of educational quality, produces a scenario in which ideas such as improving quality through paying attention to which teaching methods will produce the outcomes desired by stakeholders, or identifying which research inputs are associated with high research productivity, tend to be disregarded. It is now possible to see why processes which in other organisations have led to enhanced quality and competitiveness are simply not seen as relevant by many staff.

Quality and productivity in academic work

For many years quality in university teaching and research was taken for granted. In Model A of McNay's typology (p. 31), the scholar was all-powerful and academic autonomy was central. Scholars as a collegial group of disciplinary specialists had an absolute right to make decisions related to academic matters; students were novices to be inducted into the discipline, whose inner workings were obscure to the tyro, surrounded by mystifying jargon and unclear expectations, and whose knowledge was gained incrementally. Scholarly activity was intimately related to good teaching. Higher education was producer-orientated, specialist, elite, concerned with reproducing itself, and directed towards the interests of its staff rather than those of students, employers, and governments. It was nevertheless a high status activity whose academic staff could feel confident that they were respected and accepted on equal terms with the most privileged sections of the community. Quality went without saying.

As we have seen, this sheltered world has gone forever, for most academics anyway. Academic productivity and quality is now everyone's interest. The meaning of quality in research and teaching relates to where one stands, but does not entirely depend on it; a traditional academic view may be directly opposed to the view of an employer, but it is not necessarily so. One useful analysis (Harvey, 1995a) distinguishes five different views of quality in higher education:

- the 'exceptional' view (quality is synonymous with excellence, and by definition attainable only by an elite)
- the 'perfection' view (quality is consistently flawless outcomes)
- the 'fitness for purpose' view (quality is fulfilling a customer need)
- the 'value for money' view (quality is value for money in terms of return on investment)
- the 'transformation' view (quality is a change from one state to another)

Harvey prefers the last of these views, as far as teaching and learning are concerned. Most business enterprises, as well as higher education institutions, would draw on many if not all these conceptions in their understanding of quality; they would want to employ exceptional graduates, for example, but would focus on customer needs in marketing their services or products. It is perhaps more significant, however, that the exceptional view is characteristic of an elite university value system and congruent with the culture of higher education represented by the McNay 'collegium', while the transformation view is congruent with ideas of accessibility, opportunity and student focus characterising mass higher education and the enterprise university.

In spite of the significance of the different conceptions of productivity which I noted above for measuring the effectiveness of higher education, it is easy to make too much of the division between academic views and those of the broader community when it comes to defining higher education's desirable outcomes. Though there are differences in emphasis, there is a general level at which academics, employers and students agree on what should count as the outputs of higher education. Research and scholarship should be of sufficient quantity and high quality – although academics stress the primacy of quality in research, they also accept that measures such as numbers of publications, especially peer-reviewed publications, have an important part to play. Similarly, there is general agreement that students should learn not only quantities of knowledge, and expertise in a discipline, but also the power of 'the imaginative acquisition of knowledge' (Whitehead, 1932, p. 145). Academic staff themselves emphasise the importance of developing critical thinking, an understanding of principles, link-ing theory and practice, and acquiring lifelong learning skills (Entwistle and Percy, 1974; Knapper, 1990; Candy, Crebert and O'Leary, 1994). Employers similarly desire flexibility, ability to solve problems, communication and analytic skills (Kogan, 1985; Harvey, 1993).

There may be substantial agreement between stakeholders and those who deliver higher education on desirable ends. But this is a very different thing from saying that the goals thus represented are in fact achieved. A critical question for academic leadership to address is whether existing outcomes and the outcomes of the recent past are satisfactory. We have already noted the demoralised and embittered spirit of many academics and its objective correlates. But what of the quality and quantity of research and teaching? What are the standards we should be trying to encourage?

Productivity in teaching and learning

In the last decade public funding for higher education in the UK has declined by about 40 per cent. In the simplest sense of pro-ductivity, academics as educators are now much more productive than they were ten or twenty years ago. Student–staff ratios have deteriorated and more graduates are produced by fewer staff. Many lecturers, I have suggested, seem to think that the opposite is true: they believe that quality has suffered in direct proportion to the reduction in resources that have been invested. But even if we adopt the view that teaching productivity can be improved by maintaining outputs and decreasing costs, the issue of whether the standard and quality of teaching is satisfactory cannot be avoided. Does it satisfy students and employers? Is the learning that occurs 'fit for its purpose'? Does it involve 'transformations' in students' understanding?

People have been criticising the standards of teaching and the outcomes of university education for many years. Students and graduates consistently complain about:

- Poor quality of assessment processes (especially inferior quality and amount of feedback on student learning; and assessment that does not test understanding)
- Failure to encourage active, independent learning; over-depen-dence on teachers
- Unclearly specified aims, objectives and standards
- Ineffective and unenthusiastic delivery; too much 'lecturing' and not enough 'talking' with students

43

Williams and Loader's survey of administrators, teaching staff and students in UK higher education distinguished five types of complaint: lack of lecturers' enthusiasm for their subjects; inadequate presentation skills; lack of active student participation; failure to provide prompt and detailed feedback to students; and failure to put knowledge of learning principles into practice. Universities were criticised for not encouraging collective discussion of good teaching practice, for not recognising teaching skills, and for not supporting innovation in teaching (Williams and Loader, 1993).

In Australia, McInnis and James (1995) found that a high proportion of their national sample of first year students disapproved of the quality of some essential aspects of university teaching. These included clarity of explanations, making subjects interesting, and the quality of feedback on assessed work. Less than a quarter of them believed that academic staff took an interest in their progress. As one said,

> I don't think they care whether you pass or fail, that's *your* problem – that's the difference with university. At school the teachers wanted you to pass. At university they generally don't want you to fail, but they don't care whether you fail or not.
>
> (McInnis and James, 1995, p. 59)

The picture from graduates' perceptions is no better. In the national Graduate Careers Council of Australia survey of 80,000 recent graduates in 1994 (Ainley and Long, 1995), 31 per cent (or 24,800) respondents said that their course had failed to developed their ability to work as a team member. Forty-two per cent (or 33,600) reported that they had received feedback on their work only in the form of marks or grades, and 27 per cent (21,600) that staff hadn't made a real effort to understand problems they had had with their work. As many as 28,000 felt that their courses contained too much to comprehend it all fully, while 20,800 said that staff had not made it clear what they expected from students. Over 11,000 graduates reported low levels of satisfaction with their courses (see Table 3.1).

A striking conclusion from the Australian data is that positively and negatively rated courses are spread widely across universities. The programme of study rather than the university is the only sensible level of aggregation. No one group of universities – whether old, new, regional, or metropolitan – has generally better teaching. The variation is within fields of study: the highest rated mechanical engineering course may be in a university with the

Table 3.1 Dissatisfied graduates in Australia, 1994

	% dissatisfied
Generic skills:	
Course developed ability to work as a team member	31
Course developed ability to solve unfamiliar problems	14
Teaching and assessment:	
Feedback only in form of marks/grades	42
Staff put a lot of time into commenting on work	39
Staff gave helpful feedback	28
Staff made real effort to understand problems with work	27
Goals and structure:	
Too much content to comprehend it all	36
Staff made it clear what they expected from students	26
Workload too heavy	24
Overall satisfaction:	
Satisfied with quality of course	14

Source: Adapted from Ainley and Long (1995)

lowest rated history programme. A second important observation is that consistency in graduates' perceptions occurs from year to year. In other words, if last year's graduates reported that the teaching was good and they were satisfied with the course, it is highly likely that this year's and next year's graduates will think the same way. (Exactly the same phenomenon is noticeable for research performance. The highest-rated psychology departments for research quality in 1996 will almost certainly be the highest-rated in 2001. Quality changes very slowly in higher education).

Has the introduction of formal procedures for improving and assuring the quality of teaching in higher education exposed the serious problems which students and others seem to have identified with the quality of teaching? Probably not. In Australia, notwithstanding several years of national quality assurance processes linked to funding, affirmations by government that the results indicated the global excellence of Australian universities, and a graduate tax scheme through which customers pay for their education, academic staff remain sceptical of the quality of teaching across the system and especially whether good teachers are recognised for their achievements (Ramsden and Martin, 1996). In England, Wales and Scotland, relatively few – in fact, a tiny proportion, about one in a hundred – departments had been rated 'unsatisfactory' at the time of writing. This result flies in the face of all anecdotal evidence and indications from student and graduate surveys.

Entwistle has speculated that the substantial skew towards high ratings may be due to panels of assessors who review the work of their peers being more ready to focus on positive indications and to find reasons to excuse negative indications (Entwistle, 1995).

In 1996 Anna Tobin, a recent UK graduate, did not share the same rosy perception as the quality assessors. For her, variation in teaching quality was one of her biggest concerns; she 'endured lecturers with IQs to match Einstein's, who have written a series of theses and libraries of books, but who could not teach a dog to sit . . . this appears to be a nationwide problem'. Each semester she assiduously filled out evaluation forms, but the completed forms seemed to be ignored – the same teacher returned the next semester with the same failings (Tobin, 1996). Nor did a relative of mine from Australia find the standard of customer service in the UK to be adequate in 1997. Arriving to spend a year abroad at a highly-reputed college of a world-class research university in the UK, he discovered that two of the course units he had planned to study were cancelled at short notice, necessitating attending classes at another college. To add insult to injury, at the first class, the lecturer did not turn up. At the second, the departmental secretary appeared; she was sorry, but Dr Piercemuller was ill this week. At the third, he did not turn up again. Needless to say, both departments had received excellent ratings in the teaching quality assessment process.

Frequent complaints from students, employers and graduates are made about poorly-developed communication skills and teamwork skills. If these generic skills are desirable qualities of 'graduateness', then universities need to do more work on ensuring their development. Harvey (1993) found that UK employers rated oral and written communication skills, time management, the ability to summarise key issues, and problem-solving ability high in importance, but were relatively dissatisfied with graduates' capabilities in these areas. As we saw above (Table 3.1), in the Australian Graduate Careers Council Survey of 1994, nearly a third of graduates were unhappy with the extent to which their courses had developed their ability to work as team members. In a survey of Griffith University recent graduates in 1994, one in five reported that their course had not developed their creative capacity, and 30 per cent said that they had not developed teamwork skills.

The most telling criticisms of the quality of teaching in universities derive from research studies of what and how students learn[1].

1 The section that follows incorporates material from Ramsden (1992) pp. 21–37 and 60–85.

'Bad teaching', said Sawyer in 1942, 'is teaching which presents an endless procession of meaningless signs, words and rules, and fails to arouse the imagination'. This kind of teaching leads to what Sawyer called the learning of 'imitation subjects'. If the evidence from the research into university students' learning is correct, many students continue to experience university teaching which encourages superficial ways of learning, which in turn results in poorly understood key concepts, a lack of awareness of what learning in a discipline or professional field consists of, and weakly-developed transferable skills.

A dismal picture emerges from numerous studies of the quality of students' understanding in academic disciplines and professional subjects (Ramsden, 1992, chapter 3). It seems that many students often do not change their understanding in the way their lecturers would wish. Higher education is frequently unsuccessful in helping students to change their understanding of, for example, the nature of the physical world, or to grasp the nature of the scientific process. It has become clear that:

- Many students are accomplished at complex routine skills in science, mathematics and humanities, including problem-solving algorithms
- Most have appropriated enormous amounts of detailed knowledge, including knowledge of subject-specific terminology
- Most are able to reproduce large quantities of factual information on demand
- Most are able to pass examinations
- But many are unable to show that they understand what they have learned, when asked simple yet searching questions that test their grasp of the content. They continue to profess misconceptions of important concepts; their ideas of how experts in their subjects proceed and report their work are often confused; their application of their knowledge to new problems is habitually weak; their skills in working jointly to solve problems are frequently inadequate.

In summary, this research indicates that, at least for a short period, students retain vast quantities of information. On the other hand, many of them soon seem to forget much of it; and they appear not to make good use of what they do remember. They experience many superficial changes but they still tend to operate with naive and erroneous conceptions. Moreover, many students do not know what they do not know: they have not developed self-critical awareness in their subjects.

The research on student learning enables us to explain why problems with the quality of university teaching such as inadequate feedback on progress lead to unsatisfactory outcomes. It helps us to understand the vital importance of improving course structures, delivery methods, and assessment processes. The source of poor outcomes in all fields of study has been reliably identified as the student's *approach to learning*. In brief, a university student's intention (to understand or to reproduce) interacts with the process of studying he or she uses (to maintain the structure of the subject matter of the learning task, or to distort it). These processes and intentions are reflected in the quality of understanding reached. *Deep approaches* generate high quality, well-structured, complex outcomes; they produce a sense of enjoyment in learning and commitment to the subject; they are related to self-reports of the development of generic skills, as well as to higher grades. *Surface approaches* lead at best to the ability to retain unrelated details, often for a short period. They are related to lower levels of academic performance and more limited development of generic skills.

Approaches to learning are intimately connected to students' perceptions of the context of learning. Perceptions of assessment requirements, of workload, of the effectiveness of teaching and the commitment of teachers, and of the amount of control students might exert over their own learning, influence the deployment of different approaches. Deep approaches are encouraged by teaching and assessment methods that foster active and long-term engagement with learning tasks, excellent feedback on learning, clearly-stated goals, and opportunities to exercise responsible choice in the method and content of study. Surface approaches are encouraged by assessment methods emphasising recall or the application of trivial procedural knowledge, assessment methods that create anxiety, cynical or conflicting messages about rewards, an excessive amount of material in the curriculum, poor feedback on progress, and lack of independence in studying.

Figure 3.1 illustrates these general relationships and gives a specific example. Table 3.2 depicts the relationship between some aspects of students' perceptions, their approaches to learning, and the outcomes of their learning. Figure 3.2 shows the effects of different levels of experienced good teaching on graduates' reported development of generic (transferable) skills.

These studies teach academic leaders two definite lessons. First, there is a strong relationship between perceptions of effective teaching, approaches to learning, and learning outcomes. If it is possible to change students' experiences of courses and teaching, we can enhance the productivity of higher education by ensuring

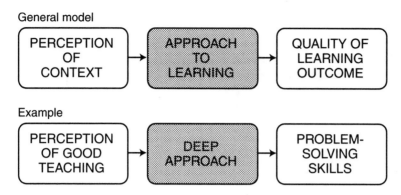

Figure 3.1 Students' perceptions of the context of learning influence the outcomes of their learning

Table 3.2 Correlation coefficients between students' perceptions of the learning context, approaches to learning, and learning outcomes

	Deep approach	*Surface approach*	*Academic achievement (Grade Point Average)*	*Generic skills development*	*Overall course satisfaction*
Experience of good teaching	24	−34	47	46	64
Experience of clear goals and standards	12	−29	46	33	55
Experience of inappropriate assessment	−21	47	−36	−35	−47

Decimals omitted.

Source: Wilson *et al.* (1997).

that more students develop the qualities of lifelong learning and of high disciplinary competence. These outcomes are not in opposition, as some people seem to believe, but are complementary; improving teaching will help improve both. It is as relevant to the development of a new generation of research scientists as to increasing the employability of students in vocational programmes. As Whitehead expressed this,

> There is not one course of study which merely gives general culture, and another which gives special knowledge. The subjects pursued for the sake of a general education are

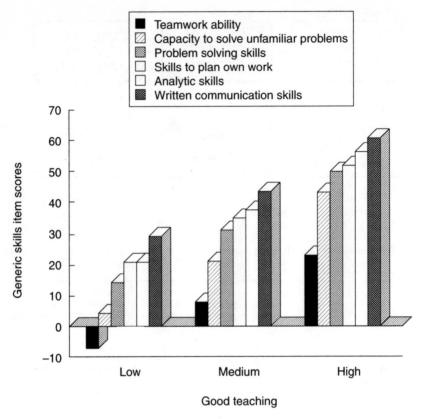

Figure 3.2 Effect of good teaching on the development of six generic skills
Source: Data from Ainley and Long (1995)

special subjects specially studied; and, on the other hand, one of the ways of encouraging general mental activity is to foster a special devotion. You may not divide the seamless coat of learning

(Whitehead, 1932, p. 18)

The second key point is that there is substantial variation in effectiveness across academic courses and departments. Despite the optimistic results of quality assessments, some courses are clearly experienced as unsatisfactory by many of their students, and these courses are ones where the quality of learning, and hence productivity, is lowest.

Academic leaders now need to consider the following questions:

- What characteristics of the academic environment encourage good teaching? Is it possible for me to influence how academic staff go about their teaching?
- What leadership qualities and actions, such as recognition of achievement and modelling good teaching in one's own practice, might be associated with better teaching?
- How can we achieve a proper balance of rewards for teaching and research? (Currently, individual and institutional rewards for excellence in teaching are so small that only the most enthusiastic teachers can be expected to devote effort to improving its quality.)

Productivity in research and scholarship

Very similar questions to these arise in relation to research and scholarship. It is useful to consider these endeavours in a broad perspective. Several years ago the late Ernest Boyer (1990) pressed for a reconceptualisation of academic work to allow greater recognition of its diversity, arguing for institutions and individual staff to adopt varying mixes of 'four scholarships': the scholarship of discovery (original research and the advancement of knowledge); the scholarship of integration (connecting ideas and synthesis across discipline boundaries); the scholarship of application (assembling knowledge through an interaction between intellectual and 'real world' problems of practice); and the scholarship of teaching (transforming knowledge through bridging the gap between the scholar's understanding and the student's learning). In all these forms of scholarship, certain activities and products constitute academic outputs.

Some of these are difficult or impossible to quantify. Who would presume to capture in numbers, for example, the intellectual climate that surrounds a disciplined and creative research laboratory and the inspiration that its graduate students derive from working there? 'Not just the outcomes, but the process, and especially the passion, give meaning to the effort. The advancement of knowledge can generate an almost palpable excitement in the life of an educational institution' (Boyer, 1990, p. 17). It is equally hard to tie down many of the products of scholarly service to the community and commerce, the consequences of a brilliant integration of existing facts, and the uncelebrated effects of exalted teaching on future careers. Nevertheless, there is again a broad consensus that scholarship in each area incorporates activities such as consultancies, grant applications, reflection, editing, writing, supervision, peer reviewing, and conferences. It covers products such as performances, patents, creative works, articles and papers, books, lectures, and trained research students.

It is impracticable to assay the worth of all these things, but it is possible to gain some general idea of scholarly output by examining the quantity of material and numbers of activities performed. Although it is far from being a one-to-one relation, the quantity of research produced by a department or an individual staff member is highly correlated with peer estimates of the department's or individual's research quality. There is a large world literature on research productivity (including integration and application as well as discovery) and its correlates. From it can be deduced four conclusions. First, there has been an exponential growth in research output during the last thirty years. Second, that despite this fact, average output does not seem to be very high. Third, this output is extremely variable, or skewed, across institutions and individual academics. Fourth, there are multiple effects on levels of productivity.

Clark's essay on substantive knowledge growth (Clark, 1996) summarises the proliferation of academic knowledge. Examples include the observation that the combined world output of historians from 1960–80 was equal to all that was published from Thucidydes' time to 1960; that more chemistry articles were published in two years of the 1990s than throughout history before 1900; and that output in science disciplines now typically doubles in a period of 10 to 15 years. Alongside this explosive increase is the rapid expansion of specialist fields of knowledge mentioned in chapter 2. Needless to say, these changes are not the result of greater accountability through research evaluation exercises. The increases reported from the 1992 to the 1996 Research and Assessment Exercise (RAE) in the UK cannot justifiably be attributed to its effects – they would have happened anyway.

Boyer's national survey of US faculty in 1989 found that a third of staff had not attended any professional meetings in the last twelve months, that 82 per cent received no federal funding for research in the same period, that 56 per cent had never published a book, and that 29 per cent had never published an article. Even in research and doctorate granting universities, only about half had published eleven or more papers in their careers. In the UK, Halsey (1992) found that in 1989, 42 per cent of university staff, and 70 per cent of polytechnic staff, had never published a book; about half the university academics and ten per cent of polytechnic academics had produced 20 or more articles (including non-refereed papers and chapters in books) during their careers. In his study of economics department staff at 18 Australian universities, Harris (1990) found that each member of staff produced research output over the period 1984–88 at a rate of four 'publication points' per annum (equivalent to less than one article in a first rank journal every two years). Twenty four per cent produced no output in the 1984–88 period. An Australian review of science and mathematics teacher education found that 34 per cent of staff had not published in the last five years (Department of Employment, Education and Training, 1989).

My own investigation of Australian research productivity indicated a median output of about five refereed articles in the previous five years across the system (Ramsden, 1994). Three quarters of respondents in the older universities published no books, sixty per cent no book chapters, and twenty per cent no articles during this period. Slightly higher figures were reported by UK academics in Halsey's study (Halsey, 1992): respondents had published on average about four publications (of any type) in the last two years. However, around one in ten staff in the older universities produced nothing of any kind in that period, and less than half the whole sample had produced more than ten papers in their entire careers.

These figures do not suggest very high levels of average output and tend to disconfirm the view that academics are generally very prolific publishers. As to the quality of research, about a third of Halsey's respondents believed that it had declined in their discipline over the last decade. I noted in chapter 2 the perception that standards in UK higher education have generally declined in comparison with other countries.

The reality of research productivity is that a small proportion of staff produce most of the work. Table 3.3 illustrates this phenomenon for the staff in the older universities in Australia. Using a composite measure of productivity (including books, papers, chapters and conference papers), it shows that half the sample produced 87 per cent of the total output, and that 14 per cent of the sample produced half of it. Equivalent distributions for the newer universities were even more skewed, with ten per cent of staff producing half the output. These results resemble very closely those of US studies (see Fox, 1983), and the same kind of distribution is evident

Table 3.3 Percentage of publications produced by percentage of academic staff in older Australian universities

	Percentage of academic staff			
	10	14	40	50
Percentage of total output (all publications)	36	50	80	87

at departmental level. It seems that we do not need to concentrate research support in productive departments and productive individuals; it is already concentrated in them.

There is clearly room in these figures for progress, both in terms of absolute productivity and its distribution. Studies of the correlates of research productivity provide important clues for academic leaders. An early interest in research, involvement in research activity, satisfaction with reward systems, and seniority of academic rank are important influences. For example, highly active researchers produce on average more than five times as many publications as the least active group; dissatisfied staff are around half as productive as satisfied ones. Staff reporting high levels of intrinsic academic motivation (that is, those who tend to agree with statements such as 'I find most new topics in my subject area interesting, and often spend extra time trying to obtain more information about them' and 'I become increasingly absorbed in my academic work the more I do') are twice as productive as the least intrinsically motivated. By far the best structural predictor of individual output is the academic's membership of a highly active research department. He or she is, statistically speaking, four times more productive than his or her colleagues in one of the less vigorous units. Active research departments, with a strong culture of research quality and support for staff to develop research careers, produce more publications for their size than less active ones. Size itself is a poor predictor of research outcomes.

Table 3.4 and Figures 3.3 to 3.5 illustrate aspects of the important relationship between research activity and productivity. Table 3.5 refers to individual staff research activities and output and shows the potent effect of higher levels of activity on quantity of publications. Figure 3.3 illustrates the same relationship at academic department level, using data from the same study of Australian academics. Figure 3.4 brings together results at individual and departmental levels from this investigation to illustrate a model of how individual staff research output is associated with both personal and structural factors (Ramsden, 1994). Staff perceptions of a cooperative departmental climate (a phenomenon I will examine in the next chapter) combined with location in a research-focused university predict higher levels of total departmental activity; this increases the likelihood that an individual member of staff will be an active researcher. Individual variables such as level of appointment, an interest in studying one's subject for its own sake, and an early interest in research, combine with these structural characteristics to predict higher individual rates of scholarly publication. The Australian results support a causal model based on Fox's theory

Table 3.4 Weighted publications index for last five years by amount of research activity

Number of research activities reported[1]	*Publications index*[2]
less than 4	1.8
4–7	5.1
8 or more	10.9

1 Including 'Received an external competitive research grant', 'Refereed one or more articles for a journal', 'Supervised one or more PhD students'.
2 One unit = one refereed journal article.

Source: Additional results from 1989 survey of Australian academic staff (Ramsden, 1994)

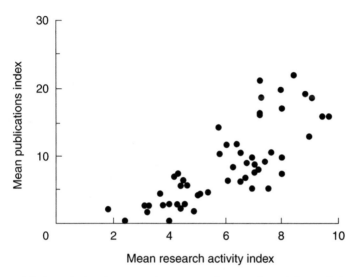

Figure 3.3 Association between departmental research activity and departmental publication rate
Each point represents one academic department.
Source: Ramsden (1994)

(Fox, 1992) that individual and environmental factors work together to influence research productivity. Research activity at aggregate level is influenced by the nature of the perceived environment. In its turn, aggregate activity influences individual output through individual activity.

Finally, Figure 3.5 takes data from the 1996 UK RAE aggregated rankings (Times Higher Education Supplement, December 1996) to show the interesting association between the proportion of staff entered for assessment – a rough indicator of the concentration of research activity in a department – and the university's ranking when all departments are aggregated together. The relationship

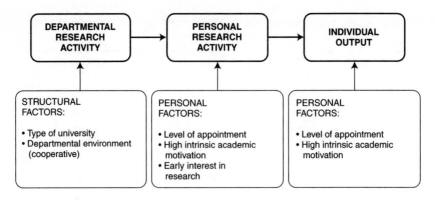

Figure 3.4 Structural and personal factors related to individual research
productivity

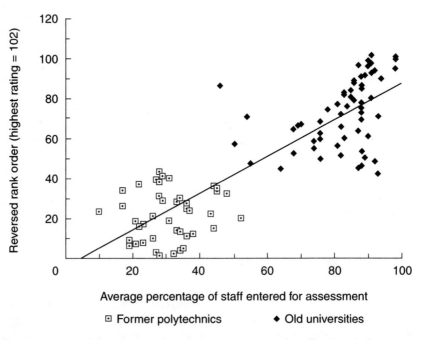

Figure 3.5 Association between average percentage of staff entered for assessment and rank order of university in 1996 RAE 'league table'
Source: Data from *Times Higher Education Supplement*, December 1996

between the proportion of staff assessed and rank is quite strong
within the old universities group, much less so in the former
polytechnics and colleges, and (because of the effective separation
of the system into research universities and a non-research univer-

sities) very strong indeed when both groups are combined. Again, the influence of an active research environment on productivity is clear.

'The constant improvement of productivity is one of management's most important jobs' said Drucker (1955). These correlates suggest some strategies for enhancing research productivity such as providing opportunities and rewards for greater levels of research activity and encouraging academics' intrinsic commitment to their work.

The general conclusion from the evidence discussed in this chapter is that levels of productivity in higher education – especially in the area of educating undergrdauate students – leave little room for complacency. What can be done to increase research activity? How should we help staff to deliver courses that reach the highest standards? I shall look in the next chapter at evidence which suggests that departmental leadership and the intellectual climate of an academic work unit can influence both research output and the effectiveness of teaching, and begin to delineate the distinguishing characteristics of forms of academic leadership which enhance productivity.

4

INFLUENCES ON ACADEMIC WORK

> The quality of scholarship is dependent, above all else, on the vitality of each professor. Colleges and universities that flourish help faculty build on their strengths and sustain their own creative energies, throughout a lifetime.
>
> Ernest Boyer (1990, p. 43)

We have seen how academic productivity is associated with the processes of academic work. The outcomes of higher education seem to be highly variable within systems and across departments as well as between individual staff. At the same time, variation in quality between academic work units is remarkably stable from one year to the next. Excellence tends to be concentrated rather than dispersed. Whatever the reason for this, it is not mainly an effect of redistribution of funds due to relatively recent accountability processes. Where good teaching occurs, it is closely related to high quality student learning and desirable graduate outcomes, both academic and vocational. High levels of research activity, themselves linked to intrinsic interest in research and an early commitment to a research career, as well as to the department in which an individual staff member is employed, are associated with greater academic productivity. Other scholarly and service outcomes are almost certainly influenced in the same way.

In a previous book, *Learning to Teach in Higher Education* (1992), I tried to show that students' approaches to learning can be thought of as responses to the academic environment in which they study. Students' *experiences* of teaching and assessment are a vital component of their *approach* to learning; and their approach influences the quality of their learning outcomes. Applying a similar logic, we might conceptualise the approaches used by lecturers in their academic work as responses to their experience of the academic environment where they work; and then we might consider the outcomes of higher education as being in part influenced by these approaches. Just as teachers are a primary constituent of the academic context for students, so academic leaders are a key part of the academic environment for lecturers.

In this chapter and the next one, I want to explore this idea by relating the second component of our presage-process-product model of academic leadership to the third. What characteristics of academic departments are associated with desirable products of academic work? Does academic leadership make a difference? What do academic staff themselves say about it? The environment for academic work is only one of the things that influences academic productivity. But it is one thing over which academic leaders at all levels have some practical control. The purpose of this chapter is to introduce readers to the substantial amount of evidence showing that academic environments profoundly affect academics' work processes, morale and productivity.

Effective schools and educational leadership

For Whitehead, 'The justification for a university is that it preserves the connection between knowledge and the zest of life, by uniting the young and old in the imaginative consideration of learning . . . the task of a university is to weld together imagination and experience' (Whitehead, 1932, pp. 139–140). It should hardly need saying that the central activity of a university is learning. Ernest Boyer's model of academic work as encompassing four scholarships, summarised in chapter 3 (Boyer, 1990), underlines the point. Original research, integration of knowledge, application of knowledge to practice, and teaching as a process of helping students to transform their understanding – all these four aspects of academic endeavour share a common thread of learning. It is therefore relevant for our purposes to examine the results of studies of other organisations whose core business is learning. The largest group of such institutions is, of course, schools.

Not all readers of this book may be aware of the huge amount of research evidence which has been sedulously compiled on school effectiveness in the UK, USA and other countries. 'Effective schools' are those where children learn well and enjoy a secure environment. They are also places where the staff take pleasure from their work. Table 4.1, derived from Reynolds *et al.* (1996), summarises the features which have been found to make British schools effective.

Perhaps the most consistent finding of this research into school effectiveness is that the quality of leadership is a distinguishing factor that separates more from less effective schools. Her Majesty's Inspectors' report on *Ten Good Schools* (1977) declared that 'without

Table 4.1 Factors that make some British schools effective

Professional leadership by the head
Strength of purpose: proactive management, consistency of purpose; appropriate recruitment.
Sharing of leadership: involving the deputy head and staff in policy decisions.

Shared vision and goals
Consensus on aims and values.
Consistent practice reflecting these aims and values.
Collaboration and teacher involvement.

A learning environment
Orderly atmosphere.
Attractive working environment.

High quality teaching and learning
Maximum time devoted to learning and interaction with students, in comparison with time spent on administrative activities.
Academic emphasis.
Frequency of opportunities for students to learn.

High expectations
Intellectual challenge and communication of high expectations for learning.

Positive reinforcement
Fair discipline.
Positive feedback on performance.

Monitoring student progress
Sound record keeping.
Cycle of programme evaluation and improvement.

Student rights and responsibilities
Good staff/student relationships.

Purposeful teaching
Structured teaching sessions, limited focus within sessions, encouragement of student independence.

Source: Adapted from Reynolds *et al.* (1996)

exception the most important single factor in the success of these schools is the quality of leadership at the head'. The first key factor of twelve in Mortimore's study of the effectiveness of English primary schools was 'Purposeful leadership of the staff by the headteacher' (Mortimore *et al.*, 1988). An outstanding head influences the behaviour of everyone in the school through his or her imagination and personal behaviour. Leaders like these communicate a vision about the future that is shared with the staff, pupils and parents. They ensure that this vision is reflected in the day-to-day educational activities of the school as well as its long-term policies (Beare, Caldwell and Millikan, 1989). They not only know what they want the school to achieve: they help teachers to work together towards these goals. They are primarily interested in solving educational problems; although they see administrative problems as important, they are not allowed to dominate. Pupil learning and welfare are their central concerns. They focus on the value of caring about students as a critical aspect of what the school does. They actively use knowledge and ideas from outside the school to improve what goes on within it.

These effective heads are also very visible; they 'walk the job'; they behave as they expect their teachers to behave in their classrooms, with a high emphasis on achievement, continuous monitoring of practice, an orderly environment, and clear rewards for good performance. They are good delegators and they encourage teachers to talk, observe, and explore ideas together. One study reported that these principals 'shared a genuine belief that their staff members as a group could develop better solutions than the principal could alone' (Leithwood, 1992). They understand both the teacher-student relationship and the principal-teacher relationship as a communicative partnership, not a one-way exercise of power and knowledge transmission.

Effective schools place a high value on both the process and the outcomes of self-evaluation. By collaborative means their heads create a climate where continuous improvement through self-evaluation is seen to be normal and is rewarded. These principals enable staff to achieve their own educational goals as well as those of the school (Donaldson, 1991; Harris, Jamieson and Russ, 1996).

The environment of effective sixth forms:
teachers' and students' perspectives

In the late 1980s, my colleagues and I studied the characteristics of 50 sixth forms in Melbourne in an attempt to understand more about the association between student performance and the educational environment. We measured educational effectiveness using inventories of approaches to studying as well as external examination performance, and we followed a sample of the students into their first year of higher education to see whether different schools influenced successful adaptation to university study. We studied the features of the educational environment of these schools by interviewing heads and asking both students and teachers about their perceptions of the culture and ethos of the schools (Ramsden, 1991; Ramsden, Martin and Bowden, 1989).

One of our important findings was that the quality of students' learning was associated with the perceived climate and leadership of the school. Teachers from the more effective schools believed that they were places where staff were encouraged to discuss issues concerned with teaching and its improvement, and where the management was collaborative and open. Teachers in these schools were also more committed to good teaching and its improvement. These same schools were seen by pupils to be places where teachers were concerned about their progress, which emphasised both high levels of achievement and independence in learning, and which had a supportive culture and ethos. In the schools where teachers experienced a collaborative environment, where decisions were jointly made and staff discussed teaching problems among themselves, there was a higher commitment to good teaching. This commitment was reflected in pupils' perceptions: the higher the teacher commitment, the better the ethos (Figure 4.1).

Principals of these schools repeatedly emphasised the role of the teacher as an autonomous expert who helped students towards autonomy in study and interest what was being learned. Pupils in their schools were more likely to be successful in their examinations and more likely to carry forward into university study habits of

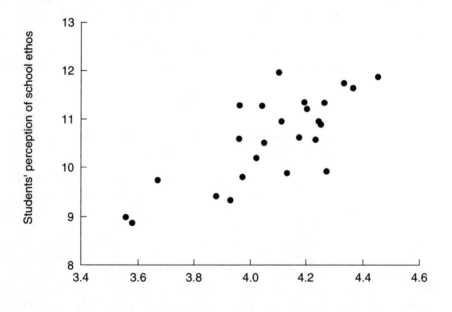

Teachers' commitment to good teaching

Figure 4.1 Relations between student perceptions of school ethos and teacher reports of their own commitment to good teaching, for 25 Melbourne sixth forms
Each point on the graph represents one sixth form

independent learning and a commitment to understanding (Ramsden, 1991).

In Peter Senge's (1990) terminology, the effective schools in this study were like 'learning organisations'. They provided an environment which was perceived by both teachers and students to be one where information was freely shared, where teamwork was habitual, where discussion of problems in teaching and learning was encouraged, and where mistakes were seen as opportunities for learning and development. The teachers' perceptions of the environment could be seen as important indicators of the climate established by the principal.

Effective academic departments, effective courses and educational leadership

There is evidence that the environment of academic departments – including their leadership – influences the quality of teaching and learning in universities in the same way, and that very similar processes affect research. Again, the key factor in the equation is the staff member's perception of the context of academic work.

Effectiveness of teaching

In 1992–3, Wright and O'Neil carried out a survey of people responsible for teaching improvement activities on over 300 campuses in Canada, the USA, the United Kingdom, and Australasia (Wright and O'Neil, 1995). Respondents included members of academic staff, administrators, and instructional development personnel. They were asked to rate a series of items in terms of their potential to improve the quality of teaching in their university. The category 'Leadership of Deans and Departmental Heads' was ranked as the most important by respondents in all countries except Canada, where it was ranked second.

The authors compared their findings to those of Massy, Wilger and Colbeck (1994), who undertook an interview study of faculty in 20 US colleges and universities. Their respondents also stressed the crucial role of the head of department in 'creating an environment conducive to effective teaching' (Massy *et al.*, 1994, p. 17). In our own study of 1500 Australian academics, as we have already seen, the most endorsed strategy for improving teaching quality was 'Creating a working environment in which staff can gain intrinsic satisfaction from teaching students', while Green (1990) emphasised the need for good teaching to be a university leadership priority if its quality were to be enhanced.

What is the link between effective academic leadership and good university teaching, and what are the lessons for academic leaders? Studies of university teaching and research performance throw light on staff experiences of the environments in which they work and help us to understand the significance of academic leadership. In *Learning to Teach in Higher Education* (1992) I argued that university lecturers espouse different ideas about what teaching consists of, that these differences are reflected in their practices as teachers and assessors, and that the quality of student learning is ultimately influenced by lecturers' understanding of what it means to teach. There is an analogy between what student learning research says about the effect of the context of learning on approaches to *learning* and the effects of the academic environment on approaches to *teaching*. Just as perceptions of good teaching can encourage active engagement with academic content, so perceptions of good leadership might encourage staff to give their best to their students. Good academic leadership should help create an environment for academics to learn how to teach better: an environment where interest in teaching is nurtured, and where solving educational problems collaboratively is routine.

Researchers in higher education began the systematic study of academics' conceptions of teaching in the late 1980s. In a series of studies, Keith Trigwell and Michael Prosser identified different ways of thinking about university teaching among science lecturers which were similar to the 'knowledge transmission' and 'facilitating learning' conceptions of teaching that other researchers in this field had previously described. Prosser and Trigwell found that university teachers hold qualitatively different conceptions of teaching and learning, and approach their teaching in qualitatively different ways, which are themselves systematically related to those conceptions (Trigwell and Prosser, 1995, 1996). For example, conceiving of teaching as being about the transmission of syllabus information to students was associated with an approach to teaching which was teacher-focused (the 'Information Transmission/Teacher Focused Approach' to teaching). Conceiving of teaching as being about helping students to change and develop their understanding was associated with an approach to teaching which was student focused (the 'Conceptual Change/Student Focused Approach'). These researchers discovered that approaches to teaching are also related to staff perceptions of the teaching environment (Prosser and Trigwell, 1997). For example, the student focused approach to teaching is associated with a perception that the teacher has some control over how and what is taught, that the class size is not too large, and that the department supports teaching. Finally, Trigwell and Prosser noted in a preliminary study a possible association between the way teachers approach their teaching and the way their students approach their learning. Teachers who adopt transmission oriented approaches have students who adopt surface approaches to their learning, while teachers who adopt conceptual change approaches have students who report deep approaches to their learning.

In the Prosser/Trigwell model, the effects of university teaching on students can be conceptualised as a series of shells of influence (Figure 4.2). The inner shell is teacher strategies – the things university teachers actually do in their teaching, which are closely linked to students' experiences. The second, or middle shell, is teacher planning, which connects conceptions and strategies. The outer shell is the teacher thinking or conceptions level. The way university teachers think about teaching is the limiting or the liberating factor in teaching and the quality of student learning (Trigwell, 1995a; Trigwell, 1995b).

Subsequently a team including Trigwell, Prosser, Martin and myself investigated relations between academic leadership and management, staff perceptions of the teaching environment and their approaches to teaching, and students' perceptions of the learning environment and their approaches to learning. A central hypothesis in the study of academic departments was that different ways of thinking about university teaching, like students' approaches to learning, were related to the perceived academic environment and the leadership which conditions that environment. This argument is summarised in Figure 4.3.

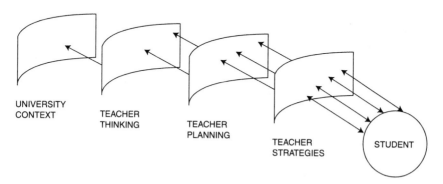

UNIVERSITY CONTEXT

TEACHER THINKING

TEACHER PLANNING

TEACHER STRATEGIES

STUDENT

Figure 4.2 Relations between perceptions of the teaching context, teaching and learning
Source: Trigwell (1995b)

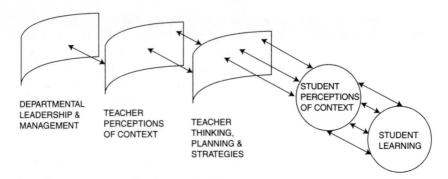

Figure 4.3 Relations between academic leadership, perceptions of the teaching context, teaching and learning

Interview studies of heads of departments and subject coordinators across four fields of study showed that leadership of teaching is conceived of in qualitatively different ways, containing elements of imposing, negotiating and enabling, with a focus on the department's organisation, on the leader's responsibilities, on the subject, on teachers, and on students' experiences (Martin *et al.*, 1997). Examining the coordinators' responses to a questionnaire in which they rated the importance of several leadership factors, we found that units in which the coordinator rated 'transformational' leadership (see below), firm and fair management of staff, and recognition and development of staff as high priorities were more likely to contain teachers who reported student-focused approaches to teaching. They were also less likely to report teacher-focused approaches. Moreover, students in these units rated the teaching more highly (Table 4.2).

In the part of the research which examined staff perceptions of leadership using questionnaire scales, the four dimensions we used to describe the academic environment derived from theories of leadership in business and educational settings (Burns, 1978; Bass, 1985; Leithwood, 1992) and were developed from the earlier work on upper secondary teachers' perceptions of their workplace and the principal's management style summarised earlier in this chapter.

Transformational leadership is a form of leadership which is held to be appropriate to the dynamic environment of the 'learning organisation' in an external context of rapid change. It is a value-driven form of leadership which engages followers through inspiration, exemplary practice, collaboration, spontaneity, and trust. *Clear goals and contingent reward* is an attempt to measure perceptions of 'transactional' leadership, an aspect of a leadership which may be seen as

Table 4.2 Associations between course unit coordinators' leadership, lecturers' approaches to teaching, and student perceptions of the quality of teaching in that unit

	Staff conceptual change — student focus	*Staff information transmission — teacher focus*	*Students' perceptions of quality of teaching in the course unit*
Coordinator's rating of importance of transformational leadership	0.29	−0.25	0.27
Coordinator's rating of importance of firm and fair management of staff	0.26	−0.34	0.28
Coordinator's rating of importance of staff development and recognition	0.30	−0.35	0.28

Correlations for 39 course units in four fields of study.

a complement to transformational leadership. It involves providing clear expectations and rewards in exchange for effort and loyalty.

Teacher involvement describes perceptions of a course or departmental environment where staff freely share ideas and discuss their learning needs. *Collaborative management* represents an aspect of the environment related to perceptions of openness and empowerment. These two dimensions were derived from the study of sixth forms described earlier in this chapter.

Sample items from the four dimensions of the questionnaire measuring the academic environment are shown in Table 4.3. Table 4.4 presents the dimensions of lecturers' approaches to teaching, their evaluation of the departments' commitment to helping students to learn, and two scales from the students' subject experiences questionnaire.

The results from individual teachers were aggregated to give a departmental result for both their approaches to teaching and their perceptions of the leadership; the results from students, including both their perceptions of the teaching and assessment they experienced and their approaches to learning, were similarly aggregated. We can see in Figures 4.4 to 4.6 how the variables were related in the first 12 departments in the study. The correlation between perceptions of transformational leadership and perceptions that a

Table 4.3 Study of academic departments and teaching: academic environment dimensions

Dimensions	Sample items
Transformational leadership	The head of this department enables you to think about old problems in new ways.
Clear goals and contingent reward	You usually have a clear idea of what's expected of you as a teacher here.
Teacher involvement	Academic staff in this department spend a good deal of time talking to each other about their teaching
Collaborative management	The head delegates responsibility fairly and consistently

Table 4.4 Study of academic departments and teaching: lecturers' and students' approaches to teaching and perceptions of teaching quality

Dimensions	Sample items
Lecturers: Student focus/Conceptual Change	In my classes for this subject, I try to develop a conversation with students about the topics we are studying
Lecturers: Teacher focus/Information transmission	In this subject, I concentrate on covering the information that might be available from a good textbook
Lecturers: Commitment to student learning	The staff here make a real effort to understand the difficulties students may be having with their work
Students: Good teaching	The teaching staff of this subject motivated me to do my best work
Students: Generic skills	This subject has developed my problem-solving skills

department was strongly committed to student learning is shown in Figure 4.4. More importantly, staff in departments where the leadership was perceived to be transformational (and where management was perceived to be collaborative, and discussion between colleagues about teaching was encouraged) were more likely to approach teaching as a way of 'making student learning possible' (Ramsden, 1992, p. 5) – with a focus on conceptual change and student learning rather than information transmission (Figure 4.5).

In turn, students doing courses in these departments perceived the teaching to be more effective (Figure 4.6). Other results, not shown here, indicate that in these environments students also

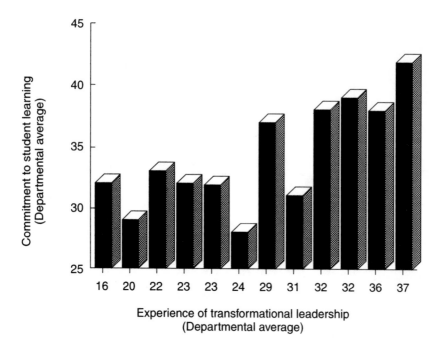

Figure 4.4 Transformational leadership is associated with lecturers' perceptions that a department is strongly committed to student learning

reported greater development of generic skills such as the capacity to work independently and communicate clearly, and approached their learning with a focus on understanding and the long-term retention of knowledge (a deep approach) rather than simply trying to succeed, in a minimal way, in passing assessment tasks (a surface approach).

Bringing together these results with the work on school effectiveness and studies of key influences on teaching improvement such as Wright and O'Neil's (1995), it is evident that the effectiveness of teaching and learning in a university department is associated with a supportive environment where dialogue about teaching is encouraged and good teaching is modelled in practice. An important element in this environment is a course leader's and a head's active advocacy for and commitment to teaching. Academic leadership influences the quality of teaching and learning through academics' perceptions of the nature of the environment in which they work.

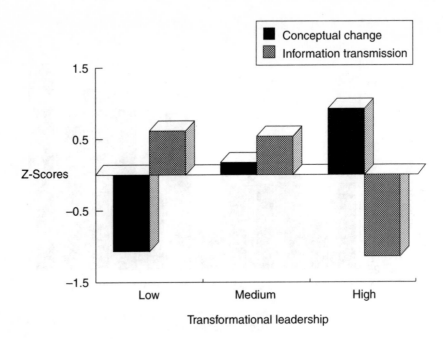

Figure 4.5 Transformational leadership is associated with lecturers' approaches to teaching

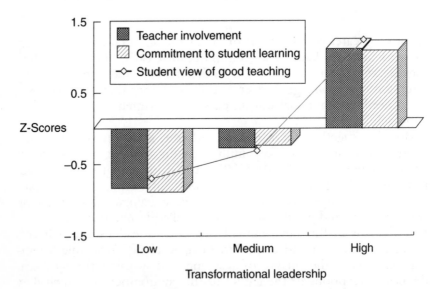

Figure 4.6 Effect of low, medium and high transformational leadership on lecturer involvement, lecturers' perceptions of commitment to student learning, and students' perceptions of teaching quality in 12 departments

Scholarly activity and research productivity

These are studies of teaching and learning; does leadership influence research effectiveness? We saw in chapter 4 that research activity (carrying out research projects, writing for publication, gaining research funds, supervising graduate students, editing journals, attending scientific meetings, and so on) is related to individual factors such as early interest in research and intrinsic motivation to carry out scholarly activity. Level of activity largely determines level of output. But it also appears that influences of leadership and the academic environment influence lecturers' research activity and productivity. Among the multiple factors affecting individual and departmental research output, staff experiences of the context in which they work have been consistently identified as exerting an influence on research productivity, after the effects of other variables have been taken into account. There have been an array of investigations of the phenomenon of departmental and university influence on research performance: among them, Long and McGinnis (1981) established the effect of different types of institution on productivity, while Blackburn *et al.* (1978) stressed the key role of the departmental environment on output; Blackburn and his colleagues also found frequency of academic communication also correlated with productivity and research activity.

Based on literature searches of the large American research databases covering the last three decades, Bland and Ruffin (1992) identified some of the environmental variables associated with high research productivity. They selected relevant publications from keyword searches and analysed them to produce the following list of twelve common characteristics of a productive research environment:

- clear goals that serve a coordinating function
- research emphasis
- distinctive research culture
- positive group climate
- assertive participative governance
- decentralised organisation
- frequent communication
- accessible resources (particularly human resources)
- sufficient size, age and diversity of the research group
- appropriate rewards
- concentration on recruitment and selection
- leadership with research expertise and skill in both initiating

appropriate organisational structure and using participatory
management practices

(Bland and Ruffin, 1992, p. 385)

The list is notable for the several items it contains related to
environment and leadership, and you will see correspondences
between these and the academic staff questionnaire in the study
of university teaching described above (p. 66). For example, group
climate, frequent communication, and participative governance
resemble the 'Teacher Involvement' and 'Collaborative Leadership'
dimensions.

Here, then, is further evidence that staff views of effective leadership are associated with actual academic performance. Departmental contexts perceived to have clear goals, a climate of respect, and
cooperative authority structures provide optimal conditions for
professional activity and productivity. Moreover it seems that similar
types of academic environments are conducive to higher quality in
both research and teaching (although this does not imply that
productive research departments are better at teaching students,
or vice versa, any more than excellent teaching inevitably leads to
excellent student learning outcomes. The environment provides the
conditions; other factors are needed as well).

My work with Ingrid Moses on Australian academic staff attitudes and output provides extra support for the argument that
research performance is associated with perceptions of the academic environment. I showed in chapter 3 how a conspicuous
feature of academics' research performance is the large range of
activity and output, with around 14 per cent of staff producing 50
per cent of the publications. Individual correlates of productivity
included an early interest in research, engagement in research activity, seniority of academic rank, and field of study. For example, staff
who reported an early interest primarily in research rather than
teaching were three times more productive than those who reported
that their early interest was primarily in teaching. By far the best
structural predictor of individual output was the academic's membership of a highly active research department. An active research
environment is a critical determinant of individual research productivity, explaining more of the variation in output than can be
accounted for by the individual academic's own research activity
alone. A staff member who was a member of one of these very
active departments was on average four times more productive than
his or her colleagues in one of the less vigorous units. The model
illustrated in the previous chapter (Figure 3.4) indicates the way in

which environmental and personal factors interact to influence research productivity.

For our present purposes the most significant finding of this study was the effect on research productivity and activity of staff perceptions of the degree to which their department provided a cooperatively managed and participative environment (Ramsden, 1994). In the more cooperative environments, staff were more likely to show high levels of intrinsic motivation for academic work, were less likely to be dissatisfied with the reward system, and were less likely to show low levels of commitment to academic work. In terms of the student learning ideas, it could be said that they reported deep rather than surface approaches to research and scholarship. Crucially, their research activity and output was higher than would have been predicted from knowledge of the other factors such as early interest in research and seniority.

This applied to both the old universities in the sample and to those institutions – formerly the equivalents of polytechnics and central institutes in England and Scotland – which were designated universities after the investigation was carried out. The effects are illustrated in Figures 4.7 and 4.8. In Figure 4.7, we see how there is an association between the average research activity in a department

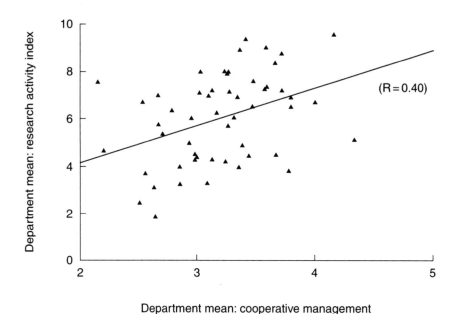

Department mean: cooperative management

Figure 4.7 Effect of perceptions of cooperative management on research activity (52 Australian academic departments)

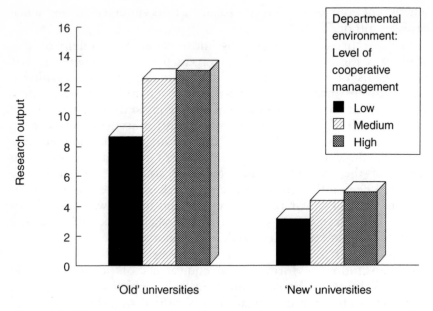

Figure 4.8 Effect of perceptions of cooperative management on research
        productivity

(including competitive grants received, memberships of journal
editorial boards, conference participation, postgraduate students
supervised, and refereeing activities) and how its academic staff
perceive it. It is evident that, although the effect is not large, the
more cooperatively-managed departments are more active in
research. In Figure 4.8, the departments are classified into three
groups in each sector (old and new universities), and the most
cooperatively-managed can be seen to have the highest productivity
in each case. The cooperatively-managed departments were ones
where staff agreed that:

- Staff are consulted on matters of policy even when they are not
  directly affected
- Staff in the department often discuss research issues together
- Teaching loads are negotiated cooperatively among staff
- There is plenty of discussion on teaching and curriculum issues
  among academic staff
- There is little professional jealousy among the academic staff
- Good teachers are highly respected in this department

It would be overstating the case to say that a cooperative academic
environment simply causes higher research productivity. On the

contrary, it might well be true that a group of highly active and committed researchers helps to create a context in which cooperative management is more easily practised. The association does suggest, however, that a focus on effective management and leadership of academic departments may be an important strategy for enhancing academic output.

Staff morale and satisfaction

The third main 'output' of an academic work unit, after teaching and scholarship, is an internal one: the job satisfaction (essentially a person's feeling of well-being in work) and morale (essentially their feeling of commitment to the unit and the university, including their perceptions of the fairness of the reward system). In very broad terms, it seems that most academics today remain relatively satisfied with their work while being increasingly dispirited, demoralised, and alienated from their organisations (Halsey, 1992; McInnis, 1992).

There are many reasons for work dissatisfaction and low morale, and perhaps no academic reading this chapter wants to be reminded once more about the changes that have led to the 'humbled' workforce described by Halsey and others, or to be told why lecturers might be feeling less than joyful about their university environment when we already know why. It is true that some senior leaders have reacted with extreme dispatch to external pressures on institutions in a way that one writer has called 'the Rambo style of university management . . . accompanied by aggressive language – talk of kicking heads, 'fingering' people, colourful threats and curses' (Baldwin, 1996). But that is not all there is to be said. Manifestly, some environments are better than others. Why?

Relationships between morale, satisfaction and productivity in academic life are complex and the directions of the effects are unclear; are people who are more satisfied more productive because they enjoy their work, or are productive people more positive about their work environment because they are productive? Probably both. What is very clear is that academics' commitment to their institutions and their departments is related to their perceptions of reward systems, and that these are ultimately associated with academic leadership. The least productive staff, both in research and teaching, in the Moses and Ramsden study of academic work were those who felt most alienated and excluded by the promotion system; they also rated their own performance low. However, these dissatisfied and relatively less effective academics were also likely to be members of academic departments where they *and their colleagues* rated the department's level of cooperation, discussion and participation low. Cooperatively-managed departments appear to be ones where staff morale is higher.

Recognition of teaching and staff morale

A critical aspect of staff alienation from their universities is their feeling of lack of reward and recognition for academic work, especially teaching. Several studies have pointed out the special problems of academic morale related to inadequate rewards and recognition for good teaching performance (for example, Gray, Froh and Diamond, 1992; Gibbs, 1995b; Halsey, 1992; Ramsden and Martin, 1996). There seems to be a discrepancy between the values of academics and the organisational culture of universities in relation to the recognition of teaching. About three-quarters of Halsey's sample of UK lecturers agreed that 'promotion in academic life is too dependent on published work and too little on devotion to teaching'. Gray *et al.* surveyed over 23,000 US faculty: they were found to favour a balance between research and undergraduate teaching, but they also believed that universities were moving in the direction of giving greater value to research (quoted in Lucas, 1995, pp. 97–8).

We observed earlier in this chapter how effective school principals minimised the difference between what they said they wanted their staff to do and the way they behaved themselves. The critical factor influencing satisfaction with promotions systems and morale in general is a perceived gap between rhetoric and reality. When organisations tell one story to the world, while their employees feel part of a different narrative, staff quickly lose faith in their leadership. The *Recognising and Rewarding Good Teaching in Australian Higher Education* project provided eloquent testimony to the truth of the statement that good teaching in universities is often unrecognised, despite universities' pronouncements to the contrary, together with an array of incentives such as teaching awards, and requirements for student evaluation. To many academics these strategies are only meaningful if they are part of a coherent system that ensures genuine rewards – especially promotion – for commitment to good teaching.

This study also found that lecturers who were least satisfied with the promotions system in their university were most likely to think that more effective management and leadership would improve the quality of teaching. Women were especially positive about the potential effects on teaching of more supportive environments and correspondingly critical of management styles and university career structures which restricted opportunities for advancement through the scholarship of teaching. Staff from the older universities in our sample were generally more satisfied with the rewards provided for teaching and research, regardless of subject area or gender; a possible explanation is that the more established universities provided a more collaborative environment for academic work.

Significantly, we found that many Australian academics attributed the lack of recognition for teaching, and their sense of frustration that their commitment to this central aspect of academic work went unrewarded, to inadequate leadership and management. As some of our respondents put it:

> The head of department demonstrates through example that teaching doesn't count! (Respondent from large research university)

> I think there's a lot we could do to improve management and leadership at the middle level . . . It's not their fault they don't have the skills; they have never been trained and they have very demanding jobs. If we do something with that then I think you'll find that academic staff will start to feel better about their teaching and feel that their good work is rewarded. (Technological university)

> Good teachers are rewarded by regular attention to their efforts at local level as much as by the odd promotion. Good teaching is built up by people in the department seeing on a daily basis that it is seen to be important. You have to have that, not just the promotion stuff. (Multi-campus, amalgamated university)

> You have to have some enthusiasts on the ground . . . You have to have committed men and women who know something of the joy teaching can be and you have to get them in there to be a champion. I think one of our problems is that we have often promoted those who are the good managers, often particularly the good money managers. I don't think that's always a wise step if you're aiming to focus on good teaching. (Multi-campus, amalgamated university)

The implications of these findings for developing leadership skills will be explored in chapter 9.

Conclusions

Summarising the results presented in this chapter, we can say that:

- Effective schools and effective academic departments share similar characteristics so far as student learning and teacher morale is concerned
- Departments which are effective in terms of teaching place student learning at the heart of their work; they provide a simultaneously challenging and supportive environment that raises the expectations of both staff and students, and encourages staff to seek better ways of teaching through interaction
- Scholarship and research is facilitated in departments which are conspicuous for their cooperative environment, clear vision, and high levels of discussion and consultation
- Academic staff report higher levels of satisfaction in more collaborative environments. There is an international phenomenon of strong dissatisfaction with the rewards and recognition provided for good teaching in universities.
- The style of management and leadership in a department is of primary importance in an effective academic environment
- 'Transformational' leadership appears to be an important ingredient of an environment for effective university teaching.

The evidence that academic work depends to some degree on what academic leaders do is surprisingly uniform. There are numerous additional influences on academic work which I have not explored here, including perceptions of workload, resource allocation and administrative support. But it does look as if some heads of departments and course coordinators may succeed in creating an environment that allows academic work to proceed more effectively, while others do the opposite. It also seems that a capable leader can increase output and satisfaction through building on collaboration and academics' natural propensities to be independent, self-motivating professionals. The old convention that academic management and leadership is unnecessary or unhelpful is not supported by these results. They would, on the face of it, seem to justify our efforts to enhance leadership effectiveness.

But, you might say, most of the results presented in this chapter are statistical associations, and not very strong ones at that. Are they enough to convince me that I should change my way of working with staff in my department or school? Isn't it the case that committed researchers and good teachers will say that the leadership is inspirational and efficient – just as successful students will praise whatever teaching they experience? Perceptions of a cooperative environment with good leadership may accompany high productivity – but wouldn't these people be highly productive in any environment, whoever the leader was? Is there any hard evidence that academics are affected by different approaches to leadership?

To answer these questions, we must listen to what academic staff themselves say about the characteristics of effective leadership and its influence on their work.

5

LEADERSHIP FROM THE ACADEMIC'S PERSPECTIVE

To get others to come into our way of thinking, we must go
over to theirs; and it is necessary to follow, in order to lead.
Hazlitt

Academic leadership as a conversation

In chapter 4 we saw how academic productivity appears to be
related to the environment in which lecturers work. What can
academic leaders do to shape that environment?

The three stage model of presage, process and product is a useful
device for thinking about how to improve academic leadership, but
it is limiting if we think of it as a one-way causal flow in the
direction of time's arrow. As I indicated in chapter 1, it is perhaps
more helpful to think of it as a 'system' in which outcomes influence presage factors and processes of leadership and well as being
influenced by them. What we can do depends on the group we are
leading. We shape the environment, but it also shapes us. This way
of looking at the problem opens out the domain of academic
leadership and emphasises its conversational nature.

Leadership is a quality that grows from a dialogue between
people. An academic leader's principal resource is other academics.
How the leader brings them into a relation both with each other
and with physical and financial resources will determine his or her
success. From this point of view, leadership is not fundamentally
about the attributes the leader *has*, but about what the leader *does* in
the context of an academic department, research group, or course.
An important part of that context consists of the perceptions of
colleagues or 'followers'. Being alert to their experiences of the
context of academic work is fundamental to leading them well.

This implies an important principle. Just as good teachers actively
listen to their students, so good academic leaders listen to what
their colleagues say about their experiences of the academic environment and academic leadership.

What do people want from academic leaders?

In 1993, Karen Seashore-Louis reported the results of an investigation of American senior high school teachers' perceptions of the qualities of an effective principal (Louis, 1993). Her findings indicated that, in these teachers' eyes, these principals were people who participated in the life of the school and were prepared to spend time on the details of providing good teaching and ensuring high quality learning. They focused their leadership on educational values; they put a strong emphasis on caring about students and their development. They brought new ideas and knowledge about teaching into their schools from the outside world, and they modelled risk-taking in their own practices. They were visible, they communicated a vision, they obtained resources, they recognised achievement, and they managed in a way that was consistently participative and empowering.

These characteristics, particularly the focus on explicit educational philosophy and links between these values and behaviour, are reflected in the organisational environments of successful schools, as we observed in chapter 4.

Lecturers' expectations

There are a few research studies that have addressed the question of what academic staff expect from heads of university departments. Summarised by Middlehurst (1993), they include a report of academics' expectations of heads in nine Australian universities (Moses and Roe, 1990); a small-scale investigation of four departments at one British university (Startup, 1976); and surveys of US faculty (Hammons, 1984; Falk, 1979).

The American investigations indicate that university and college staff value leaders who display characteristics similar to several of those of the preferred principals in Louis's research: a focus on change, participative management, recognition of performance, expertise in teaching and curriculum, participation in research and teaching, resource acquisition and management, listening to staff. The other studies focused more on tasks and skills than on valued qualities, but also highlighted the importance of setting and maintaining standards, consultation, selection, administrative skill, advocacy for the department, vision, and evaluation of performance. None of these studies, however, provided evidence that the qualities and skills delineated in them influenced academic performance.

These desired characteristics of academic leaders recall themes already examined in chapters 3 and 4. I will return to them when I look at work on employees' perceptions of managers and leaders in other organisations in the next chapter.

International survey:
What do outstanding academic leaders do?

During 1996 I asked 100 heads of departments in the UK, Singapore, Hong Kong, New Zealand, and Australia a series of questions about academic leadership (see chapter 1). The questions included this one: 'Please think of someone you know personally who has done an outstanding job of providing effective academic leadership. Could you please describe, in as much detail as possible, exactly what this person has done that constitutes highly effective academic leadership?' Before looking at the responses, perhaps we should heed the warning given by one survey respondent:

> This is an all too obvious question . . . If I could think of such a person, what they did would be far too complex – if it were impressive – to describe in this reductionist kind of a way. Drawing up ideal types for this kind of endeavour inevitably leads to looking for the impossible, including walking on water. It is this line of approach that will lead us away from academic leadership, rather than towards it.

She is right. Any attempt to manufacture a picture of a perfect academic leader by distilling the elements of good leadership qualities is hazardous and probably misconceived. 'I don't believe there's a formula and it would be disastrous to generalise', as another head of department put it. Leadership cannot be reduced to an exact method; by trying to simplify it in this way, we may lose the very essence we seek to capture. And we may set unrealisable targets for ourselves that doom us to failure in the process of learning to lead.

It is nevertheless beneficial to examine what university staff themselves think about effective leadership. How else can we hope to establish their trust and reach their needs? As I have implied, the focus here should be on what a good academic leader does, rather than what he or she is; we cannot change what we are, but we can do things differently.

Vision, imagination, and academic integrity combined with efficiency

These 100 academic heads believe that good academic leaders use their imaginative, creative powers in the service of others. They are people who show they know what they want to achieve and know where they're going. They 'set agendas'. They 'come up with good ideas regularly'. Their vision for the future is credible ('She has a vision of the strengths of people and of how the University might best contribute to the creation of greater knowledge and well-being').

The credibility of their vision springs from the fact that it is in harmony with the aspirations of academic staff, which in turn arises from them being academics themselves. They foster academic work through demonstrating that they understand its nature and by sympathising with the needs of their colleagues. They have the capacity to see beyond immediate problems, and the courage to be more than simply reactive to the demands of senior managers and governments. They lead by example ('He set very high personal standards and did not excuse underperformance. I admired him and have sought to emulate him'); they are respected teachers and/or researchers themselves with a concern to achieve the highest quality; but they are also ready to forego their own academic work to help and support their colleagues. They treat their colleagues in a principled and honourable way ('He is manifestly fair in dealings with staff and students'). They are efficient managers, who get things done, but they balance this with sensitivity to academic values and hopes.

> He has been prepared to sacrifice some of his own prime academic research interests in order to help his staff achieve. He is an outstanding teacher, who leads by example – always teaches 'difficult' Stage 1 classes.

> [This person] performs tasks well and is fair and equitable in exercising leadership. Lacks selfish motivations (at least, isn't too selfish), is able to delegate, and listens to others.

> The person I am thinking of has very effectively created an environment in his department which facilitates highly effective scholarly activity (writing, research grant applications etc); recognises different strengths and weaknesses of staff and utilises them accordingly and to the department's advantage; rewards good performance by putting staff forward for promotion or recommending merit increments etc., operates by example i.e. attracts research grants and studentships or publishes in refereed journals of the kind that he is urging his colleagues to use, has created an effective and devolved administrative structure in the

department for the management/delivery of the teaching programme and research activity (including postgraduate research) in the department.

Fairness, honesty, setting an example, efficiency, integrity and sympathy are values and behaviours which occur again and again in the replies.

Networking, political activity and strategic alignment

According to these heads, outstanding academic leaders are also risk-taking, forward-looking and entrepreneurial. Skilled politicians, they seek resources and generate new opportunities for staff in the department, both in teaching and research. They 'hire the best graduates to position the department at the top'; they 'seek new graduate students aggressively'; they exercise 'creative management of available budgets and resources, and have a good awareness of the climate within which we work at micro and macro levels'; they 'keep the ship afloat, while leading it into new waters'; they 'see the way things are going quicker than the rest of us'; they 'develop a strategy to deal with change and implement it despite vested interests'.

> He successfully melded a diverse group of people and academic units into a coherent organisation that is well positioned to become the undisputed leader in ... of information technology education. His strongest attributes have been his long experience in and depth of knowledge of the discipline and the IT industry, a considerable degree of fair mindedness and integrity and the capacity to inspire respect and loyalty.

On the other hand, they don't forget they are leaders of academic staff and academic work: 'She is a good manager and politician, but places politics in an instrumental role'; 'He combines the highest intellectual standards of scholarship with good political skills'.

Inspiration, confidence and hope; communication and collaboration

Outstanding academic leaders, these heads say, are men and women who bring people together and help them work towards a common ideal. They are people who are positive about the future and the changes it will bring. 'They project a high level of confidence that they know where they are going; therefore you know how you can dovetail your own plans and strategies with the bigger picture', said one respondent. 'They can direct, encourage and stimulate staff along new lines of investigation', said another.

They inspire trust and have developed personal skills to work effectively with other people and survive setbacks:

> [This person] has quiet wisdom, projects a confidence which appears both sympathetic and listening, but with an ability to make up his mind and not lose sleep over past (and inevitably sometimes wrong) decisions, a congenial person-ality, ability to impress in committees, ability to make clear written submissions . . .

> [This person] has courage and confidence to make judge-ments based on what is always inadequate evidence.

> He is willing to stick by decisions, even when it hurts.

> [This person] maintained a positive outlook to all activities, and sheer enthusiasm in spite of difficulties, and motivated others to achieve at higher levels.

My respondents frequently emphasised the collaborative and egalitarian nature of effective academic leadership. Good university leaders 'engender a feeling of partnership and collective responsi-bility'; they 'collaborate equally with peers and seniors'; they 'listen to points and incorporate them in their thinking (or explain why they are not incorporated)'. They build teams with a sense of scholarly purpose:

> She spends a lot of time talking with people, makes a serious effort to accommodate differing viewpoints, ensures that even the most junior academic staff are involved in the department, ensures that the general staff are appreciated and involved, makes every effort to bring postgraduate students into departmental concerns, is available to under-graduates and other students with problems, and is firm but responsive to pressures from outside.

> He or she has gone to a lot of trouble to involve others who might be affected in the decision-making process, communicated all the intermediate steps in arriving at

new procedures, and has been decisive in implementing these.

Recognition, performance management and support for staff learning

Having set up structures which inspire and enable their staff to contribute fully to the life of the department or similar academic work unit, outstanding academic leaders help their colleagues to give their best by recognising and rewarding their achievements. They link individual goals and expertise to departmental and university needs. They are also much occupied with providing opportunities for staff to enhance their skills and knowledge; effective leaders for these respondents are people who give junior colleagues responsibilities that help them to learn and develop their careers.

Thus they 'encourage junior staff and students on a personal basis', 'support hard-working achievers', and 'set up structures where everyone can contribute and be rewarded'. They 'encourage younger staff members to be more active and promote academics based on excellence, regardless of age'; they 'establish an environment which recognises and supports those making important contributions and those with the potential to do so'; they 'recognise and use to best advantage individual talents (and limitations!) in support of corporate needs as well as individual fulfilment'.

These emphases on managing performance and recognising achievement are important when seen in relation to the prevailing criticisms of university management for inadequate recognition of academic work and the still widespread view that management of academic staff performance is not desirable or necessary for proficient academic work.

Interview study of academic leaders

Similar findings emerged from a series of interviews of 20 academic leaders at one Australian university (see below). This study differed in two ways from the survey described above. First – bearing in mind the rule that leadership is not the exclusive province of people in management positions – it included staff at levels of seniority, ranging from a pro vice chancellor to a junior lecturer with responsibility for part of a course unit. Secondly, we asked people to identify what they thought poor academic leaders, as well as what good ones, did.

GOOD UNIVERSITY LEADERSHIP FROM THE PERSPECTIVE
OF 20 ACADEMIC LEADERS

- Being innovative and orientated towards change
- Wanting one's department to be a major force
- Knowing when and how to compromise, and how to accommodate dissenters
- Asking what we are trying to do, and why our methods for doing it may not be as successful as they should be
- Focusing on students
- Questioning 'sacred cows' (for example, traditional teaching methods)
- Doing things differently (for example, employers participating more in course design)
- Giving people freedom so that new ideas can surface
- Being able to change your leadership style when necessary (from 'consultative' to 'coercive', for example)
- Building a small group who think like you do in order to launch new ideas
- Being an example to one's colleagues
- Being a person who networks and knows what's going on
- Relating to people in a congenial way
- Understanding where people are coming from
- Getting feedback from your constituents
- Knowing the boundaries of what you can achieve
- Having a clear vision which is flexible and open
- Being a good manager of resources
- Being strategic and knowing about the wider system
- Being able to talk people into doing things (especially the case in academic leadership, because academic culture gives people a lot of hiding places)
- Working in teams
- Having good planning skills and a strong sense of direction
- Planning ahead, not just being reactive
- Being determined, but not rigid
- Being skilled at motivating and enabling people through identifying their needs and fears
- Creating mechanisms for implementation informally before making it happen formally

- Fighting complacency
- Finding out what people want to achieve, and helping them achieve it
- Acknowledging people's work
- Helping staff learn and develop
- Learning from your own mistakes

POOR UNIVERSITY LEADERSHIP FROM THE PERSPECTIVE OF 20 ACADEMIC LEADERS

- Being unclear about what you want to achieve
- Not listening to people
- Being authoritarian
- Being weak and defensive
- Not having an interest in people
- Not thinking about what you do
- Bending too many rules, without consultation
- Favouring one area to the exclusion of others
- Trying to push things forward without resources
- Doing deals behind the scenes without regard for equity and values
- Not looking into what worked and what didn't work on previous occasions before doing something new
- Being dictatorial
- Being too self-interested
- Communicating poorly
- Giving directives with no explanation
- Staying in the job too long
- Not being able to admit your mistakes
- Not having the respect of your colleagues because you don't have academic credibility
- Staying hidden in your office
- Following rules because you are insecure in your ability to do things independently
- Being unable or unwilling to delegate

Leadership feedback questionnaires

The qualities and activities summarised above concentrated mainly on academic leaders in different countries and at different levels. They are the perspectives of people who have had some experience of academic leadership. Do academic staff in general agree with their views?

During 1996 and 1997 members of staff in leadership roles such as course coordinator, head of research team, director of centre, deputy vice chancellor and head of department at a number of Australian and New Zealand universities used a *Leadership for Academic Work* feedback questionnaire. They invited their colleagues to provide confidential comments on their perceived strengths and weaknesses.

The first set of findings comes from an analysis of open responses to the questionnaire. The things these academic staff most admired and wanted in their heads, deans, course coordinators and pro vice chancellors can be summarised as:

- A vision for scholarly endeavour; enthusiasm for research and teaching; clearly-stated goals; commitment to the job
- Leading by energetic example as a teacher and scholar
- Honesty, integrity, fairness
- Open and participative decision-making; listening to staff and valuing their opinions
- Efficiency as a manager; getting things done with minimum fuss and maximum effectiveness
- Developing and mentoring staff through delegation and support for learning
- Encouraging initiative: rewarding and praising good performance and not accepting poor performance
- Commitment to change and innovation

And the things these colleagues least liked or wanted in their leaders were:

- Arrogance and self-interest – assuming they know everything and being critical of those who have lesser abilities
- Excessive leading from the front: trying to do everything themselves ('I'll do it myself because it's quick and efficient') – not delegating or encouraging teamwork
- Being uncommunicative
- Being adversarial and confrontational; dominating meetings
- Complaining about what can't be changed; being negative

- Not standing up for the department when its interests diverge from those of senior management
- Putting excessive emphasis on entrepreneurial activities and external ventures to the detriment of the department
- Favouritism – responding to a 'favoured few' staff and not the majority; supporting some sections of the department over others
- Secretiveness
- Making decisions without consultation
- Isolating themselves and being inaccessible
- Being disloyal

It's immediately obvious that there is a good deal of overlap between the views of leaders and followers about what constitutes effective and less effective academic leadership. For both groups, there are aspects which are particular to academic work, such as commitment to and understanding of teaching and research, and aspects which appear to be more generic, such as being a person with good 'people skills'.

By now you should be able to make out a picture of the expectations of academic staff for an academic leader and compare it with your own views. Results of the analysis of the answers to the closed questions (rating scale items) in the *Leadership for Academic Work* questionnaire may help to make the picture even more distinct. Statistical analysis suggested that there were seven dimensions which staff used to evaluate their colleagues as academic leaders (Table 5.1). (The complete questionnaire appears in the Appendix). Again these are a mixture of specifically academic leadership qualities and more general management and leadership capabilities.

An important result from the analysis of the *Leadership for Academic Work* questionnaire was that people are more comfortable with academic leaders who act in the ways described by the seven dimensions shown in Table 5.1. Respondents to the questionnaire were asked to supply an overall rating of how satisfied they were with the target person's leadership. Each of the dimensions in Table 5.1 turns out to be associated with greater reported satisfaction with the person's academic leadership. This is illustrated in Figure 5.1, where I have divided the scale responses into the lowest 25 per cent, the middle 50 per cent, and the highest 25 per cent, and then plotted them against the average satisfaction scores (which are on a 0–100 scale). The largest differences between the most and least satisfied scores are in the areas of fair and efficient management, and transformational and collaborative leadership.

Of specific interest here is the fact that academic staff expect

Table 5.1 Dimensions of the *Leadership for Academic Work* questionnaire

Dimensions	Meaning	Sample items from the questionnaire
Leadership for Teaching	Perceived effectiveness of the person's leadership of teaching and teachers	Brings new ideas about teaching into the department
		Conveys a sense of excitement about teaching to colleagues
Leadership for Research	Perceived effectiveness of the person's leadership of research and researchers	Provides guidance in the development of scholarly habits and practices
		Inspires respect for her/his own ability as a researcher
Fair and Efficient Management	Perceived efficiency and fairness of human and other resource management	Conducts the business of the work unit in an organised and efficient manner
		Delegates responsibility fairly and consistently
Strategy and Vision	Perceived emphasis on future direction of work unit and positioning for future advantage	Works to create a shared vision of the future direction of the department
		Advocates the interests of the work unit to rest of the University
Transformational and Collaborative Leadership	Perceived inspirational qualities; capacity to motivate and to promote cooperation between colleagues	Motivates people to do more than they ever thought they could
		Encourages people to share ideas and learn from each other
Development and Recognition	Perceived support for career development and recognition of colleagues' achievements	Helps good people develop their skills
		Praises and supports colleagues' successes

Table 5.1 continued

Dimensions	Meaning	Sample items from the questionnaire
Interpersonal Skills	Perceived openness, concern, and capacity to work effectively with colleagues (negatively scored)	Doesn't show a lot of concern for the people with whom she/he works Has an inflated sense of her/his own importance

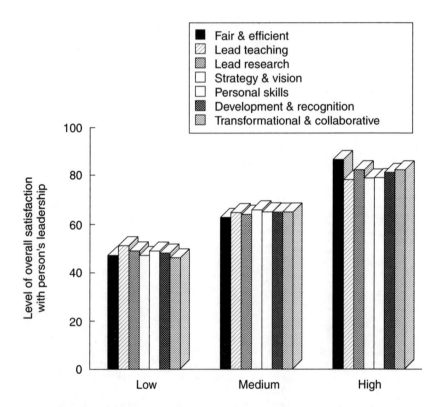

Figure 5.1 Association between seven leadership qualities and satisfaction with leadership

their heads and deans to be effective managers as well as inspiring leaders. Efficient management is complementary to capable leadership, not the opposite of it. This is an issue I will return to in the next chapter.

Relationships between leadership and the effectiveness of academic work

The results summarised above suggest that there is remarkable agreement about what kind of leadership enables academics to do their work well. The interview and questionnaire material tends to confirm the statistical associations described in chapter 4, but expands the picture considerably to include aspects of interpersonal skills, efficient management, and staff development as well as collaborative and inspirational leadership. Several of these aspects are apparent in the studies summarised by Middlehurst (1993) and outlined above.

How is the effectiveness of academic work related to the quality of academic leadership? Perhaps the best way to answer this question is to attend once more to what lecturers themselves say. The comments that follow come from many sources, including research interviews and open responses to questionnaires. These experiences can be usefully examined at a number of different levels. The extracts can be divided into three groups:

- Academic leadership as seizing opportunities and realising them in practice
- Academic leadership as leading the way
- Academic leadership as teaching

These may be seen as three broad academic leadership functions. They clearly overlap with the questionnaire dimensions and the categories from the surveys of academic leaders. Essentially they represent the vision and goals – or lack of them – provided by leadership; processes of motivating, inspiring, communicating and enabling (and their contrasting negative aspects); recognition of achievement and support for continuing professional development (and the opposites). Each can be seen from the evidence of academic staff experiences to influence how they go about their work, their responsiveness to change, and the outcomes achieved. Underlying the categories are general qualities of honesty, caring for people, an orientation to the future, listening and learning, and setting an example.

It is a worthwhile exercise to compare this evidence with the results of studies of academic environments presented in the previous chapter. One important issue raised in the comments is the way in which attempts to do things differently interact with central academic values such as autonomy and diversity. This is related to the issue of innovation and change in academic work. Several comments show that academic leadership may be ineffective if it does not challenge academic norms that work against new forms of doing academic work, especially innovation in courses and teaching. A culture that endorses very high levels of individual autonomy and permissive supervision tends to discourage change unless the views of individuals coincide with those of the leader and other staff. Note also, in those extracts which describe negative experiences, the recurrent themes of lack of feedback, poor interpersonal skills, and lack of commitment to ensuring that a vision is realised.

Leadership as seizing opportunities and realising them in practice

The central idea here is that academic work is facilitated through clear goals and a vision for the future which is consistently pursued and communicated with integrity, an understanding of individual needs and fears, and energetic commitment. An effective academic leader does not just have some good ideas and lofty goals; he or she is able to translate ideas into action by working on the ground to make the ideas become real (Donaldson, 1991, p. 189). The effect is to bring academics together and provide them with a sense of shared purpose:

> She has a clear vision for a better course, a better department, which is focused on a different breed of students, a more differentiated group with less science background but who will become scientists, some of them outstanding scientists. She knows where we're going and where we're going is down the flexible learning and technology road, and why we are doing it is to make sure we become the best place to do this course. I feel a part, we each feel a part of this conception. It's made real because she's aware of the practical skills needed to make it happen. She has a vision but knows it has to be worked out on the ground with staff who may not see in the same way. (Science lecturer)

> [This person] came into the department where I was working with a brief to increase our research profile and make more academics 'research active'. Instead of talking to people about other people to get information when he came in, he looked at our CVs, talked to us individually about where we wanted to go, and where we saw ourselves in the future. And then he gave you his view of what he saw and where he wanted you to be. I found this generally supportive and very

encouraging. He'd say: 'Yes, that's a great idea, you could do that'. So he not only gave you work but set up opportunities for you to show that you could perform. What a poor academic leader does is say that you've all got to perform this way, and if you can't there is something wrong with you. They have great ideas but they don't get people on side and get their consent. Whereas this person looked at people and started thinking about what kinds of opportunities might help them. (Engineering lecturer)

When this process does not work, it is seen as forcing change through without reasonable consultation, and its effects on academic work are demoralising:

The new head of department had a mission to give it an even stronger research orientation. A very bright, charming and confident person with a very good research reputation. We looked forward to working with her. But it became clear that her way of getting change was to force it on people. She would confront and threaten respected and competent people whom she had targeted because of what she saw as their low research performance. They would come to me to seek guidance. Staff felt threatened already because things were changing so much in the university. She would call their academic credentials into question publicly.

(Interviewer: What effect did it have?)

People became utterly miserable and even less productive. It affected their teaching and their interest in students as well as their research. I asked her if she was aware of it. She was quite upfront. 'I'm doing it because I want them to leave, and I want the rest to know that that's what will happen to them if they don't keep up to speed'. There were two of her – one an entertaining, pleasant and committed leader, running a tight ship as a manager and brooking no slackness – a very effective person for making change occur, fantastic. And the other – a vindictive and vicious person. She could present a public face of collaboration and cooperation, but then ignored the results of collaborative planning. Staff then just stopped being collaborative with each other and went back to doing their own thing. Some very good people, good researchers and good teachers, left the department

because they couldn't tolerate the environment any longer.
(Social science lecturer)

In the following comments, the unhappy effects of having a
vision for a course and not pursuing it by inappropriate appointments and failing to control academics' propensity to demand
complete autonomy are evident:

M. [the head of department] had a significant role in conceptualising the subject, but in terms of actually delivering
it, it was B. and I that did it. We worked on a set of
assumptions and teaching principles which M. had encouraged us to hold about the department. The course was
holistic, cumulative, and integrated theory and practice.
The rhetoric was my ideal professional course! Unfortunately, M. had all the right ideas but no idea of how to
actually go about it. The staff appointments subsequently
made were inconsistent with the ideal; many new staff had
no interest in it. It got to a point where we could see the
ideals being frittered away, where people could do what they
liked, which was unfair to students because they don't know
what to expect.

I'll never forget M. drawing his model of leadership – it was
that he would move wherever the staff in the department
wanted him to move. But that isn't right, if you want a
vision to happen. If it turns out to be wrong, you look at it
then, you at least try and do it once. As time went on more
and more was put into question, the conflicts got bigger,
the meetings got less productive and more aggressive with
people saying academic freedom meant they could teach
how they liked . . . I'm a great believer in diversity, but not
diversity for its own sake. There's got to be some kind of
shared vision about what you're trying to achieve. He was
employing people who fundamentally disagreed with the
educational model he was trying to realise. This kind of
laissez-faire model does not work if you want good teaching. It was frustrating and alienating, it sapped your motivation and it impacted negatively on the students; people did
not want to learn from each other. Being academic means
you should think critically about what you do and learn
from others, not being free to do what you like.

Leadership as leading the way

Academic staff describe certain experiences of leadership which variously inspire, energise and arouse them to teach well and pursue scholarly activities more vigorously. The essence of this category is the traditional idea of leadership as 'showing the way by going first':

> Jack, the coordinator, is extremely approachable. He has legendary status as a teacher. That's why I came here. His whole life's devoted to teaching and to improving teaching. I was inspired by Jack's reputation. I was only here for a week and I realised that this was where I wanted to stay. I'm still inspired. Like him I believe it is the best to motivate students and show them why they should be learning something, showing the relevance of it for the rest of their lives, why it should be relevant to them for every day for the rest of their lives. It's a matter of them learning something that's going to be relevant to them and it's going to be important to the patients they're looking after as well. There's no way out of learning the absolute exact anatomy of the area for some procedures. But they learn the meaning of it, rather than just going through the motions of rote learning it. (Health Sciences lecturer)

> [She has a clear vision for a better course, a better department which is focused on a different breed of students] . . . She wants people to feel they've achieved and feel committed. Everyone feels the excitement of new ideas and works that much more vigorously and it's a good department to work in. (Science lecturer)

> She still sets the standard in research despite her other admin. commitments. The fact she is world famous and was at one time tipped to be the university's best chance for a Nobel Prize means that you feel there's something to live up to. Being in the same department stimulates those of lesser talent like me to try that bit harder. (Science lecturer)

Related to these inspirational qualities are a perceived willingness to model good practice and to encourage new ways of approaching academic work, again with sense of honesty and openness, and the skills to make it work:

His first move was to accept the assignment that nobody wanted – the first year service course with around 500 students most of whom don't want to be there and don't have the background to do it properly anyway. He even asked people to come into the lectures and give him comments on his performance. I learned from just observing that you can do amazing things with impossible students. I learned it didn't matter if you risked something and it turned out wrong. (Business Studies lecturer)

She started the idea that everyone in the department should circulate early drafts of papers for comment. This was to help less experienced researchers. We spent some time in a staff meeting working out what kind of feedback. We decided it would be focused on the paper's main concepts, the ideas, what it was trying to tell people. The comments were to be only on the idea not the details at this stage. This worked well and I found I got useful feedback and it ended up that I was able to write a good collaborative paper with a senior colleague as well as one with only my name on it – two papers in six months that I wouldn't have produced at all without this system. (Arts lecturer)

A couple of times I've been in a meeting with staff and there's been a fair amount of conflict. What he does is confront the conflict. He says something like 'Well, I'm aware that there are these issues and that there is conflict here'. And then what he does is suggest ways of moving forward from the conflict, like 'These are the things I suggest we do to move forward'. So he won't just let the conflict go on. He won't let it degenerate. He enters into the process but he does it in a constructive way so that people feel supported. Then they go away and feel stimulated to solve the problem. (Social science lecturer)

It's now not only just OK, it's actually expected that people get together to talk about their teaching in this department. Before everyone sat in their rooms and you know what engineers say, teaching is one of the most private things in a university after sex. But she created a different atmosphere, an atmosphere where it was all right to admit mistakes and share problems. She invited people into her own classes. You could trust her. She understands what it is to be out at the sharp end and makes you feel she understands you. She made an environment where it was both safe and necessary to chat about students' needs, learning, how to assess, what the evaluation questionnaire results meant, what to do about it, what the rest of the university was doing about quality in teaching, etc. We meet formally now and again as a group but we also meet more informally and just talk about the students and the problems rather than bottling it up and worrying about how to get out of some more teaching next year. (Engineering lecturer)

The other side of this picture is that academic environments shaped by academic leaders are too often disempowering and disabling. The leader who is seen to model poor practice (by, for example, representing administrative convenience as having priority over educational process) may encourage minimal commitment; the department which provides no guidance or expects no dialogue about teaching may leave junior staff with a feeling that their questions are unimportant:

We'd worked feverishly for months to get [the new unit for a graduate course] up and running, burning the midnight oil, getting the thing through the committees, finding the students. The first morning, the first class, it's the starting time, I'm just going in the room and full of apprehension. My head of department stands outside and chooses this time of all times to tell me that there are some students enrolled without his permission, and what am I going to do about it, and why didn't I inform him? I'm livid with him, he's already admitted with some self-satisfaction that he's a shocking teacher in a staff meeting, and now he's trying to torpedo my class, shake my confidence and I have to go in there and tell someone they're not supposed to be there. (Social science lecturer)

The first time I became aware of academic leadership as an issue was after I'd been teaching in a university for a few years. It was a small, new faculty. I was given subject outlines and told to go away and teach. All I knew about teaching was that I didn't like the way I'd been taught. After a couple of years of flying by the seat of my pants, I felt there were questions I couldn't get answers to. My Dean would occasionally say 'Don't worry if you have a few students who don't like you, if you get a few negative student evaluations'. It was basically 'Do whatever you want, but don't expect the rest of us to do what you do, and don't expect us to answer any of your questions' . . . I eventually left when it was clear that there'd be no possibility of leadership in teaching, and no hope of being helped to learn to do it better. (Lecturer in professional subject)

Leadership as teaching

The conception of an academic leader as a person who helps her or his colleagues to learn and develop is the third category into which these experiences of academic staff may be classified. The concept is closely associated with the idea of helping people through change and providing a vision for the future. It is related, too, to the idea of effective leaders as being lifelong learners themselves. It reflects an established notion in the mainstream literature on management and leadership – that effective leaders act as educators who help others to learn, and provide institutional as well as personal support for people to develop their skills. By these means credible leaders 'turn followers into leaders' (Kouzes and Posner, 1993, p. 156). And according to Drucker:

> Whether [the manager] develops his subordinates in the right direction, helps them to grow and become bigger and richer persons, will directly determine whether he himself will develop, will grow or wither, become richer or become impoverished, improve or deteriorate . . .. The function which distinguishes the manager above all others is his *educational* one.
>
> (Drucker, 1955, pp. 415–18)

This is, of course, an even more significant idea in the context of the university as an organisation devoted to learning through research, scholarship and teaching. Again the comments of academic staff indicate that the practice of leadership as teaching can influence their productivity for better or for worse. And once again we can see that the exercise of leadership is not confined to people in formal positions:

> I remember the first year of my teaching here as being the most formative of my academic career. I started to see wider connections between my teaching processes and my content; it was a whole new dimension. This was entirely because of an outstanding senior colleague who listened to my ideas and prevented me from reinventing the wheel. I'd

100

always thought that an interactive process was important, but I couldn't see why – now because of her guidance I can see that as a teacher I am trying to help students change the way they see things by having a different frame of reference. I can see now that teaching is a conversation, not a one-way communication. My interest in communication in political institutions is reflected in my classroom teaching . . . It was a form of apprenticeship. She sensitised me to differences in the student body, and the need to draw on a range of different strategies to suit different students . . . she showed all this reading to me; I watched how she taught; it took a long time; I remember specific conversations such as the one about assessment, where she explained the difference between assessment to help students learn and assessment for certification in relation to a particular assessment task I was planning. (Lecturer in a professional subject)

Probably the worst experience I've had of leadership is where a deputy head actually folded his hands across his shirt, stuck his feet out in front, looked at me and said, 'Do you really think you're an academic?' This actually happened in an official capacity. I find that sort of belligerent adversarial approach entirely inappropriate for his role. Completely demonstrating in my view a lack of understanding of how to manage people in general and women in particular . . . I asked for some feedback, but he said I couldn't have it. There's this idea that academic staff should automatically know what to do and what's good without getting appropriate comments. (Arts lecturer)

I am someone who has had a mentor in my academic life, never anything explicit but someone for me has been a role model. He taught me about resource-based learning and also a way of managing committees which is very thorough. He was good at giving you something you just couldn't *quite* do, but you could if you kept at it. He put opportunities my way like . . . , which involved managing budgets, and thinking about tendering processes, which I wasn't very good at, and had had no contact with, and going to meetings I wasn't confident at. There have been three people here who could chart their career in relation to that single mentor. It isn't just self-sacrificing, it's productive for the mentor as well, it's working as a team. If I'd had something like him in my research career, who could model good practice and had helped create opportunities for me just a little bit ahead of what I was doing, I'd have done a lot better. (Arts lecturer)

I am on the lowest rung in this department and don't have my PhD yet but I work with probably the most productive group in terms of scientific endeavour. I was called in by the head and he said it had come to his attention that I was doing research supervision of a couple of Masters students. To cut a long story short he said I could not continue doing it, even though it was within the university's guidelines. He said that a staff meeting had agreed to it, but I checked and this wasn't the case. I was then faced with having to tell two masters students I couldn't keep supervising them. None of the other staff had a particular interest in the area, so it was difficult to find a replacement. I was very upset after the meeting because I knew I was good at the work and enjoyed getting the experience and responsibility and here I was being rapped over the knuckles. It underscored for me what my position was in the department. I was being made little again. He said it was to protect the students and ensure them the best possible supervision. But I would never have taken on the task if I hadn't felt I had what it takes to do it. Contrasted with this is . . . , who takes a more respectful, non-rule-bound and collegial approach. For example, I recently did a presentation of some research results, in a particularly difficult area, and was quite angry that some people had been highly critical and insensitive in their comments in the seminar. He contacted me and we talked about it; I really felt he cared about the problem and about me. I trust him. He is very knowledgeable and a brilliant conceptualiser and is consultative as well; a good teacher and colleague who encourages you to go on your way, explore, and learn to be a fully competent academic. (Science tutor)

If the head grabs everything, and takes it away from you, you don't learn anything and can't go on to perform so well as an academic. On the other hand if they leave it all to you, then when you make mistakes, if you get no direction on how to avoid them, you perform less well for that reason. It's a balance between autonomy and support. In the early days of the new programme here, my role was curriculum development. He gave me complete autonomy, but was always there to guide. I'd come up with the 'perfect' course structure. He'd sort of say, 'Yes, but what if . . . isn't that going to create a problem?' And I would go back and re-work it. There was always support there but also total free-dom. (Science lecturer)

I applied three times for promotion and was never success-ful. So I went to my head of department and said, 'What's going on here?', and all he said to me was, 'Keep doing what you're doing, I value you. I think your work is good'. But in fact that was incorrect. The work I was doing was not being valued. I was doing a lot of work in developing continuing education projects in areas where there was a perceived market demand. The courses were extremely popular and generating a high level of income for the department. But the system at the time was that those courses were in addition to teaching load, so I was teaching about twenty hours a week in those programmes in addition to my normal teaching. In fact the continuing education programs were not valued at all. And if he had of said to me when I first came, 'Laura, I want you to attract research money', I would have done that. I work hard and all I wanted was direction. There was a huge inconsistency in the advice. So the con-sequences of that leadership were that I lost my motivation, I was extremely unhappy, very disappointed in that person, and very angry towards the organisation . . . While this is my own story I'm afraid that I'm not alone. The conse-quences of inconsistent advice and secretiveness about per-formance have been low morale, and fanatical competitiveness between staff. The department is successful from an external point of view because they're attracting a lot of big research grants, but it's at a cost. (Health sciences lecturer)

As a junior staff member, I used to avoid the head of department, run away from the guy. Because I didn't have the knowledge base that he had, and I always felt that he expected me to have it. It was abysmal leadership, because what it did was to make me feel incompetent. My produc-tivity as a researcher went down. I can't give you an answer as to what the problem was, but he would not acknowledge any new development which would take us forward, so our organisation became backward in the way it was doing things, and other groups were moving farther ahead of us. That failure to identify change, and the benefits of change was part of it. And a total inability to deal with individuals, an ability to be able to relate to people when needed. That's something managers have got to have . . . What he developed was an environment of inadequacy. Except for a couple of individuals who had a very extroverted nature, who could challenge him at his own level. A whole group of people who felt totally inadequate, who felt that it didn't matter what they said, it wouldn't be acknowledged, nothing would happen. Frustration breeds inertia, which is very hard to overcome. I was actually branded as being a non-performer . . . I went from that type of environment to here, working with the chap I was referring to, where everyone's in control because the boss is in control. The boss makes it very clear what direction we want to move in. And that was the feature about the other guy. There was no direction set for the department. Peter puts people in control and improves their performance by giving them the confidence that he's expecting them to do every academic task well. You asked me whether leadership matters to academics and affects their work. I think you can see why I think it does. (Engineering lecturer)

Conclusions

From the perspective of academic staff, leadership is a complicated business. It presents itself as a series of forces ranged in different directions, a balancing act where equilibrium is fugitive and temporary. There seems to be no ideal model to be captured and rendered down into a series of competencies and skills that we could set as objectives for aspiring leaders. But equally, there can be no doubt that academic people can distinguish good leadership from bad, and that the process of leadership influences the outcomes of their work. At its best, academic leadership can inspire lecturers to achieve more than they ever thought they could.

As we saw in several accounts by academics of how the departmental context influenced their behaviour and outlook, a determining factor in successful university leadership is the way in which the leader responds to and negotiates the imperatives of the academic culture. This culture is one aspect of the first factor in our original model of academic leadership. Handled in some ways by leaders, academics are telling us, it prevents change and disempowers staff, rather than enabling them to work well. Proficient academic leadership is an active process which must sometimes confront the negative aspects of academic culture. Only in this way can it forge

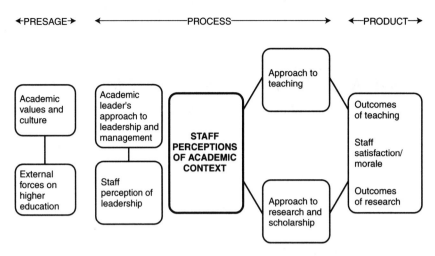

Figure 5.2 Perceptions of the context of academic work in relation to presage, process and product

a departmental environment that contributes to good academic work and an orientation to development through cooperation, support, vision and inspiration. Figure 5.2 redraws the model originally presented in chapter 1 to emphasise the centrality of staff perceptions of academic leadership in the process of transforming presage into product.

Is there something special about leadership for academic work which distinguishes it from leadership in organisations other than universities? To complete the picture of effective leadership and supportive contexts for academic work, we need to address the question of whether proficient academic leadership is really any different from expert leadership in other types of organisations.

6

LEADERSHIP AND ACADEMIC LEADERSHIP

> Reason and calm judgement, the qualities specially belonging to a leader.
>
> Tacitus

The special character of academic leadership

The last two chapters have shown how research evidence and the voices of lecturers combine to provide a representation of the kind of academic environment that facilitates academic work. The predominant theme has been the idea that academic work gets done better when the leadership is enabling, coherent, honest, firm, and competent; when it is combined with the efficient management of people and resources; and when it blends a positive vision for future change with a focus on developing staff – a focus on helping them to learn. I showed that there was a powerful similarity between the views of academic leaders and academic followers about what a good academic leader does. Effective leaders in universities do not conform to the stereotype of being functionaries whose main role is to react to academic demands.

A striking thing about this material is the resemblance between competent academic leadership and good university teaching. There is an analogy between what research into university students' learning says about the effect of the context of learning on approaches to *learning* and the effects of the academic environment on approaches to *teaching and scholarship*. Good teaching is responsive, but it is also proactive. It combines clear goals, intellectual challenge, imaginative explanations, concern for students, appropriate assessment, reflective evaluation, and student independence to create a context that encourages effective learning. Just as good teaching can encourage active engagement with academic content, so good leadership can encourage staff to give their best to their students and their subjects. Good leadership helps create an environment for academics to learn continually, to make the best use of their knowledge, to solve problems in research and teaching collaboratively as well as individually,

106

and to feel inspired to overcome the obstacles presented by change and upheaval in university life.

I explained in chapter 2 that the presage factors of academic leadership comprise both external and internal aspects. An increasingly unstable and demanding external environment for higher education, a decline in the status of academic work, and an academic culture which emphasises collective decision-making and autonomy combine to present a potent set of dilemmas for academic leadership. When we add to this blend the similarities between leading academics and teaching university students, it is easy to understand the appeal of the idea that academic leadership is quite different from leadership in other organisations.

Many readers will be aware that, as commercial organisations strive for success in today's internationally competitive markets, leadership has become a topic of surpassing interest in the world of business and industry. Leadership development is big business. Several thousand books, articles, manuals and training videos have been published on the subject of leadership in the last ten years. What kinds of leadership are typical of successful organisations – organisations which provide higher quality products for their customers, and more satisfying work climates for their employees? Is any of this knowledge relevant to learning to lead in universities? Is the academic culture unique, and therefore in need of an entirely original model? The purpose of this chapter is to explore the differences and similarities in the context of some recent ideas on leadership; to determine whether there are any useful principles that are common to both universities and other organisations; and to draw some conclusions from this analysis about implications for learning to lead in universities.

Leadership or management?

So far in the book I have used 'leadership' as shorthand for 'leadership and management'. I have assumed that 'leaders' are also 'managers'. One principal recent contribution to mainstream thinking in the field of leadership uses the distinction between leadership and management as its central structuring principle (Kotter, 1990). But in other respects John Kotter's work conceptualises leadership in exactly the same way as I have in this book. It is a process of directing and mobilising people, rather than as a description of the group of individuals occupying formal positions in a company.

Kotter's ideas are important because they help us see beyond the clumsy notion that leadership is a difficult and noble art while management is a simplistic, unnecessary and bureaucratic process that damages academic endeavour. Things are more complicated than that. He points out that 'management' is a fairly recent idea; it is a response to the need to handle large and complex enterprises in a way that brings consistency and conformity to the delivery of products and services. It is a way of imposing regulation on the incipient chaos of the large firm and its multiple suppliers and customers. It is a way of keeping companies on time and on budget. It is the essence of rationality. Managers plan, organise, staff, and solve problems. Management is about 'doing things right'. The concept owes much to the insights of Frederick W. Taylor, who was one of the first people to study human work systematically, and to separate the activity of planning work from doing work.

In contrast to management, leadership in Kotter's model is about movement and change. Leaders produce change; effective leaders produce 'constructive or adaptive' change to help people and firms survive and grow. They establish direction, align people, and motivate them. Leadership is about 'doing the right thing'. Leadership foresees and enables, enabling people to adapt to change rather than to resist it. This is precisely what Taylor's 'scientific management' signally failed to do. In Taylor's concept, workers were meant to do, not to know or to plan or to learn; their natural resistance to change was amplified by a system which actively encouraged people to focus on components of a job rather than the whole job (Drucker, 1955, p. 341). Lurking in the shadows of many academic complaints about 'managerialism' is the ghost of Taylor, whose ideas nourished the ideology that a management elite should think, know, and plan while the workers should get on with doing the job. We hear occasional echoes of the opinion that thinking should be divorced from doing in some senior university managers' assertions of their 'right to manage'.

A central idea in Kotter's work is that the two systems – management and leadership – are complementary and equally necessary to a work unit or organisation's success. Excessive management produces compliance, passivity, and order for order's sake; it discourages risk-taking and stifles creativity and long-term vision. But excessive leadership without the compensating force of strong management produces inconsistent, delayed and off-budget results, while emphasising change for change's sake. Confusion and cults reign. In this case the whole organisation is threatened with destruction as deadlines, budgets and promises fail to be delivered.

According to Kotter, in most organisations today the balance is too far towards management; leadership is not sufficiently well-developed. At a time of significant change in the external environment, resolute leadership is essential to help people adapt and to ensure survival. But substituting leadership for management is not a sensible solution; both systems are needed. Kotter's examination of how a combination of capable leadership and resourceful management is associated with more productive, happier work environments is compelling.

We can readily see how valuable Kotter's ideas are to understanding leadership in today's academic environments, and with a little imagination can think of instances in our own experience where leadership and management have both been weak, or where one has dominated the other. Strong leadership without strong management is a characteristic and disruptive failing of innovative courses in traditional academic contexts, for example. Weaknesses in both systems have characterised several departments, in my experience, in which the head has assumed that academics can 'manage themselves'. Evidently, strong management without strong leadership contributes to the sense of disempowerment and irritation, and the corresponding culture of compliance and minimal desire to change, which has accompanied numerous attempts to introduce accountability measures and performance management systems in universities and higher education systems.

Correlating the views of academics presented in the previous chapter with the idea of these reciprocal systems also illustrates the desirability of an emphasis on both management and leadership. It corroborates the general applicability of Kotter's deceptively simple model. Clearly, people in universities believe that firm, fair and efficient management which gets things done effectively is different from inspirational leadership, but equally desirable. They undoubtedly do not think that all management is a conspiracy to cripple academic freedom. In universities, as in other organisations, systematic processes which produce orderly results are required to balance the imaginative ideas that produce change. These processes do not necessarily have to be informed by a Taylorist view of the separation of planning from doing. There are analogies with scholarly activity and with the process of teaching and learning itself: in universities, as Whitehead once more so succinctly put it, 'Imagination is not to be divorced from the facts; it is a way of illuminating the facts' (Whitehead, 1932, p. 139).

At the same time, the academic culture presents both problems and opportunities in implementing Kotter's four strategies of creating an agenda, developing a human network for achieving this agenda, carrying out the plan, and achieving desired outcomes. It is perhaps helpful to re-visit some of the aspects of academic values and beliefs which we described in terms of contrasting management and academic cultures in chapter 2, but this time using Kotter's

	Managers	**Leaders**
Create an agenda	plan and budget	set direction
Develop a human network	organise and staff	align people and groups
Execute the agenda	control and solve problems	motivate and inspire
	↓	↓
Impact	*create order*	*produce change*

Figure 6.1 Comparing the tasks of management and leadership
Source: Derived from Kotter (1990) p. 139

model. His matrix (Figure 6.1) tabulates the four essential organisational processes described above against the functions of management and leadership. Academic culture presents many opportunities for misunderstanding and conflict between leaders and academics. Tables 6.1 and 6.2 compare the Kotter matrix with the darker side of academic culture and the lighter side respectively, emphasising both the difficulty and the facility with which these ideas can be applied in an academic environment.[1]

Transformational leadership and leadership credibility

The idea of leadership as transformation and the leader as an agent of change is as old as time. When there is a strong need for direction, as in times of crisis, the emotional appeal and power of leadership which is based on charisma or a 'godlike gift' is well known (Weber, 1946; Hollander and Offerman, 1993). James Burns (1978) developed the idea of *transformational leadership* as a moral process whereby both followers and leaders were raised to higher levels of motivation and virtue. Such leadership, he said, ought to

1 For the conceptualisation of academic culture in terms of light and shadow, I am indebted to Alf Lizzio.

be distinguished from the older, Hobbesian view of leadership as an exchange based on rewards and driven through followers' self-interest. The quasi-religious, moralistic tone of the 'new leadership' represented by Burns's model imbues many of the recent texts on the subject.

Burns made a distinction between transformational leadership and transactional leadership which reflects the management–leadership difference described above. Unlike Kotter, however, he saw these two processes as opposite ends of the same continuum. Subsequently, Bass (1985) revised Burns's concept to recognise the fact that transactional strategies such as rewards for good performance were not incompatible with inspiration, emotional arousal, personal consideration for followers, and intellectual stimulation. Bass developed a questionnaire to measure these qualities of transactional and transformational leadership, and later authors such as Sashkin and Rosenbach (1993), and Kouzes and Posner (1995), extended the idea to identify types of leadership behaviour and attitudes from studies of exceptional leaders. Kouzes and Posner's list of five types of behaviour, below, has been particularly influential.

FIVE PRACTICES OF SUCCESSFUL LEADERS

1 Challenge the process
'Experiment and take risks; learn from making mistakes'

2 Inspire a shared vision
'Vision is the force that invents the future'

3 Enable others to act
'Effective leaders turn followers into leaders'

4 Model the way
'Lead by example. Live your values'

5 Encourage the heart
'Celebrate achievement'

Source: Adapted from Kouzes and Posner (1995)

Table 6.1 How academic culture makes managing and leading harder

Kotter's task areas	Management	Leadership
Create an agenda	Planning and budgeting requires detailed steps, timetables, resource allocation	Establishing direction requires a vision of the distant future and strategies for producing the changes needed to achieve the vision
	BUT academics are suspicious of formal planning, distrustful of management, and often inexperienced as administrators	BUT academics tend to be orientated to the past, and their culture is often fragmented (highly discipline-based) in its world view
Develop a human network	Organising and staffing requires establishing a structure for achieving plans, delegating responsibility, developing procedures to guide people, monitoring implementation	Aligning people requires communication of direction and developing teams that accept the validity of the vision
	BUT academics value self-determination of priorities and individual expertise, believe in academic freedom, and resist external accountability	BUT academics are 'cosmopolitans' with low commitment to corporate goals. They value individuality and are trained to question and criticise joint agendas, not accept them
Execute the agenda	Controlling and problem solving requires monitoring results against the plans, identifying deviations, and reducing the deviations	Motivating and inspiring requires energising people to overcome barriers to change by satisfying basic human needs
	BUT academics typically find quality processes intellectually uninspiring, distracting, trivial and routine	BUT academics inhabit a relatively protected environment, have low responsiveness to innovation, and are suspicious of enthusiasm
Impact	Strong management produces order, consistency, and predictability; key results expected by stakeholders are delivered	Strong leadership produces change, often useful change to enable the organisation to create new markets and be more competitive
	BUT academics believe that they produce consistently high quality results by virtue of their expertise and long training, without the need for 'being managed', or consulting stakeholders	BUT academics value tradition, are sceptical of change, and dubious about the need to adapt to different external environments

Table 6.2 How academic culture makes managing and leading easier

Kotter's task areas	Management	Leadership
Create an agenda	Planning and budgeting requires detailed steps, timetables, resource allocation	Establishing direction requires a vision of the (distant) future and strategies for producing the changes needed to achieve the vision
	AND academics are skilled at planning their own work and meeting deadlines	AND academics are highly trained thinkers, used to imaginative, long-term planning
Develop a human network	Organising and staffing requires establishing a structure for achieving plans, delegating responsibility, developing procedures to guide people, monitoring implementation	Aligning people requires communication of direction and developing teams that accept the validity of the vision
	AND academics value self-determination of priorities and individual expertise, and have the skills of independent learning which enable them to create effective processes	AND academics have high intellectual curiosity; they can constructively criticise unworkable procedures, they enjoy working in collaborative modes, and they can actively find better ways by searching among their colleagues in other institutions
Execute the agenda	Controlling and problem solving requires monitoring results against the plans, identifying deviations, and reducing the deviations	Motivating and inspiring requires energising people to overcome barriers to change by satisfying basic human needs
	AND academics enjoy the intellectual challenge of linking theory to practice and are often skilled at project implementation and monitoring effectiveness	AND academics are typically intrinsically motivated, enthusiastic about their subjects, committed to new ways of understanding the familiar, and enjoy communicating their ideas to others
Impact	Strong management produces order, consistency, and predictability; key results expected by stakeholders are delivered	Strong leadership produces change, often useful change to enable the organisation to create new markets and be more competitive
	AND academics are self-regulating, believing that consistently good results are essential but that over-management and control by stakeholders or others may diminish rather than enhance quality	AND academics can interpret the future in the context of enduring qualities; they are lifelong learners who can take change in their stride; as public intellectuals, they can scrutinise the underlying values and the practicability of political decisions

The same authors subsequently developed the associated idea of leadership *credibility*, a concept which seems particularly important in lecturers' experiences of effective academic leadership (see chapter 5). Credible leaders are honest, forward-looking, inspiring, and (academically) competent. People must be able to believe in their leaders; must assume that when they say something, they can be trusted to do it; must agree they are personally enthusiastic about the direction in which the group is going; and must feel that the individual at the helm is capable of taking them in that direction. You will remember that there was a positive association between the leadership qualities measured by the *Leadership for Academic Work* questionnaire and academics' satisfaction with the leadership they experienced (see p. 92). Kouzes and Posner studied the correlation between followers' perceptions of their immediate managers' credibility and their attitudes to the organisation. They found that perceptions of credibility were linked to being proud to tell others they were part of the organisation, having a strong sense of team spirit, being committed, and having a sense of ownership of the organisation. Lower credibility was associated with saying good things about the organisation publicly, but criticising it privately, and feeling unappreciated and unsupported (Kouzes and Posner, 1995, pp. 26–7).

The idea of transformational leadership and its associated behaviours is of course generally reflected in the results presented in the previous two chapters. The work of Leithwood (1992) supports the idea that transformational educational leaders pursue three fundamental goals: they help people develop and maintain a collaborative, professional culture; they foster staff development; and they help their people to solve problems together more effectively. The strategies they use include actively communicating educational values and beliefs, involving staff in cooperative planning, celebrating joint achievements, and using management mechanisms such as staff selection to support cultural changes. It would seem that effective transformational leaders in educational contexts are good managers as well as inspirational guides. Like good teaching, in which both clear objectives and independence are important for good learning, good educational leadership requires directive strategies as well as enabling ones.

The goals and strategies informing transformational leadership are implied in academic staff perceptions of effective heads and other academic leaders. For example, the items in the *Leadership for Academic Work* questionnaire related to transformational leadership are:

- Motivates people to do more than they ever thought they could
- Works to create a shared vision of the future direction of the work unit
- Enables you to think about old problems in new ways
- Gets people moving collaboratively towards a common purpose
- Talks about change in a positive way

A similar scale was used in the study of leadership of teaching teams reported in chapter 4. Clearly these items make sense to academic staff and, where such activities are practised by an academic leader, their colleagues feel they have a positive impact on the quality of academic work and on staff morale. The practices represented by these statements were also evident in the survey and interview comments of both academic leaders and followers concerning effective leadership.

Transformational leadership provides encouragement for followers to try and improve their way of working. Since its authority rests on the exercise of consensual rather than top-down power, it would seem to be of critical importance in helping academic staff to welcome and take control of new challenges such as increased accountability and different kinds of students. Vision and energy sustain hope in times of transition (Kouzes and Posner, 1995, p. 26). Transformational leadership, moreover, is about sharing leadership. The management literature is clear on the point that shared leadership leads to more productive organisations. It is not only in universities that collaborative forces operate to maximise activity and morale; in this sense, academic leadership is not at all a special case.

The idea is, however, also in harmony with basic processes of scholarship. Although there are discipline-specific variations, there is a sense in which discovering, integrating and applying knowledge can be seen as *transforming* existing ideas about the world. Higher education is also about helping to change students' understanding of the world around them; it is about transforming and empowering students through enhancing their knowledge and skills (Harvey, 1995b; Ramsden, 1988).

Students follow teachers they can believe in, who are personally delighted by the subject they profess, and who keep their promises; academics follow academic leaders who are personally enthusiastic about the route they are travelling and who do what they say they'll do. The idea of transformational leadership, then, together with the closely-associated idea of credibility, is another concept from the mainstream literature on leadership which appears to be useful in helping us to learn how to lead academic staff.

'Followership'

The concept of transformational leadership underlines the idea we have repeatedly encountered that leadership is a shared enterprise dependent on a relationship between followers and leaders. There is no such thing as one-person leadership; without followers, a leader is useless. Leadership and followership are inextricably linked.

There are several critical points in the concept of followership that are relevant to developing academic leadership. The first is the recognition that academic leadership, like other forms of leadership, does not have to be conceptualised primarily in terms of control and power over others. On the contrary, its effectiveness depends on developing and enabling colleagues to contribute to the goals of the department and the university. Leaders and followers are partners in the same firm.

But two warnings are necessary. First, academic leaders and their staff are not entirely equal partners. We are not talking about the older, reactive model of the department head as a reluctant administrator who does not exercise leadership or practise management. Rather we need to recognise that nothing useful can be achieved in these endeavours without the commitment, expertise and loyalty of staff. While these qualities are encouraged through collaboration, not 'managerial' imposition, collaboration should be tempered by forward vision and a readiness to endure dislike. Like good teaching, good academic leadership is not a popularity contest. Liking and helping people are not sufficient qualifications; sometimes not getting along with people is necessary not only to command respect but also to get things done as a manager (Drucker, 1955, p. 416). This is a theme I will explore in subsequent chapters.

A related warning is that leadership and followership are not identical. Kouzes and Posner (1995) asked senior managers to specify qualities of ideal leaders and ideal followers. The former were described as honest, competent, *forward-looking and inspiring*; the latter were described as honest, competent, *dependent and cooperative*. Sometimes we have to make a choice between being a follower and being a leader; academics often find it hard to choose to play the cooperative follower role. But few effective leaders are not effective followers as well. As far as my own experience is concerned, it was only when I accepted that universities operated on exactly the same principles as other organisations in terms of leader and follower expectations that I felt I began to have any real influence on my seniors, or to feel that I was getting on top of the job of being an academic head. The two aspects of my own development proceeded hand in hand, just as leadership and followership are two qualities that cannot be understood except in relation to each other.

Finally, we should not forget Kotter's distinction between leadership as a process and leadership and a description of the group who occupy the top jobs. Leaders are not inevitably in formal 'leadership' positions, either in universities or in other organisations. Everyone needs to be a leader to help a company succeed in a stormy environment. A far-sighted organisation will try to turn all its people into leaders. Levi-Strauss & Co., for example, recognise the need to create a work environment in which staff can develop their own goals and develop shared responsibility by providing leadership training for all their 31,000 employees. As the Australian study of recognising and rewarding good teaching in higher education (see chapter 4), showed, leadership for good teaching needs to be exercised at every level of the university. A junior lecturer can inspire and motivate his or her colleagues to try new ideas in teaching and assessment, and lobby the head to provide resources to support them and the skills development needed to make them work. A vice chancellor can put the quality of teaching at the top of her or his list of priorities for the university, and through personal demonstrations of that commitment can energise staff to pursue the vision. Educational leadership is an organisational quality as well as an individual one.

The learning organisation

> We say school is about learning, but by and large schooling has traditionally been about people memorizing a lot of stuff that they don't really care too much about . . . deep learning is a process that is inevitably driven by the learner, not by someone else. And it always involves moving back and forth between a domain of thinking and a domain of action . . . the principals I know who have had the greatest impact [on changing this situation] tend to see their job as creating an environment where teachers can continually learn.
>
> Peter Senge, quoted in O'Neil (1995, p. 20)

The key point here is the understanding that learning by *academic staff* is fundamental to achieving successful educational environments. Effective academic departments increase the power of their staff through providing them with opportunities to lead, develop skills, and have their achievement, their learning, and their responsibility recognised.

Universities that encourage and reward learning and development in their component academic units resemble 'learning organisations'. Peter Senge popularised the concept in *The Fifth Discipline* (Senge, 1990) and it has become a primary theme of modern management literature. In Senge's terminology, a learning organisation is an organisation where people at all levels work collectively to enhance their capacity to create things they want to create. We are certainly not as good at this as we should be in higher education. Two of the behaviours in the *Leadership for Academic Work* survey questionnaire that respondents were least likely to say their leaders displayed were 'Actively works to develop others as leaders' and 'Encourages people to regard mistakes as opportunities for learning'. In a learning organisation, failure signals an opportunity for learning, for understanding the gap between vision and reality, between theory and practice. It isn't about inferiority or impotence.

For academic leaders the concept is significant because, as Senge's comment above makes clear, it brings into sharp focus the theory that effective educational leadership is comparable to (and indeed requires) us to apply the principles of good teaching. Good teaching makes a certain sort of learning possible for students – the kind of learning which relates the theoretical and the practical, existing knowledge with new knowledge, personal experience and the key concepts of a discipline. Most of us in universities would regard this as the best kind of learning for our students (Ramsden, 1992, chapter 3). Effective leadership makes such creative learning possible for academics. There is also an important link with the research process, especially in the idea of failure as signifying an opportunity for learning and the idea of a fruitful tension between current reality and future vision. Effective academic leadership, seen through the prism of the learning organisation concept, also comprises characteristics of scholarly research.

As we have observed, people who work in academic environments favour a climate where staff development and learning is supported and recognised by academic leaders. 'Leadership as teaching' was a recurrent theme of the interviews in which staff were asked to describe their experiences of how the environment created by academic leaders had influenced their work. This learning environment is not created simply by developing individual skills through activities such as teaching workshops and conferences, but by daily attention to the collective and individual responsibility to learn and improve.

The view of leadership as a phenomenon distributed through an organisation, rather than being concentrated among an executive group, is also important in Senge's view of the learning organisation. 'Local line leadership' consists for Senge of 'individuals with significant business responsibility and 'bottom-line' focus. They head organizational units that are microcosms of the larger organization, and yet have enough autonomy to be able to undertake meaningful change independent of the larger organization' – a fair description of many university departmental heads. 'Executive leaders' – something like pro vice chancellors – support and serve line leaders, championing their improvement projects. 'Internal networkers' have no positional authority, but can be effective for precisely the reason that they have none. Their effectiveness comes from the strength of their convictions and the clarity of their ideas for change and development. There are evidently many staff in universities who can, or could, fulfil this role as facilitators and networkers, who carry out local experiments in better teaching or more effective research processes and then help staff in different departments to share ideas.

Two other axioms in the concept of the learning organisation are important for academic leadership: the notion that organisational and individual learning are linked; and the premise that leadership in learning organisations focuses on building shared visions, challenging existing assumptions, and linking intrinsic goals such as setting one's own standards of quality with extrinsic ones such as finding new student markets. This idea is also compatible with what we know about effective academic leadership and environments for productive academic work. It stresses the role of the leader as an agent who designs systematic processes whereby staff can reflect on what they are doing, and work collaboratively to solve educational problems.

These characteristics once again illustrate the common features of effective leadership and work climates in universities and in other organisations. It is not only in universities that perceptions of excessive managerial control and top-down decision-making, lack of intellectual challenge, imposed quality assurance procedures, and aggressive administrative tactics that stifle the desire to learn, are disempowering to staff. If the contemporary literature is right, most such efforts are misconceived and are likely to imperil an organisation's survival – any organisation's survival – through encouraging a compliance mentality and inhibiting the entrepreneurial and innovative inclinations of its staff. There is reason to believe that, in an increasingly competitive external environment, universities which fail to recognise the danger will be similarly threatened. Our proclivity to think we are more special than we really are is at least as dangerous as the belief that there are no differences between academic organisations and business ones.

The special character of academic leadership revisited

I have looked at a tiny proportion of mainstream contemporary thinking on leadership and management, and have chosen to high-light some key ideas which, because they accentuate the similarities between academic institutions and other organisations, may enable us to see the differences more clearly.

As far as desirable leadership qualities are concerned, the con-clusion from the evidence presented here and in the last chapter must be that the correspondence between higher education's needs and needs elsewhere is remarkable. What academics want from leaders is an academically-inclined version of what people in most organisations want, and what they would like their heads of depart-ments to do is close to what school teachers would like principals to do. The qualities identified in the leadership literature as effective ones are applicable to leadership in the university. Table 6.3 com-bines and summarises a selection of these matching qualities from the literature and surveys to which I have referred in this and previous chapters.

Most aspects of leadership expertise can ultimately be derived from one simple and quite unoriginal principle. *Leadership's unique function is to bring out the best in people and to orientate them towards the future.* The effective academic leader provides clear goals and seizes new opportunities; manages both people and resources in an orderly and efficient way; motivates and inspires staff to perform; educates and develops her people; and continually listens to staff in order to learn how to improve her own performance. She does these things with integrity, energy, drive and spirit; for without these things, she will never be followed. Deep down we know that not all academic staff are excellent teachers or researchers; most of us are average. Anyone can help brilliant students and brilliant staff to perform superbly. But only an outstanding teacher or leader can help average people do excellent things. It might be said that the art of leadership is to transform the ordinary into the extraordinary.

The skills of academic leadership consist in those qualities which encourage one's colleagues to strive towards common goals and confront change with enthusiasm. The future for higher education, in so far as anyone can predict it, is one of diversity, growth, responsiveness, and external accountability. The ideas of transfor-mational leadership and the learning organisation speak directly to us in framing a solution to the difficult problem of managing these changes in a way that maintains independence, encourages hope,

Table 6.3 Similarities between effective leadership in universities and other organisations

Kouzes and Posner (1995)	*Kotter (1990)*	*High school teachers' views (Louis, 1993; Donaldson, 1991)*	*Australian, UK, Singapore, Hong Kong university staff views (my surveys, 1996)*
Honesty and integrity	Credibility, trust, commitment	Sincere focus on educational values	Tolerance, genuineness, consistency, academic integrity
Knowledge, competence	Efficiency, good management, clarity	Knowledge, persistent emphasis on activities central to learning, good management	Clear conception of the discipline, integrating ideas, efficient and fair management
Forward-looking vision, challenging the process	Vision, risk taking, challenging conventional wisdoms	Bringing in new ideas	Pushing forward frontiers, scanning the environment, networking, strategic alignment, vision, academic leadership as seizing opportunities
Enabling others to act, encouraging the heart	Focus on recognition & feedback, focus on people's self-esteem, devolved leadership	Delegation, empowerment of teachers, staff as partners not instruments	Freeing people up to achieve, respect for autonomy, development and recognition of achievement
Inspiration, enthusiasm and excitement	Motivating and inspiring	Inspiring emphasis on caring about students	Encouraging, motivating, challenging, inspiration, hope, academic leadership as leading the way
Modelling	Role modelling and coaching	Participation and time on details, fostering continuous self-evaluation	Academic leadership as teaching
Knowing your followers, listening, communicating	Communicating, aligning, teamwork	Collaborative decision-making, teamwork, sense of community	Being a good listener, consulting, combining ideas, teamwork

and enriches the working lives of staff in the university of the future.

Thinking in the wider field of leadership is moving towards a view of leadership and organisational development that resembles Scott's third stage of mass higher education, or McNay's model D (see chapter 2). However, some universities still seem to be focused on earlier models, in which combinations of assertive management and rationalised administrative processes are used to help control an increasingly complex system. In Kotter's terms, universities and their leaders have discovered that without strong management, they cannot deliver on time and on budget. Good; but what we may not have fully realised is the complementary need for strong but supportive leadership. Leadership isn't better than management; but management cannot replace it. Ideally, such leadership is not of the kind which imposes a personal vision for the future on a university, and which safeguards compliance by maintaining a constant state of crisis. It is one which invites a shared commitment to a desired future which staff may enter into of their own free will. This is as true at the level of the academic department as at the level of the institution.

Academic people in particular understand change. The process of discovering and reinterpreting knowledge is itself an uncertain process of restless variation with which all academics are familiar. Few academics are unsympathetic towards innovations that benefit their work and are likely to ensure its survival and growth; it is how the process of introducing such changes is managed and led that is the essential leadership challenge. Much of the scepticism, mistrust and cynicism of academics towards change in universities can be traced to leaders underestimating resistance and not attending to the need for gaining shared consent within a culture that so values autonomy and cooperative decision-making. Addressing these problems must be a central focus of the curriculum of our programme of learning to lead.

Academic leadership learning

There's a question mark over how distinctive academic leadership is from other forms of leadership. You have to have appropriate academic credentials and particular kinds of intellectual training if people are going to place reliance on your judgement where it bears upon academic matters. There are issues of content that are important and specific to managing intellectual resources. But as much as we should recognise that there are issues distinctive to universities, we should also recognise that the overlap between the forms of leadership and management that are called for in universities and other organisations is increasing. The task for training university leaders and managers of the future is to produce people who are adept at operating in that zone of overlap. That means having to unlearn a good deal, having to forget the earlier kinds of management and leadership associated with the professorial figure. Where you've got that kind of leadership, universities are ossified.

A senior academic in an Australian university

As universities have become more open to the environments in which they operate, the skills needed for leaders in a university have changed. The answer to the question posed at the beginning of this chapter about the differences between leading academics and leading staff in other organisations can be expressed in the form of a paradox. Academic leadership is both identical to leadership in other organisations, and idiosyncratic to university environments. It has some special characteristics, chiefly related to the values and beliefs espoused by academics, and to the nature of 'academic business', which is essentially concerned with transformation of people and ideas. However, it can be understood within the framework of broader ideas about management and leadership – especially the contemporary thinking on these subjects. In this sense it is not fundamentally different. To see it like this may help to overcome some of the problems that universities now face in the management of academics, as well as providing a framework to which we can refer in developing our own leadership.

Mapping the territory

The association between individual learning, organisational climate, and leadership effectiveness which is particularly clear in the concepts of transformational leadership and the learning organisation now provides an indication of the extent of the territory of academic leadership development. Relating these ideas to the demonstrated importance of a collaborative academic environment for more productive academic work (chapters 4 and 5) provides some maps of the country we are traversing.

One map can be drawn which shows the country as having three related regions: *Personal leadership development, Leadership for academic work*, and *Leadership in the university and beyond* (Figure 6.2). The first region focuses attention on our own development as academic leaders and managers. It is about acquiring a commitment to lifelong learning

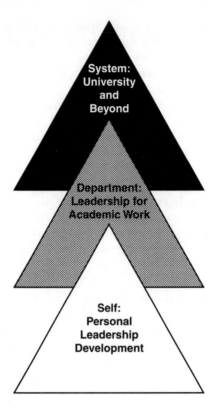

Figure 6.2 Three levels of academic leadership

about academic leadership, survival skills, reflection on achievements, successes and failures, and application of our past experiences to enhance future ones. This underpins our second zone: the
work of the department or similar academic work unit. This is
about providing an enabling environment for academic work and
academic people, and applying tools and concepts that will help us
manage them for maximum effectiveness and satisfaction. The third
zone is the university itself and, beyond it, the environment in
which it operates; here the challenge is to connect the development
of people and departments with the growth and future of universities and the higher education system, economy and society of
which they form a part.

This map also emphasises the importance of understanding leadership development in the university as a learning organisation to
be a process that occurs at multiple levels: organisational, work unit,
and individual.

A second way of conceptualising the field is to consider Kotter's

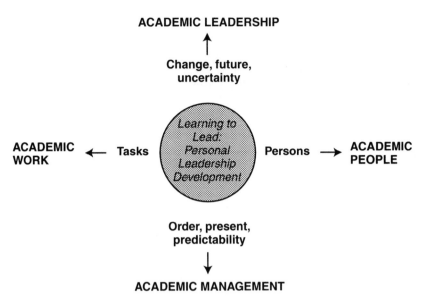

Figure 6.3 The domains of academic leadership

distinction between management and leadership in relation to academic people and academic work. Figure 6.3 shows that this enables us to divide the territory into four quadrants[2], held together by the leader's own programme of continuous personal development. The top left hand sector is the realm of academic entrepreneurship and the skills of influencing senior staff and other decision-makers: a world of risk, calculation and strategic behaviours. To its right is the zone of leadership of academic people: a region of transformational leadership and many of the skills of interpersonal relationships. The bottom right-hand quadrant encloses the region of people management, with a focus on supervision of staff and their efficient organisation through selection, delegation, rewards and performance management. The lower left quadrant contains the region of management for academic tasks, including planning and budgeting, quality assurance, and effective administrative processes. Finally, the centre of the chart incorporates the personal development of the academic leader, which both draws on and informs experiences in each of the quadrants.

Naturally, most of the practical skills of leadership and the

2 For an earlier version of the tasks–persons dimension, see Blake, R.R. and Mouton, J.S. (1964) *The Managerial Grid*, Houston: Gulf Publishing. The four quadrants model is similar to a scheme developed by Farey; see Farey, P. (1993) 'Mapping the leader/manager', *Management Education and Development*: 24.

qualities of effective academic environments we have identified in Part I of the book cross the boundaries of the zones identified in these theoretical maps. As we shall see in Part II, the leadership challenge in universities involves much more than addressing each issue listed in the maps. It also requires us to maintain the tension between the contrary forces implied by them. The common feature of both maps is the area of reflection on experience, self-assessment, application of what has been learnt to new ventures, management of oneself, and continuous personal improvement through lifelong learning. In Part III I intend to explore this area and show how its examination can help us to lead more effectively across the other regions as well.

Conclusions:
the principles of academic leadership

It is appropriate to conclude Part I by drawing together the main ideas presented in this and previous chapters into a simple series of principles of academic leadership.

1 *A dynamic process* The first principle of academic leadership must be that it is a dynamic process or it is nothing. It involves creatively managing opposing forces. These include tensions such as tradition and change, clear goals and the independence to pursue them, management and leadership, executing tasks and looking after people, sympathising with academic values and coping with external forces, short-term objectives and long-term visions. To focus on one of these pairs to the detriment of the other is to take the path to misfortune. And there is no possibility of a right answer to the dilemmas they represent. It is precisely their tension that maintains the structure of an effective context for academic work.

2 *An outcomes-focused agenda* 'Power and leadership are measured by the degree of production of intended effects' (Burns, 1978). The second principle is that academic leadership is properly focused on outcomes. Its processes exist to transform 'presage' into 'product'. By its effects, rather than by the leader's possession of competencies, it should ultimately be judged. Its purpose is to create conditions that enable high quality research and teaching, and to raise the awareness of staff so that they can welcome change. Academic leaders are teachers who try to expand options, develop their staff, and listen attentively to how well they are meeting the needs of their staff – in order

that they can achieve changes in their own understanding and the understanding of their students.

3   *Multi-level in its operation* The third principle is that academic leadership is a phenomenon that exists at multiple levels. The higher education system, the university, the department, the individual staff within it, the leader's own development – these different layers must be coordinated and equally attended to by a proficient academic leader. Organisational development and individual development become different aspects of the same picture when leadership is understood in this way.

4   *Relational* Like other forms of leadership, academic leadership is about both the leader's qualities and behaviours, and those of his or her followers. It occurs in a context; it is always 'situational'. Your colleagues determine whether you are a leader. No leader can ignore the experiences of their colleagues; good leaders learn from these experiences.

5   *About the leader's learning* An academic leader is a learner. Leaders can't learn unless they develop others; equally, no development of staff and improvement of their performance is possible unless leaders are also constantly transforming their own understanding. No one can do this transformation except themselves. They will draw on personal experience as well as theory and research about universities as organisations in order to learn. They will quickly recognise that the core principles of effective leadership and management apply across different types of organisation, and are not unique to universities.

6   *Essentially transformative* The final principle is a 'higher order' one that could be seen to encompass and condense all the previous four. It is that academic leadership is *transformative*. The presage-process-product 'model' of leadership, inadequate though it is, represents the idea of transformation in the succession through which presage is changed into product through process. Academic leadership is transformative in more than one sense. First, it is about helping ordinary people to do extraordinary things. Leadership is the lifting of a person's vision to a higher plane, the raising of achievement beyond what might normally be expected (Drucker, 1955, p. 195). Second, it is about helping academic people to embrace change with alacrity, an attitude which is a primary requirement of the enterprising university in a turbulent environment. Third, it is about transforming one's own performance through reflection: no-one who is not developing themselves can teach others how to change and develop.

Fourth, it takes place in an organisation whose fundamental purpose is learning – where 'learning' is conceptualised not only as the adding of more knowledge, but as a continual series of changes in understanding.

Part II

LEADING ACADEMIC WORK

7

VISION, STRATEGY AND PLANNING

Vision is the art of seeing things invisible.

Swift

Introduction to part II:
applying academic leadership theory to practice

In Part I we looked at an extensive range of material linking academic leadership and management to change in higher education. I hope you now feel more familiar with the connections between the quality and quantity of academic work, the processes of academic leadership and management, and the contemporary context of higher education. We have seen how academic culture and values, together with massive change in the nature and size of universities, combine to provide a exceptional challenge for academic leaders, a challenge which is particularly severe for staff with responsibilities at the level of head of department.

Nevertheless the picture is far from being a disheartening one. We also observed how the experiences of lecturers, coupled with modern ideas about leadership in other types of organisation, can help establish principles of effective academic leadership. Some practices and some environments conduce to higher productivity and commitment. Listening to the views of academic staff tells us why and how. Their combined experiences tell us most of what there is to know about leadership for successful and satisfying academic work.

Academic leadership shares its basic qualities with other forms of leadership. It differs not in its fundamentals but in the way in which these fundamentals are realised in the context of higher education's core business. The six principles summarised at the end of the preceding chapter highlight the features of competent academic leadership. It is dynamic and outcomes-focused, and concerned with change and development. It is essentially optimistic, energetic, outward-looking, and supportive of academic endeavour. It involves the recognition and development of university staff; it is a kind of support for staff learning. It includes establishing direction and managing complexity. It requires a focus on both tasks and people, and a commitment to one's own learning and self-management as an academic leader. It demands the confidence to influence change and the skills to help people recognise the need to change for themselves.

How can we use this understanding to learn how to lead better? It might be helpful to break the problem down into convenient parts. In the practice of improving university teaching, there are five issues that we as teachers need to address (Ramsden, 1992, pp. 123–4):

- *Goals and structure*: What do I want my students to learn and how can I express my goals clearly to them?
- *Teaching strategies*: How should I arrange teaching and learning to help students achieve these objectives?
- *Assessment*: How can I find out whether they have learned?
- *Evaluation*: How can I estimate the effectiveness of my teaching and thereby enhance it?
- *Accountability and educational development*: How should the answers to these questions be applied to measuring and improving quality in higher education?

A surprisingly similar set of issues has to be tackled in the practice of academic leadership. This topic has four aspects:

1   What do I want my work unit to achieve, and how can I enlist the support and resources I need to pursue these goals? This is the problem of *vision, strategy and planning*.
2   How do I provide the means for my staff team to achieve these objectives? This is the problem of *enabling academic people*.
3   How can I help my colleagues to develop their skills and align their personal goals with those of my work unit? How do I monitor their progress and assess their achievement? This is the problem of *recognising and developing performance*.
4   What do I need to do to survive and grow as an academic leader? How can I improve my own performance – and my university's performance? These are the closely related problems of *learning to lead* and *improving university leadership*.

These four issues constitute the four central academic leadership responsibilities. All four incorporate aspects of what Kotter (1990) defined as leadership (focused on coping with change and uncertain futures) and management (focused on coping with complexity and consistent outcomes). To reiterate: when I speak of 'leadership' in an unqualified way in this book, I intend to imply that management is included as well.

The leadership responsibilities can be linked to the leadership maps previously introduced (Figures 6.2 and 6.3 in the last chapter) as well as to the problems of improving teaching summarised above. Figure 7.1 makes explicit the comparison between problems of teaching and responsibilities of university leadership, while Table 7.1 summarises

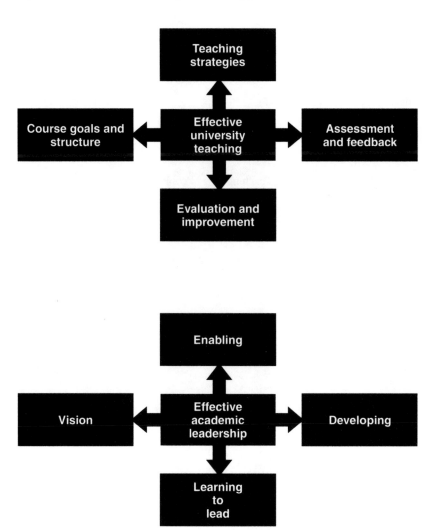

Figure 7.1 Problems of university teaching compared to responsibilities of academic leadership

Table 7.1 Four responsibilities of academic leadership

Academic leadership responsibility	Levels of operation (see Figure 6.2)	Corresponding aspects of university teaching (see Ramsden, 1992, pp. 123–4, and Figure 7.1)	Primary and secondary focus of leadership and management (see Figure 6.3)	Examples of functions
Vision, strategic action, planning and managing resources	The system (the university and beyond) and academic work unit	Goals and structure of course	Tasks and people	Forward thinking; positioning in university and in system; operational planning; new research and teaching directions and projects; enlisting staff in the vision
Enabling, inspiring, motivating and directing	Work unit	Teaching strategies	People and tasks	Collaborative leadership and team building; efficient, effective, and fair management; leadership for research; supporting effective teaching
Recognising, developing, and assessing performance	Work unit	Assessment of students	People	Feedback to staff; monitoring of progress; developing and mentoring others as academics and as leaders; delegation; performance management
Learning to lead and improving university leadership	Self, work unit and system	Evaluation and improvement of courses and teaching	Yourself and your university	Lifelong learning as an academic leader; personal survival skills; developing more effective university leaders

the academic leadership problems in terms of four responsibilities and shows how these are connected with the earlier maps, illustrating their levels of operation and their primary and secondary focus. For example, *enabling academic people* is concerned chiefly with the level of the academic work unit; its primary focus is people and its secondary focus academic tasks; it corresponds to the problem of *teaching strategies* in the practice of improving university teaching.

The present chapter and chapters 8 and 9 tackle problems one, two and three. Part III will take up the question, implicit throughout this and the next two chapters, of our personal survival and growth as academic leaders in the context of improving university leadership.

At this point I should remind readers that our programme of learning to lead is both eclectic and outcomes-focused. The methods used to organise and direct academic work are secondary to the degree to which they produce intended effects. I have no agenda of particular techniques and ideologies which I want to raise above other methods, and no commitment to specific methods of leadership education such as action learning, skills training, or mentoring. I have, however, assumed that among the effects we desire are a motivated and committed staff who derive pleasure and benefit from their university work. If you are unable to share this assumption, then there is little point in pursuing an academic leadership role. I have also assumed that the connection between our practices and the responses of those whom we seek to support is contingent and uncertain. We cannot escape from the responsibility of making decisions about how to manage and lead in specific circumstances. The best training for making these decisions correctly is practice in applying principles to real situations.

Establishing clear expectations

When you began your academic career, how clear were you about what was expected of staff in your department? To what extent did the head create a shared view of what staff were trying to achieve in research and teaching? For many staff the answers would be the same as mine – I had very little idea of what was expected, and I began with a feeling of puzzlement and uncertainty. I was not sure whether my ideas about what my courses and teaching methods should be achieving, for example, were similar to, different from, complementary to, or opposed to the majority of staff or the views of the head – or indeed whether it mattered. Only after a lengthy period did it become clear what the expectations were, and what room for manoeuvre there was. I do not think that I ever found out whether there was a shared belief in what the department stood for in its research and scholarship. If there was one, it might have been related to statements about excellence and application in the prospectus. It wasn't clear whether this was similar to or different from other departments in the same field.

Like new students in higher education, staff often do not know what is expected of them or whether there is a collective and distinctive understanding of where the work unit is going. Perhaps this signified little in an earlier, less demanding and more stable climate for academic enterprise. Each person could be expected to do things that fitted the broad direction of applied mathematics or English literature or sociology as practised in the department, and to have the independence and responsibility to be relied upon to do it.

Whether this worked out well in practice is immaterial; what does matter is that the imperatives of mass higher education, knowledge differentiation, competition and accountability discussed in Part I make it no longer feasible. We shall see in chapter 9 how performance management can be used to help address one aspect of this problem – the alignment of individual staff objectives with collective goals. The other aspect is the need to establish a clear, shared vision for all members of the group. The academic work unit that provides a satisfying environment and which survives and expands will have a strong common view of where it is going and what it believes in. Academic leaders who are admired and respected have lucid visions and make it clear what staff are expected to do. If you have any doubt at all about whether this is true, look again at the results presented in chapter 5.

Effective academic leaders will therefore want to ask as their first questions: What does my group – or department – stand for? What do we want to produce? Where are we going? They will recollect the critical principle of leadership credibility, and know that whatever the vision is, it must be sincerely held and practised with integrity if they are to win the minds and hearts of academic staff so that they enlist in it.

Seeking opportunities

As Kouzes and Posner (1995) tersely say, 'The domain of leaders is the future'. And as we have seen, university staff admire and take heed of academic leaders who are honest, highly skilled, and *forward-looking* – and in this respect they are no different from 'followers' in other types of organisation.

What does it mean to be forward-looking as an academic leader? Above all it means challenging widely-held assumptions and con-

136

fronting the status quo, whether this is in the internal operation of the department or in relation to wider issues such as research directions, contracts and new courses. It means taking risks and encouraging other staff to take risks. It means wanting change and innovation, and animating the same spirit in others. It need not involve entrepreneurial activities such as establishing new markets for courses and attracting overseas students to increase income, although it includes these kinds of opportunities. It need not be something you have personally thought of; it may be a suggestion or even a direction made by a university committee or a more senior colleague, which you have thought of an enterprising way of handling.

Seeking opportunities and being forward-looking may seem very different from a conventionally-academic way of doing things. In one sense it is, but in another it isn't: it requires a frame of mind which embraces the idea of applying existing knowledge to new situations, of finding links between ideas, of advancing new hypotheses to explain puzzling phenomena, and of transforming old knowledge into fresh wisdom. The following two examples illustrate aspects of seeking opportunities and risk-taking as an academic leader.

John Stiles changes research assistant allocations

John Stiles found that the status quo in his new department was that each research assistant worked exclusively to one or two senior researchers. The departmental norm was that RAs were individual lecturers' property. This was fine so long as RAs were generally PhD students effectively supervised by the staff member at the same time as supporting the department's research, but in recent years this had become less common, and problems arose when RAs left or were absent at crucial times in projects. As a result, a practice had grown up among one group staff of 'sharing' RAs, so that each one knew at least something about one or two other projects and could step in if necessary. But many departmental stalwarts held to the older pattern, and resolutely refused to be part of this system. As a result, projects were being held up and some colleagues were no longer on speaking terms. John challenged the existing process and pointed out the advantages of the sharing system. Confronted by the conservatives with a claim that he was being unreasonable, he emphasised the need to increase research productivity and establish harmonious relationships. From next semester the new system would be established. When the conservatives complained to their colleagues, they received little support. By the end of the semester the new system was fully operational and manifestly better for everyone. One lecturer who refused to move on from the old method attracted no sympathy, but was allowed by common consent to carry on with one exclusive part-time RA funded from an external grant.

John took a risk in the interests of his department. He might have failed, and in one sense (the recalcitrant lecturer) he did. But the larger outcome was better research and a more committed staff who appreciated his willingness to confront the problem and to solve it with firmness and sympathy.

Alana Preston takes an initiative in teaching evaluation

Alana Preston learned that the university had finally mandated a new form of teaching evaluation involving self-assessment logs and portfolios of activities which were to go to heads of schools. The response of many schools was predictable, focused on the status quo, and immediately negative: How can we go around this new accountability requirement so that it disrupts our 'real work' as little as possible? Minimalist and grudging compliance with the university's demands occurred in many schools. In a few others, heads took the excuse to introduce a requirement for student evaluation reports to be provided twice a semester and arranged special interviews with staff who scored below the school average on half the questions.

Alana took a different line. She saw at once an opportunity to present the school to the faculty and the university as a creative place with a strong commitment to quality in teaching. The scheme also provided a mechanism by which she could increase staff discussion and mutual support in relation to undergraduate teaching, while at the same time enabling staff who had complained for years about their teaching being undervalued to get some recognition for it. She set up all the accountability mechanisms with all her staff (including casual staff) during a single meeting. People had an input to the specific process used in the school, and could see that it was possible to use it not only to produce far better cases for promotion, but also to gain valuable advice and support to make their teaching a more interesting and less tedious experience.

Vision, purpose, values and commitment

Academics are not given to flights of optimism; they are trained to caution, criticism, doubt. Academic leadership, however, demands imaginative optimism. A key aspect of being creative and forward-looking is the idea of *vision*. A vision is a picture of the future that you want to produce. A vision is an ideal image, a picture of excellence, a distinctive pattern that makes your department or your course or your research team different.

'Vision' has become a debased term in management literature: it has come to refer all too frequently to one person's emotionally-inflated, empty slogan which must be imposed on others. It would be a serious mistake to dismiss the idea as irrelevant to effective academic leadership because of this devaluation. Visions are at the heart of leadership; they are about committing, animating, believing, hoping, exciting, inspiring. In all organisations, but perhaps especially in universities, a vision draws its power to motivate from being both intellectually and emotionally engaging.

Thinking about vision requires temporary attenuation of rational and critical thinking in deference to creativity and imagination. Where do you see your work unit in the future? What could it achieve? What could be really special about it? What is possible rather than probable? What can we improve? What, even with all the threats and resource constraints, might happen if we believe in it strongly enough? If we have been at all creative as academics, we will all have done this kind of free thinking in the process of thinking of new research directions or additional hypotheses to extend existing theory. It is not an unfamiliar activity. Only the application is different.

Oscar Wilde said that a map of the world that does not have Utopia on it was not worth using (quoted in Lowe, 1994). Make sure your map is worth using. The best visions are positive ones. They 'move towards a dream, not just away from pain' (Lucas, 1995, p. 55). Negative visions focus on what needs to be avoided – let's not reduce the quality of teaching, let's not compromise the integrity of our basic research programmes by seeking industrial sponsorship, let's avoid being merged with the other classics department. As Senge (1990) says, negative visions are limiting visions. They limit in three ways: by diverting energy that could be put into something new into prevention; by carrying the message that the group only pulls together when it's threatened; and by being inevitably short term. Ill-thought out responses to government pressures for quality assurance and to reductions in funding have produced a whole arsenal of visions in universities of this negative and limiting type. Visions must carry hope, not despair.

The best visions for academic work units are simple ones focused on profoundly-held commitments, purposes and values. Short unqualified statements do not necessarily come easily to us as academics, but it is a discipline worth developing. For every academic department vision or mission that is too glib, there are fifty that are so hedged around with qualifications that they are unmemorable or incomprehensible. 'We offer access to more students without compromising quality of outcomes' is a thousand times better than 'In the pursuit of academic excellence the Department of Civil Engineering will do everything within its control to ensure the highest standards of benefit to students from diverse achievement backgrounds, given the existing constraints on funding and resources, and in the context of a necessary complementarity between research, teaching and professional practice'. If you cannot come up with something more like the former than the latter your effort is wasted. Visions are about directions and orientation, not describing every stone in the road or even the distance to be travelled.

Visions should be flexible enough to permit people to exercise choice and to allow for continuing relevance when conditions change (Kotter, 1990, p. 36). Uncomplicated visions are always the best; they are easy to remember and hard to ignore. In my own centre for staff development some years ago, one of the goals that made up our vision (suggested by one of my staff, not me) also possessed this unforgettable quality: 'We want to be a focus of comfort and hope for academic staff'. Sometimes the vision is more entrepreneurial (for example: 'To become the pre-eminent School of Tourism and Hospitality in the Asia/Pacific region; to be an exemplar for the rest of the world'). There is nothing wrong with that either. Visions come in many forms. To be effective they must capture your imagination.

Securing commitment to vision and change

Vision is about change. Change is highly characteristic of all higher education institutions, and always has been. Although it has been humorously said that academics never want to be the first to do something (Tucker, 1984), it is a misconception that academic staff automatically resist change. As chapter 5 showed, staff value leaders who address change in a positive way. What lecturers resist, just like everyone else, is *being changed* (Senge, 1990).

Effective visions are by definition shared visions. Nevertheless, as Senge also says, 'the only vision that motivates you is your vision'. The apparent paradox is resolved by understanding that visions cannot be imposed; each person must genuinely hold the vision for themselves. It is, of course, this quality of free participation and collaboration that makes visions exhilarating and motivates work teams to achieve the seemingly-impossible. Unhappily, we rarely come across sincerely shared statements of vision and goals in universities; it is much more common for visions to be created by a small group and then 'sold' to staff. The effect of such a strategy is to encourage either revolt or compliance, never commitment; people may accept the vision, but they don't want it. Like students who can see little value in an assessment question that tests mere reproduction of facts, they adopt a minimalist approach focused on survival. They agree to it grudgingly and find ways to ignore it. The dynamic energy generated by change, which should be at the heart of any university, is dissipated. The academic leader's task is to create an environment in which people move from resistance, non-compliance, or compliance to commitment to a vision: in summary, from the left hand column to the right hand one in Table 7.2.

Table 7.2 From non-compliance to commitment

Non-compliance	Compliance	Commitment
People doubt the vision (or the change) and/or reject it	They go along with it	They are enrolled by choice – they personally want it
They do tasks related to the vision (or the change) grudgingly or not at all	They are 'good soldiers' – they do it willingly	They do it with energy, passion, excitement
They oppose the rules	They play by the rules	They are responsible for the game

Source: Derived from Senge (1990).

Where do visions come from? One notion is that academic visions spring from the 'collective mind' of a group of staff; the leader draws out and articulates ideas that are already latent. The opposite view is that the head has an idea and encourages staff to develop a commitment to it. The truth is somewhere in between. Effective visions arise from creative tension between the goals and hopes of the academic leader and the desires of members of the work unit and other interested parties. It is important to grasp the fact that shared visions are not the result of a series of departmental meetings called to 'develop a strategic plan'. Devising a shared vision is a chief part of the daily work of a head or coordinator; it is a continuous process requiring intense communication both internally and externally.

It is very much the task of an academic leader to do more than his or her colleagues to be apprised of the local and national environment in which the department operates, and to provide direction and focus to address challenges within this environment. This is specifically true about developing a shared vision; but it is also more generally true about introducing changes in academic work patterns. Often, lecturers are unaware of the fact that there is trouble brewing beyond the department which demands an adaptive response. The leader must be alert to this external environment and wait for the appropriate point when the internal environment can accept change (Deetz, 1992, p. 19). Doing this well is not an optional part of the job. Introduced at the wrong time, new ideas and different work practices create fear and defensive behaviour. But not reading the external signs, or ignoring them, leads to disaster[1].

Developing a vision must begin from the leader's personal perspective, and not, as some writers have suggested, start from discussions and meetings where staff express their views of where they want the unit to go and what they want it to do. Such meetings invariably lead to 'visions' which, after much debate, are remarkably general and capable of multiple interpretations; they please everybody and excite no-one. They are also often not based on wide

1 Deetz (1992) uses a surfing metaphor to contrast 'the inclination to jump in with major changes' with 'preparing for change by building relations, support and understanding':

Most troubled departments are filled with powerful faculty who cannot read environmental signs; they do not know they are in trouble. Most chairs are not good at jarring faculty into awareness, but when a clear change is in the making they can excel at helping others adapt to it. *Waiting for the appropriate moment for directing change is critical.* Chairs, no more than surfers, can make the waves they want. Effective chairs can cleverly fund and shape the issue forcing change while waiting for that wave.

knowledge of external opportunities and problems. Moreover, people may feel inhibited from being creative about the future for fear of critical and dismissive comments from colleagues. (You may recognise the voice of experience here).

This is not to say that there should not be meetings, but that they should have a different purpose. People follow leaders with strong personal convictions that they can share. A leader must be ahead and must take charge. You are *supposed* to believe passionately in the vision yourself. You are *supposed* to have an imaginative picture of the future which takes your staff beyond where they think they can go now. You are *supposed* to have ideas that exceed expectations and transcend everyday concerns. This is what makes people leaders, not the fact that they may have titles like head of department.

You should seek to test those beliefs and illuminate them in two ways. First, you need to gather additional information from stakeholders and other interested parties – chairs of relevant decision-making committees in the university, senior managers, employers of graduates, your counterparts in other universities, funding agencies – to determine whether the vision and goals will be compatible with their requirements. It is critically important to realise that the vision must appeal to all groups and individuals who can be seen as 'customers', including internal customers such as your immediate superiors, as well as to the staff in your own group.

The second way to test your conceptualisation is by asking your colleagues about their own visions for the department, especially their view of a preferred future in a few years time, and how this future might be achieved. I have found that an effective way of listening to their needs and strengthening a draft vision and strategy is to ask colleagues to be leaders themselves, and to describe their visions and strategies in the form of one page statements. These will contain common features which can be drawn upon to enhance and invigorate – and possibly radically alter – your own ideas. As we have seen, competent academic leaders are excellent and genuine listeners. They use their colleagues' insights to help improve and transform their understanding. They invite their colleagues to share the process of leadership. It is a mistake to think that visions must be *either* the product of a collective or of an individual. They are the result of a relationship between an individual leader's ideas and the collaborative thinking of followers.

Then is the time to discuss these views in a meeting convened for the purpose and to invite creative responses to the broad vision and associated long-term goals you have developed.

143

Then also is the time to ask for reactions to general strategies which you will have developed from the vision and to invite detailed written suggestions for amendments and extensions. An example of a vision and general strategies which might emerge from this process is shown in Table 7.3; the list on p. 145 summarises some advice on strategic planning. It is important to remember that vision and strategies are dynamic. They need to be in a state of change if they are to be useful in helping us adapt to change.

Table 7.3 Steps to vision and strategy

Step	Example of result
General external environment scan	Increased competition for funding, need to increase research output and attract more graduate students
Client and stakeholder interests. Internal. External.	Expectation of increase in research productivity by university, joint projects with local firms
External opportunities	No other university department in region with close connection to commerce and industry such as we have
Unit weaknesses	Department in new university: low research output, few research active staff
Unit strengths	New appointments, some from the private sector, that have strengthened applied research activity, some newly research qualified existing staff
Long-term vision (key values and outcomes)	A true university department with a broader focus on high quality research and an exciting atmosphere of scholarly commitment, higher research productivity combined with unique profile for this field of close links with local organisations
Long-term strategies	Selection of appropriate staff to help propel change, more efficient teaching, more cooperative projects with local firms, review of effectiveness in 12 months

- A strategic plan's purpose is to produce directions for change to cope with an uncertain higher education environment
- Visions and strategic plans are about *positive, desired, ideal futures*, not problems now, negative reactions, past mistakes, qualifications, reasons why something can't be done
- Consider what your department does that is unique, different, special, extra
- Listen to your colleagues; find out about their shared aspirations; search for common patterns
- Articulate these shared hopes with each other and with your own preferred direction
- The only vision people believe in is their vision
- Believe in the vision yourself
- Use powerful ideas and animated language to shape the vision
- Don't confuse plans to manage events with long-term visions
- Use the past and present to understand how you have created what you currently have
- Set some clear, realistic objectives related to the grander plans
- There is no end to the process of strategic planning. It is a process, not an event

Management and operational planning

The English architect William Lethaby declared that there were only two types of domestic architecture: the type where the chimneys smoked and the type where they did not. We might say something similar about academic environments. Some are managed with calm deliberation and the rest are not. All the visionary and stirring leadership in the world will not compensate for the necessarily mundane processes of business-like management and simple administrative procedures. It is significant that respondents to the *Leadership for Academic Work* questionnaire regarded efficient management and straightforward administration to be just as important as inspirational guidance and collaborative decision-making on the part of their leaders.

The processes of establishing vision, then, should be clearly distinguished from detailed management and operational planning. Vision is related to Kotter's idea of leadership; planning is a management process. 'The basic function of management is homeostatic: its to keep a system alive by making sure that critical variables remain within tolerable ranges constantly' (Kotter, 1990, p. 62). Management planning is 'deductive in nature and designed to produce orderly results'. Unglamorous as it may appear, good management planning is an essential complement to developing a shared vision and creating a harmonious work environment. Most of today's academic work units are too complex and the people in them are too varied to ensure that commitments are met and quality assured without systematic preparation. Operational planning is a method designed to produce routinely successful outcomes without overstraining the system and the people in it. The process must be as risk-free as possible. This book is not a treatise on financial and resource management and I do not intend to try and cover the details of these processes here. However, some general points related to project planning and resource management may serve as an introduction.

BASICS OF PROJECT PLANNING

Stage 1: Planning proper
What needs to be done? (derived from vision and strategies)

How will what is done meet the needs of stakeholders (University decision making bodies, students, other internal clients, external funding agencies, and so on?)

Who in this department, or somewhere else, has done this (or something similar) before?

Who will do it? (Who is responsible/accountable for performance targets?)

How much will it cost? How much money is available?

What is the timetable? How is it linked to peaks and troughs in resource use?

How will we know whether it has worked? (What indicators of performance?)

Stage 2: Monitor progress against the plan
Reporting and meetings during the course of the project (both official and informal)

Identify departures from plan and correct

Stage 3: Conclusion and wrap-up
Evaluate performance using agreed indicators

Summarise and record successes and failures for future reference

---

The list above outlines the basics of project planning in the form of a series of questions related in turn to planning itself, monitoring progress, and learning from the outcomes. Readers can easily supply their own examples of research projects and teaching initiatives, as well as ventures into commercial operations such as the sale of consultancies and teaching materials, to bring these cold structures to life. In fact it is possible to conceive of virtually all academic and administrative processes in a department in terms of a series of such interlocking projects. Budgets, accountabilities, personnel and timelines can then be allocated in a rational way. As each project proceeds, the inevitable departures from the plan should be noted and changes made – just like a strategic plan, a project plan should not be seen to have an immutable character. But it should have enough validity and assurance to ensure that it is followed unless circumstances alter. The activity of recording successes and failures in order to learn how to be more effective in the future is an essential component of an adequate project planning cycle.

Resource management[2]

Resource management and project planning are like sister and brother. In recent years many higher education institutions have

2 The section that follows was written in collaboration with Eva Lietzow.

devolved increasing responsibility for resource management to departments. The extent of this responsibility, and the concomitant authority for planning, varies from institution to institution. There is no substitute for detailed knowledge of local procedures. There are, however, some general strategies for the management of departmental resources of which it may be useful to be aware.

Resource management is a fundamental part of operational planning for two reasons. First, the amount of resources available, and the extent to which you can exert control over them, limits what you can do in a department. Control can exist over some or all elements and is usually greatest when it is expressed in control over money to be invested in some or all of the remaining resource categories. When this occurs, *budgeting*, or the planning for the investment of financial resources, becomes the most significant aspect of resource management. The second reason why resource management is important is that it enables you to implement long-term strategic plans and short-term projects, as well as to monitor and evaluate their outcomes. Its purpose is to allocate and monitor resources of all kinds – including money, people, equipment, furniture, fittings and buildings, services and consumables. Its aim is simply to help achieve a work unit's goals in a rational and efficient way.

If you are a newly-appointed head of an academic work unit, you may find that your first task in resource management is one of familiarisation with the budgetary and financial environment in which you have to operate. Finding out about your level of control over resources, your influence on, or authority over, financial decision making, and the university's expectations can be an intimidating task. Budgeting and financial management matters can be expressed in jargon-laden language which seems impenetrable to novices. At times it can seem difficult to obtain sufficient information. Some sources of information which may prove useful include university policies for resource management and business procedure manuals. From these, you should try to determine the answers to the following questions:

- What is the relevant level of financial authority?
- What level of control does the position have over decisions pertaining to staff, equipment, furniture, fittings and buildings, services from internal and external providers, and consumable goods?
- How is income generation defined, and what level of income generation is expected from you?
- Is the position expected to plan for long-term resource needs

such as early retirements, outcomes of pay negotiations, equipment replacement and refurbishment?

- What are the restrictions on research and consultancy income?
- What kind of role does the position play in the determination of budgets for the department?
- Can allocated or generated funds be transferred to the next year?

Planning and budgeting

Good resource management helps you to select appropriate procedures for achieving the strategic goals of your department. Important considerations are long-term responsibilities and maintenance tasks. To ensure that these, together with their resource requirements, are not forgotten, you need to articulate them early. One way of doing this is to ask three questions:

- What must we do?
- What do we want to do?
- What can we do?

The answers to the first question are most likely to reflect maintenance and long-term planning tasks. They probably will also reflect institutional expectations arising from the university's current environment. The answers to the second question predominantly reflect urgent issues arising from the knowledge and expertise of people in a particular field of study. A satisfactory answer to the third question should bring together the answers to the other two in the context of resource constraints. Through the operational planning process you will be able to identify a set of procedures which you can implement in a particular period to produce the greatest benefit from the available resources.

In practice this means that a department will have a better base for decisions if it can identify a number of different procedures for the achievement of its strategic goals. Each of these procedures will have different resource demands associated with it – some will be more time-consuming than others, some will require more or less expertise, some may demand expenditure on consumables or equipment, and some may be able to generate income. At the same time, each procedure is likely to contribute differently to the achievement of the goals, and the effects of some of them are difficult to predict. For example, marketing a course can increase student numbers but does not contribute to the quality of student learning;

a local initiative to increase the number of staff publications may or may not generate increased research income.

A department will need to decide which mix of procedures suits its individual requirements in a particular period. Developing a variety of procedures linked to identified resource requirements will provide more options for juggling competing priorities and matching these to available resources.

Monitoring of expenditure and income of projects can normally be done quite easily using a university's accounting systems. You may be able to create accounts for your separate projects. Alternatively, codes can be assigned to track expenditure for a particular project through a variety of accounts. It is best to monitor finances frequently to detect variations from planned expenditure and judge the cash-flow of a department. Monitoring information enables a department to compare actual progress, time-lines and resource usage against the plans.

Interrelation of resource categories

We can think of resources as input elements: money, people, equipment, furniture, fittings and buildings, services, and consumables. Alternatively, they can be seen in terms of the value they contribute to the department. Money contributes only indirectly through investment in other resources; people contribute time, effort and expertise; equipment, furniture, fittings and buildings contribute efficiency and effectiveness; services contribute a wide array of specialised and timely expertise (such as external consultants) or the use of other organisations' equipment. If investment in one category of resources is increased or decreased, other categories are often affected, and wise resource management will take this into account. For example, if more staff members are appointed, more money needs to be invested in equipment, furniture, fittings and buildings to use their contribution efficiently and effectively. But more work can be done in-house, thus reducing the cost of services. On the other hand, a reduction in staff often requires a greater investment in equipment and services to enhance the efficiency of remaining staff and buy in expertise that is now lacking.

Strategic orientation and political skills

'No government', Machiavelli reminds us, 'Should ever imagine that it can always adopt a safe course; rather, it should regard all possible courses of action as risky'. Beyond questions of resources and planning, the risk-taking and policy-making which are inseparable

150

from accomplished leadership lead quickly to questions of power and persuasion.

Unquestionably among the key functions of a competent academic leader are issues related to political activity and strategy. The effective academic leader links the levels of self, work unit and system (see Figure 6.2) through the wise exercise of authority. High levels of perceived strategic orientation – working to bring resources into the work unit both within the university and beyond, building its reputation, and working for that unit as much as for him or herself – were linked to high levels of satisfaction in my surveys of academics (see Figure 7.1). Eighty per cent of professors in an Australian study of heads rated 'Serving as an advocate for the department' as being of great importance; 86 per cent of their staff felt the same way (Moses and Roe, 1990). Similar findings emerged from the interviews and surveys reported in chapters 4 and 5. Middlehurst (1993, p. 136) summarises several other studies which confirm that both academic leaders and academic followers attach significance to the academic leader's role as a political strategist and promoter of the work unit's interests.

An ardent commitment to what you want to realise is as much a *sine qua non* for academic political activity as it is for enlisting others in a vision.

Followership

Elizabeth Yee's tenure as head of department started with a word from the acting head about her predecessor. 'Phil had lots of first-rate ideas about how to streamline the administrative processes of the department and the faculty, and cut out the vast amounts of time academics were spending on filling out forms and double-handling trivial requests', Malcolm said. 'But he got offside with the Dean almost from day one because he wouldn't do what he wanted when it came to taking some hard decisions, firstly about flexible learning and then about reducing casual staff numbers. Phil followed a pretty rigid agenda focused on maintaining standards and the quality of student learning. He also said he didn't have time to brief the Dean on the plans for the network on the new campus, even though he's a nationally-known specialist on Intranet facilities. He might have succeeded in getting all his ideas supported if he'd waited a bit, but he got labelled as a person who was a problem and a non-cooperator. It may be a coincidence, but sixth months later the plans for the new admin. process seemed to get lost in the Dean's office and the resources for implementing it never materialised. It's worth remembering that'.

Elizabeth's first meeting with the Dean didn't go too well either. He had a crazy idea for a new research reporting system where the staff filled in a weekly log of activities and publications. She said it would cause a riot; it was far too heavy-handed and it would mean that most people submitted empty returns in most columns every week. On returning to her office, though, she recalled Malcolm's advice. On the face if it, it looked like conceding academic integrity to obsequiousness, but perhaps . . . After ringing her partner to say she'd be staying late at work that night, she began working out a slightly different reporting process which was more consistent with the University's appraisal procedure and in fact would help staff in their preparation for their appraisal – so it would be more likely to be acceptable to them. A few days later she'd presented the idea to the Dean as a minor modification of his plan and offered to trial it in her own department. After that, and especially after she'd heard that the Dean had been publicly praised by the VC for a highly innovative approach to research reporting, things began to go much better. Several of her ideas for revitalising the department were generously backed by the Dean at the next meeting of the budget committee, and she found several more opportunities that year to offer her advice and support.

An essential part of working effectively to advance the interests of one's work group or department, curiously enough, is good followership. In this respect, an academic career often does not fit us well for leadership; we shy from the notion of being seen to fawn to more senior staff; we are imbued with the spirit of intellectual equality; we are conditioned to believe that the most junior lecturer may have an idea that can make the most revered professor think again; we like our own judgments and will defend them vigorously, especially if they are rational and supported by empirical evidence. Learning to lead in higher education requires a capacity to understand that these convictions should be pursued so far and no further. Heads of departments and course coordinators need trusty allies at more senior levels, and engaging their loyalty requires us to be seen to be trustworthy ourselves. It is no weakness or betrayal of academic values to work in this way; in fact, it may be the only means by which academically-honest objectives can be achieved. Resolutely selling a point of view which is different from a senior manager's creates a perception of uncooperativeness and disloyalty, and will ensure that your needs for your work unit will be disregarded. At all costs you must be committed to the key ideas and mission of the faculty or university, even though you may disagree with its processes and short-term objectives. And despite your qualms about not being able to do jobs properly without adequate time and resources, you must learn to say 'yes' to most requests from more senior managers.

Academic leaders desire reliable followers who are cooperative and dependable, who will not persistently complain, who will say 'yes' nine times out of ten when they need something doing, and who will not invariably seem to have a different vision. It is easy to be a good follower when you agree with your senior manager's strategy, but the testing time for followership skills is when you don't. 'I always tell my staff' said Sir John Monash, 'I don't care a damn for your loyalty when you think I'm right. The time I want it is when you think I'm wrong'. But carried too far the desire for unquestioning loyalty can inhibit organisational change and the development of colleagues' leadership skills. Once more we need to maintain a creative force between these opposites in academic leadership.

Many advantages accrue from being a good academic follower. You will have friends in more senior positions and committees who can inform you of proceedings and who may well defend you against attacks which you would not otherwise know about. At times of making decisions affecting resources, your loyalty and your willingness to say yes to assignments will be remembered. When you become known as someone who can be relied upon to solve problems for a leader, you can expect to be asked to do more and to develop your own skills by doing so. Opportunities may then arise to suggest changes to practices and policies that will benefit both your group and the university. And the more you have developed a capacity to be an effective follower, the more scope you will have to dissent and challenge on subsequent occasions. The exercise of followership is an investment in academic independence.

A sombre reality that constrains the exercise of followership in many universities is that their day-to-day administrative processes often work ineffectively. It is harder to be a good follower of one's senior colleagues when the administrative staff for whom they are responsible appear to see their role as applying rules and announcing restrictions, who delegate trivial tasks to academics, and who expect multiple handling of requests related to appointments and equipment.

Power and trust

Power can't be ignored if we want to lead effectively in higher education. Centralised power in university departments creates a lack of trust and a tendency towards compliance. It discourages commitment. In these circumstances academics act like their students do when they are given too little discretion over methods and content of learning; they become passive and over-dependent, and they concentrate attention on the signs of performance rather than the substance. But the alternative to centralised power should not be the retraction of power, or even worse, the apparent retraction of power. Many heads of departments have learned the hard way that pretending to give up control leads to misery.

What the organisational theorists call 'distributed' power, in which followers have decision-making responsibility themselves (Hollander and Offerman, 1993), is often thought to represent the traditional form of authority in higher education. In practice, sharing power between leaders and followers through forms of participative decision-making is more common than truly distributed power in a 'collegial' culture. However, distributed power through delegation and self-managed work teams is effective in enhancing people's performance in other types of organisation, and it clearly harmonises with academic values of autonomy and collaboration. For the exercise of high quality distributed power, it is critical that heads ensure that colleagues share the department's vision and goals, are involved in operational planning, and have ample information so they can make independent decisions. It is also desirable to select assistants to whom tasks are delegated with care; chronic problems may arise in academic units when inexperienced leaders assume that all colleagues are equally able to handle delegated responsibility.

These requirements support the need for a collective vision, high levels of communication associated with the vision, and confident management. Shared power is an important means of developing leadership in other staff, and we will look in more detail at enabling colleagues through mentoring and delegation in the next two chapters.

From a self-interested standpoint, the vulnerability of the academic manager's power, whether it comes from the position held, from access to resources, or from personal sources such as an international research reputation, supports a strategy of distribution. A paradox of academic leadership is that sharing power through empowering colleagues increases one's power as a leader. Empowerment commands respect for the leader's authority.

A close relation of power is trust. Confidence and trust in a leader's authority always has to be won. Trust comes from restraining motives of self-interest and carrying the same burdens as followers; and from showing fallibility and the limitations of one's knowledge. Pretending you know the answer to a student's question when you don't rapidly erodes your authority as a teacher. It is sure to impair your colleagues' respect if you appear unwilling to admit a mistake. As one academic leader put it, 'Trust of academic staff is never up front – it only follows when promises are kept. You have to say what you mean and mean what you say. Your colleagues will be amazed if you do this. And then they adjust to it, and then they will give you their power'.

Decision-making and meetings

The contradictions of authority in academic settings – in particular the requirement for control and direction balanced against the necessity of distributed power – are uncommonly evident in meetings. Committees are likely to remain important in university cultures, and since many of the political goals that we seek for an academic work unit are likely to be achieved in groups of this sort, operating at a level beyond the work unit (such as faculty or university), meeting skills are important. Chairing meetings is a key skill of an academic leader, and most of the skills of chairing are immediately applicable to effectiveness as a member. So it is instructive to address the problems of being a competent member of university committees by setting yourself the task of reflecting on the approach used by chairs of these groups.

'It's the business of academic leaders to produce a sense of direction,' a humanities Dean said. 'It's vitally important when convening and chairing meetings to put forward a sense of possible directions to go in. You don't go and say 'What shall we do?'. You go in and say 'We can do a, or b, or c – what shall we do?'.

'Chairing meetings well has as much to do with what you do before the meeting as it has to do with what you do while you are at the meeting. In the meeting itself, you are directing the discussion. If you're chairing a committee, it's your job to have thought through what the issues are before it meets and to present them to it with a sense of options. It's your duty to give them a sense of where you think things should go, and particularly your duty to do it in such a way that everyone feels they can say 'You missed this out', or 'There's another relevant point'. We are governed by discussion and disagreement, not by command'.

By far the best education for working well in academic meetings is to observe skilled people in action, and to learn from them. Effective members as well as effective chairs are able to move meetings beyond the almost-inevitable divisions of opinion that occur in academic groups towards solid proposals for action. They will often have worked behind the scenes to gain support and will often request someone else to introduce propositions which might seem self-interested if they proposed them themselves. They know the techniques of embracing opposition by inviting disputants into their confidence, or by insulating opponents. They know too that these techniques should be used with honesty and openness if they are to be productive in the long term.

I shall have more to say about conducting effective meetings and encouraging discussion, disagreement and feedback at the level of the academic work unit in chapter 8. The last word on capable meeting skills at university level related to obtaining resources and enhancing departmental reputation may be left to a head of a science department:

> You deal with resistance by working through meetings which allow people to say their piece. It's critical not to act defensively, but to follow a protocol whereby there are forms of dissent and negativity that are acceptable. Above all, if you want to try and change the rule for how decisions are made, say about new course approvals or how travel allowances are allocated, you have to use the existing rule to achieve the change.

> It's a question of meeting your audience, knowing where the debate is going, seizing the moment, being open to what others have to say. Lecturers tend towards being negative and sceptical but they also have a good eye for the shallow, unconsidered, empty idea. This can obviously work to your advantage. Being ready to talk about your plans at all levels is important. Your agenda needs to be tested but you need to stay in control of the process.

At the right moment it's essential to help bring the continuing debate to a conclusion and get something definite agreed on. If you do this well people will come in behind you, feel part of the same undertaking, and the change and support you need will be there. If you can manage to walk this tightrope between maintaining your conception and getting other contributions and criticisms, you have an excellent chance of achieving what you want, whether it's more resources to support a teaching initiative, a streamlined administrative process, or better cooperation with another department on research and graduate studies.

8

ENABLING ACADEMIC PEOPLE

A leader is a dealer in hope.

Napoleon Bonaparte

Good teaching in higher education starts from a straightforward conviction that it is what students do, rather than what their teachers do, that determines how well students learn. From this point of view, teaching is inseparable from learning. Appropriate teaching strategies encourage students to relate to the subject matter they are studying in a purposeful way. A lecturer's primary task is to help make student learning possible. High quality student learning is about now and about tomorrow: it is about transforming understanding to meet an unknown future.

Effective academic leadership starts from similar considerations. What academic staff do, not what the leader does, decides whether they will excel in scholarship and teaching. From this perspective, academic leadership is intertwined with the needs and goals of academic people. High quality academic work is also about both today and tomorrow.

I have shown how staff perceptions of the context of academic work help us to understand the kind of conditions we should try to provide. Research and teaching are enriched in contexts which staff perceive as providing high levels of dialogue, support and collaboration. Good leadership actively builds such enabling environments. In this chapter I shall try to show how that the kinds of outcome we associate with successful academic work can be achieved by building on central academic values of openness, excellence, cooperation, joint decision-making, respect for truth, discussion and dialogue – and how this work implies doing something very different from taking a reactive role. I now want to look at some of the practical ways in which the positive aspects of the academic culture, properly handled, can be applied to enhancing academic effectiveness.

158

Motivation, example and responsibility

Most management books devote many pages to processes for motivating people. The idea of 'motivating' our colleagues to perform seems to sit uneasily with the idea of academic leadership. The differences are more imagined than real. 'Motivated' in this context means no more than being energetic and enthusiastic about something to do with academic work. Fostering the commitment and power of academics calls for a variety of strategies: clearly stated, challenging goals infused by values; strong involvement of staff in decisions about these goals and how to achieve them; modelling oneself the practices desired (being positive and motivated oneself – leading by example); recognising and rewarding achievement; and doing away with environmental factors which prevent or discourage people from engaging productively with tasks (such as unfair or incompetent supervision and administrative procedures).

These strategies parallel standard advice both for motivating employees (Kotter, 1993; Adair, 1996) and for helping university students to learn through good teaching (Ramsden, 1992). Excitement and challenge inspire students to engage productively with subject matter, while excellent feedback is critical to successful learning. Moreover, a central objective of good university teaching should be to create a dynamic equilibrium between freedom and discipline, or what Whitehead called romantic discovery and precision (Whitehead, 1932); control over learning should reside both with students and with teachers if we really desire our students to become experts in their subjects. And when students share in decisions about how they will learn, they are more motivated to learn well; perceptions of choice over how to learn, and of control over which aspects students may focus on, are associated with high quality learning. Studies of graduate satisfaction with courses and reported development of generic employment skills show that powerful links exist between an emphasis on student independence, learning outcomes such as teamwork and problem-solving ability, and course satisfaction (Wilson, Lizzio and Ramsden, 1997).

Students who enjoy learning and who learn well typically describe themselves as being in environments where assessment processes do not reward reproductive learning processes, and where the amount of content to be learned is not excessive. Inappropriate assessment and immoderate workloads easily induce the adaptive response of a surface approach to learning. The other side of this coin concerns the environments that encourage approaches focused on understanding and close engagement with the material to be learned. These are much more fragile contexts, but they are evidently associated with enthusiastic, committed and inspiring teaching and an environment that encourages high levels of independence and control over learning.

We will not go far wrong in our attempts to enable academic staff if we remember and apply these principles of good teaching and effective motivation. We need to do all we can to remove barriers to effective academic work. But that is not enough; another part of our job is to build on and expand academics' inbred sense of responsibility, desire for independence, and capacity to adapt to new circumstances. We also need to assess, recognise, and reward their achievements, and help develop their skills and knowledge – matters to which I will devote special attention in chapter 9.

To encourage our colleagues' engagement with a continually-changing context for academic work it is fundamentally important that we live the values and practices of self-directed academic work ourselves. Obvious as it may seem, we must share the same hopes and dangers as our colleagues if we want them to follow us. It's fruitless to expect other people to do things you are not ready to do yourself. Each of our colleagues is constantly measuring the difference between what we say we will do and what we actually do, and evaluating our leadership on the result (Kouzes and Posner, 1995, p. 211). Xenophon declared that 'There is small risk a general will be regarded with contempt by those he leads if, whatever he may have to preach, he shows himself best able to perform'. Credible leaders minimise the gap between rhetoric and action. This is leadership as 'leading the way', identified in the interviews of lecturers in chapter 5 as a key component of proficient academic leadership. It entails resourcefulness, resolution, a sense of purpose, and a vision beyond oneself.

Like knowledge of and enthusiasm for one's subject, these are qualities that cannot be feigned, nor can they be learned from courses in management skills. Integrity and leading the way emphatically do not imply 'doing what people want'. Sometimes it is necessary to do exactly what staff do not want in order to act fairly and enable people to prepare to meet future threats. Effective academic leadership is authoritative and proactive as well as responsive.

> 'There are existing incentives for academic staff to go off into their own corner and do their work,' said a head in a new university. 'Unless we can show that there are benefits in working as a team, they won't do it. The curriculum we had here a few years ago was very teaching intensive with a lot of contact hours. I could see that with the shift to being a university that academics weren't going to survive this

amount of teaching plus research. We had to rationalise and I had to get everyone to understand that there would be new criteria for the amount of teaching, and that everyone had something to offer in the new system. I was reasonably dictatorial: 'You can't teach 16 hours a week' and I asked them for ways of cutting it down. Some people blamed me for that, weren't happy with it. They wouldn't take notice of you until they realised you were on their side. That takes time. Trust comes only after you can show that the change will benefit them. They eventually saw that other departments that didn't get their act together on teaching were the first to get the big cutbacks, and then of course the changes and the teamwork to arrive at them were seen to be the best solution in the circumstances. You have to wear it as a leader and not just do what people want. What they want might not be in their best interests in the future'.

It is not invariably sensible to share decision-making about goals. But it is generally always practicable to involve staff in determining the means by which these goals are to be achieved. The values of independence and autonomy inherent in academic culture are not unique, and difficulties may arise in any organisation employing professionals when managers attempt to exert excessive control over the means of achieving agreed ends. We frequently observed in Part I how leadership of academics, like the leadership of professionals generally, is a relationship of honesty and mutual regard. The head of department who ignores this irreducible aspect of the role does so at his or her peril. As John Adair summarises it:

> Motivating others . . . should not be confused with manipulatory practices used by strong personalities to dominate weaker ones. Leadership exists in its most natural form among equals. It is not the same as domination or the exercise of power. True leaders respect the integrity of others. Bosses demand respect; leaders give respect.
>
> (Adair, 1996, p. 139)

These characteristics of respect and integrity are of special significance in the important leadership task of helping people through change. As universities come more and more to resemble business enterprises, with an increased focus on service, responsiveness, and productivity (which, as noted in chapter 2, department heads in several universities regard as a certain prospect), so an environment of constant change becomes more and more inevitable. No one will follow you into this atmosphere unless you inspire confidence and hope by your own commitment. Academic leaders are responsible for supporting staff by providing an environment that makes change attainable. This aspect of business venture and the reciprocal responsibilities of followers and leaders in working to address change was clearly expressed by Peter Drucker, well over forty years ago, in his classic *Practice of Management*:

> There is a second demand the enterprise must make on the worker: that he (sic) be willing to accept change. Innovation is a necessary function of business enterprise; it is one of its major social responsibilities. It requires, however, that people change – their work, their habits, their group relations . . . the enterprise's demand for the worker's ability to change therefore requires positive action to make it possible for him to change.
>
> (Drucker, 1955, pp. 324–5)

The good news is that independence and flexibility of mind constitute two impressive assets possessed by academics and academic leaders in engaging with the turbulent environment of today's and tomorrow's higher education. They imply exactly the self-renewing, self-transforming ways of operating that are needed in a fast-changing market. The dominant style of academic work which relies less on applying standard procedures and more on general rules which are tested and refined against evidence is precisely appropriate to an uncertain environment.

Teamwork, dialogue and collaboration

We know how much academics honour and admire individual achievement. Like 'motivation', 'teamwork' can sound like another empty concept imported from an alien management literature. Yet a moment's reflection will show that exceptional achievements in the academic world are frequently the result of collaborative effort. We have already looked at research evidence indicating that cooperative educational environments, involving a high degree of inter-colleague communication and support, appear to nurture better teaching and research (chapters 4 and 5). In fact, success in terms of enhanced performance and increased creativity is strongly related to high cooperation in many occupational groups, ranging from business executives to research scientists and back to university students (see Kouzes and Posner, 1995, p. 154).

To understand the nature of the academic leader's task in fostering collaboration we must conceptualise our role in terms of a dialogue with staff. Like good teaching, academic leadership is not telling or transmitting information and ideas; it is a sort of conversation aimed at helping people to change and develop. In a satisfactory conversation, we listen as well as talk; we try to engage in productive dialogue; we respect the other's right to contribute; we imagine ourselves in the shoes of the people with whom we are conversing. It is by modelling these processes that academic leaders advance collaborative effort. Senge (1990, pp. 238–9) quotes the physicist Werner Heisenberg's comments on his lifetime of conversations with Bohr, Einstein and other great twentieth century scientists; these conversations 'literally gave birth to many of the theories for which these men eventually became famous'. Collectively, we can achieve more, and we can be more insightful when we work in teams that continually learn.

During the time I was preparing this chapter I attended a meeting of a research team of which I am a member. It was a meeting like others this groups has had: task-focused, productive, and enjoyable, but certainly not without conflict and debate. Different interpretations of results were presented and defended. At the same time as these discussions were in progress, another process was also going on: a kind of collective learning where members communicated their ideas openly and exposed their assumptions. The disagreements never threatened our progress; in fact, they helped it. I subsequently came to see that the processes were those described by Senge (1990) as 'discussion' and 'dialogue'. We were using conflict to be more productive, and the reason we could do it was that we respected each other and each other's competence in the field. We each felt we had something to learn from the other members.

It is an unfortunate fact that many academic seminars and research groups do not achieve this dynamic balance. Discussion involving a desire to predominate over one's colleagues, and an absence of the confidence required to make oneself vulnerable, often prevail. Our academic leadership task is to enable staff by establishing through example and coaching a team environment where both dialogue and discussion occur. A key skill of academic leadership is to help our colleagues see each other as colleagues – to bring out the positive aspect of the collegial spirit, to help them feel they are in an environment where it is safe to suspend assumptions. It is easy to be collegial when everyone agrees, but the true advantages of collegiality come from being able to work productively when there is disagreement (Senge, 1990, p. 245). As I have indicated, the bedrock of productive disagreement is mutual respect.

The most creative academic teams are constructed on the principle of shared vision and collective regard.

Table 8.1 illustrates some differences between different models of departmental organisation in relation to teamwork. Paradigm 3 represents a model of collaborative teamwork which is focused on enabling colleagues to be instrumental in adapting to change, rather than either attempting to avoid it (P1) or being reactive to it (P2). Paradoxically, academic leadership is more, not less indispensable when collaboration and teamwork is required in a rapidly changing environment. An effective leader in paradigm 3 actively helps colleagues develop co-operative goals, seek unifying solutions, and build trusting relationships (see Kouzes and Posner, 1995, p. 154).

Table 8.1 Organisational paradigms for academic departments

Paradigm 1: Traditional academic department	Paradigm 2: 'Managerial' academic department	Paradigm 3: Academic department as team
Conservative and inflexible	Bureaucratic and rule-following	Flexible and experimental
Non-interventionist leadership; management by exception	Positional leadership; authority resides in rank; compliance expected	Leader as creative coordinator, varying leadership roles determined by congruence of problem and expertise
Decision making by debate and individual power (academic freedom predominant)	Decision making by rule application or imposition (control over academics predominant)	Decision making by compromise and appeal to common needs, including fairness and equity (freedom and control in creative tension)
Discussion	Requirement	Dialogue and discussion
Rhetoric of respect for all points of view	Emphasis on one right way	Emphasis on testing ideas against demonstrated outcomes
Conflict in adversarial atmosphere; may be productive	Conflict restricted; seen as destructive	Conflict viewed as positive and comparatively comfortable
Goals vague or unspecified	Short term operational goals, reliance on algorithms	Long term fluid visions based on broad principles of problem-solving
Slow learning and adaptation	Reactive, possibly impeded learning and adaptation	Rapid learning and adaptation

It is important to re-emphasise that this does *not* imply renouncing the leadership responsibility of thinking and acting ahead. Creative teams have creative leaders: thinkers who can also act, people who can create a mental picture of where they want to go and can be relied upon to get there. Teams need leaders and academics require their leaders to exercise these qualities. Nor does leading a team mean shirking the task of making oneself unpopular when that is necessary either to help the team position itself for maximum advantage in the external environment, or to rectify unfair practices within the group. One of the greatest barriers to advancing academic leadership effectiveness is the belief that discipline and freedom are incompatible qualities of a successful academic environment. Few academic teams can operate well without a leader who is willing to make strong decisions. Paradigm 3 requires greater, not less perseverance than P1 and P2 if it is to function properly.

A lucid account of the characteristics of creative teams is contained in Antony Jay's *Management and Machiavelli* (Jay, 1970), chapter 13. Their central features are:

1 The authority of their leader is unquestioned.
2 There is constructive dialogue (see above) between members.
3 They focus on producing real output – which spurs ideas, enhances morale, and provides external feedback.
4 Their leader has a large amount of autonomy in the organisation.
5 They grow and develop, or they die.
6 If their creative leader is removed, they become extinct.
7 They define their own projects within the constraints of the organisation.

These characteristics provide a useful set of prompts for leading creative academic teams. As we shall see, they are also useful for developing creative university leaders.

Ron Lawson deals with an issue of equity in a department
Ron Lawson wanted people in his department to 'feel in charge of their own destiny'. He wanted them to be responsible and take initiatives, and believed that the best way to encourage this was to involve them in decisions and to steer a line between managing situations and trusting people. Shortly after becoming head a serious question of policy related to equity and fairness

arose. 'Within the faculty there were a number of people, mainly senior male academics, who'd been around a long time and who were pretty street smart. They knew how to subvert the system, ending up doing a lot less work in teaching than they were supposed to do. We had staff who looked as if they were doing 98 hours in a semester who by careful manipulation were actually involved in less than half that. And some of them had been teaching this course for 20 years and had the same notes they'd been using for years! They did no research either. Meanwhile there would be junior staff teaching, mainly women, large first year classes with seven tutorials a week and vast numbers of assessments to mark.

'I decided to create a policy that would work systematically against the exploitation of younger staff, who were working in a system which allowed others to rig it. I didn't solve all the problems but I knew if I solved some it would increase my support from the people who were being taken advantage of. I deliberately calculated what level of support that would be, and that if we constructed a policy that was clearly going to be opposed by these senior people, what the chances of that support being strong enough to win would be.

'One way of changing this would have been confrontation. If you did that, they'd deny it, ask you to prove it. I wanted my colleagues to achieve a solution and produce as a team a system that no-one could say was unfair. So, after consulting several people for advice, I changed the measure of teaching from hours of contact to full time equivalent students. People were left to construct their teaching time as they wished. I argued for it from the standpoint of justice without reference to particular incidents, spending a lot of time on document development and not hurrying the matter through.'

Meetings

An important leadership skill for a head is being able to run departmental meetings well. No work group can function effectively for long unless its members get together to discuss issues and address problems. Academic meetings can form useful ways of enhancing team spirit and solving difficulties creatively. They also often waste time, increase inter-colleague hostility, and paper over deep divisions between points of view (Lucas, 1995, p. 184) – as we have already noted. Lucas (1995, pp. 184–95) provides some practical advice on how to plan effective meetings, including the basics of room arrangements, agenda construction, and evaluating meeting effectiveness.

Above and beyond these skills is the question of what meetings are for and what the head's role is in running them. It is important to remember that different kinds of groups should be established to deal with different kinds of problems. The theory that a meeting of all academic staff is the best way to govern an academic work unit and deal with its manifold problems usually does not work out in practice. Think rather of different kinds of meetings for different purposes. Small advisory meetings may be used to exchange information with subgroups and are an appropriate place for heads to bring complex issues which they feel they cannot solve alone. Small groups like this can creatively develop joint policies, test them out on their colleagues and suggest improvements, and then the head can float them before the whole department; this is especially important in cases of major policy change. Most of the difficulties should have been addressed before this stage, minimising negative reactions in the larger group. If it should turn out that something has been overlooked, do not try to solve the problem on the spot but compromise by establishing a task force or working party to deal with it.

As we saw in chapter 7, the job of an academic leader chairing a meeting is to produce a sense of direction. But a balance must be struck between directing and consulting. The art to be acquired is an art of compromise. You must not work entirely behind the scenes so that people feel they are being manipulated and that departmental meetings are mere rubber stamps. On the other hand you should not suggest changes to policy and procedures without having consulted carefully beforehand, lest the changes are misunderstood and are defeated as a result.

Jane Drew overhauls her departmental staff meetings
Jane's department had used academic staff meetings, held fortnightly for three hours for all fifteen permanent staff, as the main vehicle for decision-making in the department for as long as anyone could remember. The problem was that every decision, or so it seemed, had to be made in this meeting. Bitter and furious controversy arose over matters such as the proposed

refurbishment of one office and whether the second year lecture programme should be reduced to include a visiting speaker. The last meeting had been occupied for two hours by a procedural point relating to one member's failure to have his amendment to the minutes of two meetings ago mentioned in the revised version of the minutes (He had wanted to change them to include his comment that a colleague had been 'unseemly and bullying' in her remarks and that the chair (Jane) had shown 'distressingly unacceptable and non-academic behaviour in gagging proper discussion'). Meanwhile, Rome was burning: the university had asked for the faculty's proposals for staffing and resource reductions of five per cent by next month – the Dean was breathing down Jane's neck about it – and student numbers were falling for the third year in succession.

What was Jane to do? She spoke individually to all her colleagues about the meetings, and it emerged that everyone disliked them, and only two people wanted them to continue in their present form (one of whom was the complainant mentioned above, who said that only Jane needed to change so that she 'stood by the principles of collaboration and openness she espoused rather than being manipulative and preventing legitimate academic debate'). She assured herself after meeting them privately that some of the powerful voices in the department would support a radical change.

Subsequently she put it to the staff meeting that time which all of them could ill afford to lose was being wasted, that decisions were not being made, and that the present meetings would cease, to be replaced by informal half-hour meetings every week over lunch, plus two general meetings of one hour a term with shorter agendas which allocated time to each item and listed the anticipated results. The idea was enthusiastically accepted, with one dissentient.

To improve these quality of the new group meetings, Jane began a policy of seeing individual staff regularly to strengthen relationships, and to discuss ways in which the departmental meetings could be run even more efficiently without denying the input of colleagues to decisions affecting them. She found the protocol for problem-solving in academic meetings suggested by Lucas (1995, p. 193) to be a helpful device for gaining consensus: Define the problem; generate alternative solutions;

consider the advantages and disadvantages of a short list of these solutions; select an alternative people can live with; experiment by trying the solution for a designated period; nominate one or two people who will report back to the group on the success of the solution.

Leadership for teaching

What are the messages about teaching that are being conveyed by our module coordinators and heads of departments? What is their role in providing the leadership in teaching and learning within those courses? Good teaching is an institution-wide matter that demands effective leadership. If I look at what we have done over the last few years, that is where we have probably fallen down.

A senior university manager

A paradox of academic work is the relative significance attached to research and teaching. Teaching undergraduate and course work postgraduate students is an absolutely central function of universities. For most of us it is a non-optional activity. It is the reason, in the last analysis, why the public supports universities (Anderson, Johnson and Milligan, 1996) and it is the major source of their income. Moreover, at the heart of the shift to mass higher education and the associated idea of 'enterprise' university is the concept of accountability to clients and a demand for the highest standards of customer service. The desire to serve others is a critical aspect of good teaching.

Nevertheless, teaching is still seen by many academics to be less interesting, less creative, less important, and less rewarded than research. There has been in a steady increase over the past twenty years in the proportion of staff who say that their main interest is in research, not in teaching (Halsey, 1992; Ramsden et al., 1995). Lecturers in many countries believe that career advancement is coupled directly to acquiring research funds and publication of research. While the official view of most UK and Australian universities is that excellence in teaching is fully recognised (and umbilically attached to merit in research) their staff see the situation quite differently. Effort and commitment as a teacher, they continue to maintain, is neither recognised or rewarded by their universities (Halsey, 1992; Boyer, 1990; Gibbs, 1995a; Ramsden and Martin, 1996). In the UK and Australia, present (1997) funding mechanisms appear to reinforce the view that research is a higher-status activity demanding more interest and resources than teaching. While elaborate performance-based funding schemes exist for research – and have unquestionably influenced behaviour – links between performance in teaching at university level and funding are either weak or non-existent.

This set of incongruities forms the background against which we must execute the leadership responsibility of enabling academics to teach well. Fulfilling this function successfully will require you to draw on the full depth of your leadership resources. I referred in chapter 3 to the large amount of dissatisfaction with the quality of university teaching among students and graduates, and showed how the outcomes of their learning continue to give rise to concern. Employers value the qualities that really good university courses give rise to; their complaint is that there are too few really good courses. Yet many staff think that they are competent teachers, and are likely to respond to entreaties to improve with defensiveness and lack of interest (Lucas, 1995, pp. 100–2). They don't think that there is any need to discuss teaching or examine how they might do it better. Attempts to raise the status of teaching often fail because universities, and the academics within them, are expert at responding to attempts to direct them in ways that offset the impact of change.

What can we do about it? In no other area of academic leadership is personal commitment to the goal of high quality and productivity ('modelling') more important. Simply stated, you must believe that good teaching matters. You must act in ways consistent with your belief.

We need first to address our own preconceptions about effective teaching and learning, and if we are not already aware of the substantial literature and research on the topic of effective learning and teaching in higher education, we might spend some time becoming familiar with its basic ideas and associated implications for curriculum structures, teaching methods and student assessment. Academic development unit World Wide Web sites and organisations such as the Staff and Educational Development Association (UK) provide useful starting points.

It is important to escape from common myths about teaching in higher education if we are to help our staff teach effectively. These include:

- the tradition that the characteristics of effective teaching cannot be described and the related belief that there is no firm knowledge of the principles and practice of effective teaching in higher education (Fact: There is consistent, replicated, research-based evidence that certain teaching approaches and strategies are associated with higher quality student learning)

- the belief that good teachers – unlike good researchers, it would seem – are born, not made (Fact: People change their teaching methods and their understanding of teaching, and acquire specific skills, through training and development)
- the view that teaching is inevitably a less creative activity than research (Fact: Exemplary teachers describe their teaching as a continual process of learning and liken it to creative, curiosity-driven res earch)
- the view that learning at university is actually enhanced when teaching is poor (and that students must therefore not be guided too carefully) (Facts: Poor teaching on average leads to poor learning; lack of clear structure and guidance is associated with lower quality learning outcomes and student dissatisfaction)
- the fallacy that teaching first year undergraduates is easier than teaching more experienced students (Facts: It is always harder; students are more critical of the standards of first year teaching)
- the belief that knowledge of subject matter is both a necessary and sufficient condition for good teaching (Fact: It is necessary but not sufficient)

These and similar myths (Ramsden, 1992, pp. 87–8) serve to obstruct discussion about teaching and learning. They provide excellent excuses for not doing anything to improve teaching. They permit lecturers to assert that they always 'teach for understanding' while using methods of course design and assessment that encourage students to avoid understanding. They deter innovation and the reflective, decision-making approach to work which should characterise professional practice. They imply no special determination to search out techniques of teaching for effective learning, and they permit factors other than educational ones – such as student numbers – to govern teaching and assessment methods (Biggs, 1996). They help maintain resistance to the changes which academic leaders will be keen to help their staff embrace – particularly when the standards of teaching and the outcomes of learning are likely to assume greater significance for resources and survival in a more competitive higher education environment. One of the keys to enabling lecturers to accept change in teaching is to link their fear of change and their desire for it in a creative and supportive way. Staff may be anxious about the introduction of information technology in teaching, for example, but they are also probably looking for ways to cope with larger numbers of students without reducing quality. Because simple forms of IT may provide some solutions to this problem, colleagues may see a reason for modifying their view.

The following strategies may help to operationalise a commitment to enabling academic staff to teach more effectively. They include processes which are based on empirical research into the leadership and environmental factors which academics believe would encourage better university teaching (Ramsden and Martin, 1996). The summary below lists some specific actions which academic leaders can use.

SUMMARY OF SOME SPECIFIC WAYS IN WHICH ACADEMIC LEADERS CAN IMPROVE THE STANDARD OF TEACHING

Make demonstrated teaching skill a non-negotiable criterion for every academic appointment

Conduct an audit of the factors which staff feel are making good teaching difficult in your department, including conditions such as access to teaching rooms, equipment and class size

Show your personal commitment by asking your colleagues to help you improve your own teaching

Value teaching by publicising teaching accomplishments of the department and its staff (e.g. student evaluation results, quality assessment results) and hold celebrations of successes

Expand moves towards instructional processes that demand greater teamwork among staff (such as flexible learning strategies using print-based teaching materials)

Show how innovative assessment methods can be used to give high quality feedback to larger numbers of students

Hold 'what's on top' lunchtime meetings where staff can safely explore problems in teaching (Begin with a problem of your own)

Allow staff to design their own student evaluation questionnaires rather than use standard instruments

Establish an internal email list on 'effective techniques for better teaching and learning'

Provide an incentive for participation in teaching evaluation and reporting process (e.g. £100/$200 towards travel or conference attendance)

Admit your own mistakes, misgivings and disasters as a teacher

Invite staff to compete against their own objectives for better teaching rather than against norms set by the group

Establish a student liaison forum where students can meet staff over lunch to canvass ideas and creative options for better teaching and learning

Initiate simple 'research' procedures whereby staff can collect information about student learning (e.g. The 'Three Most Important Things' exercise: Gibbs *et al.*, 1987)

Invite respected teachers from other departments or local universities to talk about how they teach, asking them to give special emphasis on the errors they have made and how they have learned to do it better

Offer to be the first person in the department to have their teaching observed by peers

Talk to staff about times when you have really enjoyed your teaching, and ask them to share similar experiences with you and their colleagues

Form a group of staff who are interested in working through key texts on university teaching at lunchtime meetings

Make links from your departmental WWW site to sites throughout the world concerned with excellence and innovation in university teaching

When giving feedback on a colleagues' teaching, provide descriptive comments not evaluative ones

Provide incentives to staff to gain a qualification in university teaching

Encourage staff to publish articles about teaching their subject in international journals

Attend national conferences and workshops on university teaching personally, and report back to your staff what you have learned and what you will do differently

Follow up some recent graduates and ask them to comment at a staff meeting about how their course might have been improved

Do the same thing with some local employers

Set targets jointly with staff for improvements in, for example, progression rates and course experience scores, and monitor progress against these objectives

Talk about learning and the quality of graduates at every staff meeting

Establish a programme of teaching skills for casual staff

Persuade your university that investing small amounts of resources for improving teaching can lead to surprisingly large returns in quality

Always say that problems in teaching are *our* problems and that successes are *our* successes

---

Be committed to good teaching yourself

I have repeatedly emphasised the significance of 'doing what you say you will do' for leadership credibility in any setting, and especially for effective academic work. Since the introduction of more rigorous quality assessment processes, every academic has heard their university sing loud and long about its commitment to good teaching. But few staff believe that their institutions are actually doing what they say they are doing. The leader's task is to help narrow the gap between the policy rhetoric and staff perceptions.

To do this you must, of course, openly express your belief in the benefits of excellence in teaching; but more importantly, you must do what you say you believe. This does not mean necessarily being the best teacher in the department. It does not mean being an expert in every aspect of pedagogical theory and practice. It *does* mean being genuinely interested in teaching, and publicly speaking out, at meetings and in less formal interactions with individual staff, about the importance of good teaching and the need to understand teaching as a professional process in need of constant self-examination. It means providing tangible support for efforts to make teaching better, including resources and time, and showing a commitment to enriching your own teaching by participating in professional development activities yourself. It means 'going first' in any programme such as peer review and observation of teaching.

The role of educational leadership in creating and transmitting a culture in which achievements in teaching are acknowledged and celebrated cannot be overestimated. In chapter 4 I reported that an international survey of instructional development personnel (Wright and O'Neil, 1995) had found that the leadership of deans and department heads was central to improving the effectiveness of instruction. Lecturers in workshops on recognising and rewarding good university teaching frequently express a desire for academic managers to learn how to lead teachers and establish strong, committed course teams. Moreover, they want them continually to reinforce the importance of good teaching in their daily behaviour. They want them to help them gain pleasure from teaching well. All the staff development and training in the world is less important than the leader's own genuine commitment to supporting excellence in undergraduate education.

'I feel very strongly' said a lecturer in one of my surveys, 'that administrators and heads of department quickly lose contact with day-to-day working conditions for their staff. They show little or no interest in what happens in classes. They have unrealistic expectations of what staff can do in the time available. They lose sight of the fact that enjoying teaching is an important factor in the quality of teaching'.

Promise yourself that your staff will not be able to say this about you.

Provide the means for good teaching through enhancing teamwork

Although research in many fields of study requires collaborative effort, teaching remains an individual and private activity in numerous departments. If we truly believe in the benefits of collegiality in a mass higher education system, we need to rework it so that it serves students as well as sustains lecturers. Teaching that advances learning is not an isolated activity. Effective undergraduate courses are typically ones where methods of teaching and assessing students are widely discussed, and new methods are openly advanced, risked, tested, and applied. Peer examination of research methodology is normal: to enable good teaching and increase its status, you need to make peer discussion of teaching and collaborative design of curricula the norm as well. The academic leader whose institution supports a shift to more flexible teaching and learning methodologies has an advantage in this respect. Flexible delivery methods in higher education, including applications of information technology and the increased use of printed materials to replace lectures, entail more teamwork and expose the products of teaching to public scrutiny, thus assisting a shift to collective responsibility for improvement.

Lecturers in our study of rewards for good teaching in Australian higher education (Ramsden and Martin, 1996) held the view that understanding teaching as a collective obligation as well as an individual one was vital to enhancing its status. More than six out of ten said that 'encouraging more collaboration and discussion about teaching among staff in academic departments' would have a powerful effect on improving teaching quality. A changed conception of the unit of innovation in teaching and learning (to include not only the individual staff member but also his or her colleagues and the larger environment in which he or she works) is part of the idea of the university as a 'learning organisation'.

Aim to get your colleagues talking about teaching in both formal and informal meetings by talking about it yourself. Encourage a spirit of trust, sharing ideas and dialogue by showing that you are vulnerable to making mistakes in working to help students acquire knowledge and understanding – and that you try to learn from the experience about how to do it better. Your goal is to establish a safe environment for experimenting with new ways of teaching and assessment. Many staff may not be fully aware that very few new ideas about teaching work right first time.

Tom Williams introduces a self-evaluation of teaching process
'I've never had a lot of faith in strategic planning of the kind that puts everyone in a department together and gets them to work out goals and ways of getting there. My 'vision' was no more than to get staff in the department talking about teaching so they would learn more about it and maybe figure out for themselves what they could do better as economics lecturers. Well that's what I came to eventually. Originally I wanted to do everything under the sun!

'I did it by focusing on a self-evaluation process which happened to be something related to what the university was trying to do at the time – to get everyone's teaching evaluated so that there would be better material for promotion committees to work on. I decided that we could do it by concentrating on the idea of a cooperative approach to evaluation where people learned from each other. I structured the meetings so that there was plenty of opportunity for social contact. At the first meeting I got staff, both lecturers and tutors, to identify areas of their teaching they would like to enhance, and distributed some resources related to 'good practice' and practical tips to improve university teaching in economics and commerce subjects, which they could try out. The staff selected their own criteria for evaluation, not mine or the university's. At a later meeting each person who had signed up presented their areas for improvement, their criteria and the sources of evidence they would use. This session proved to be a helpful forum where staff started to talk about problems in teaching and the discussions have continued ever since. I wanted to create an avenue for staff to create something substantial which they could use in presenting cases for promotion or applications for jobs.

'Some became committed and enrolled in the process, and have since gone on to do the certificate in teaching course; some realised that if they had a difficulty in teaching there was now someone to talk to about it over coffee (and I heard them doing it quite often). Some ignored it; you can't win them all. I'm thinking of different ways to reach them. But as an experiment it was a success. It helped change the atmosphere in the department to one where teaching became a topic you could openly discuss with your colleagues, and in that sense I think it was worthwhile'.

Make teaching a profession among your staff

Start by determining what good teaching means in your work unit. Your colleagues should aspire to a vision of what teaching effectiveness is, and why its practice will benefit their future. One way of advancing towards a shared view of what high quality teaching in your department or subject consists of is to begin by looking at a standard text on university teaching or teaching assessment criteria such as those produced by quality and funding agencies (of which there are now many examples). Identify key aspects you believe are relevant and circulate a draft among your colleagues. Through communication techniques such as email or internal memos, work towards a common set of educational goals, values and strategies which can be agreed at a staff meeting constantly referred to in planning curricula, teaching, assessment and evaluation. It is not necessary that every colleague becomes a world class educator for each of them to agree on the importance of good teaching for the work unit's future and to accept a joint responsibility for promoting teaching excellence. Teaching undergraduates is, after all, the job which permits most academic organisational units to survive, and survival will increasingly depend on a professional approach to helping them to learn.

Establishing a set of shared aims and methods for good teaching provides an opportunity to shift the focus of education in your work unit from information transmission and teacher-centred instruction to teaching designed to change understanding and centred on students' learning. It is possible to use research findings to help colleagues conceptualise teaching in a more professional way. For example, research showing that high quality learning outcomes, which all lecturers desire their students to achieve, are consistently linked to the latter approach to teaching (see chapter 3) may, when shared with colleagues, convince them that different methods are worth consideration.

There are other ways in which research and familiar academic procedures associated with research can be used to help manage the professionalisation of university teaching. Nowadays, every academic is expected to become 'research qualified': show leadership in teaching by encouraging and supporting staff to acquire qualifications in university teaching as well, and by rewarding staff who achieve them. Courses leading to such qualifications are now offered in an increasing number of universities, and moves to make training mandatory are supported by several bodies, including the AUT. Encourage a scholarly approach to teaching. Make it clear that you value staff commitment to carrying out research into the best ways of teaching in their subject area, and particularly that you regard grants for teaching and refereed publications on teaching and learning highly. Fund small teaching projects from your budget, or seek funds from other sources to support them. Consider introducing well-known processes related to research, such as peer review, as a normal part of evaluating and improving teaching performance. There is evidence from recent US studies of the effectiveness of processes for assessing university teaching which reflect customary research performance evaluation methods, such as the use of peer review and teaching portfolios (Gibbs, 1995b).

Appoint good teachers

'No other decision your department will make will be as important as the selection of a faculty colleague. Deliberate and careful selection of new colleagues has more to do with the growth and well-being of your department than any other action you may take' (Gmelch and Miskin, 1995, p. 19). It is easy to underestimate the seriousness that needs to be attached to recruiting staff who want to be lively partners in making teaching and learning as good as it can be. The fantasy that excellent scholars are automatically good university teachers remains all too prevalent.

It is unnecessary to specify required teaching skills in great detail when establishing appointment criteria. Skills can be acquired fairly easily; a commitment to teaching and improving it is very hard to instil if it is not already present. The three most important attributes needed are:

- A positive attitude towards students
- An ability to communicate well
- A sharp interest, and ideally some experience, in continuously improving teaching through professional reflection

These should be critical factors in assignment to any post involving substantial teaching duties. Show that you are serious about good teaching by making it a requirement for all candidates to document their teaching experience in a three-page teaching portfolio, and ask short-listed candidates at interview to give examples of how they have tackled specific teaching problems during their careers, as well as requiring them to give a presentation to a group of staff and students. Not only will these processes safeguard your students and colleagues against bad teaching – they will also establish clear expectations among new appointees that teaching is a priority in your work unit.

Develop your staff

Don't leave the task of improvement in teaching and learning to an educational development unit. As we will see in the next chapter, an academic manager must regard staff development as a top priority. Encourage constant self-examination of educational practice: continuing professional development is an indispensable part of good teaching. Aim to provide resources for travel and attendance at conferences on teaching and learning. In a large department, try to identify one or more champions of teaching among your staff to whom the tasks of building teams and developing and improving can be delegated – and ensure that their contributions are fully recognised in tangible ways.

Provide assistance for new staff and casual staff to improve their teaching skills. Studies of the experiences of new academics indicate that they generally find their teaching responsibilities to be difficult and stressful. They often feel under too much pressure (with heavy teaching loads and inadequate assistance); they are unsure about how to manage their time; they receive conflicting messages about the importance of teaching and research; and they get limited support and advice from their colleagues. They are often uncomfortable in the classroom, find communication with their students difficult, focus on delivery rather than encouraging learning, and over-prepare their sessions. They report feelings of isolation and lack of collegial support. In time they learn to cope: but they often do so in a way that has a negative impact on the quality of student learning. They learn to use strategies that are inimical to excellent student learning outcomes, and their initial excitement about teaching and interest in it declines (Boice, 1992; Martin and Ramsden, 1994).

To lessen these problems, ensure that you and your colleagues do not show indifference or resentment towards new staff who are developing their teaching skills. Support mentoring and co-teaching programmes (including peer review and observation); encourage self-assessment of teaching performance; arrange reduced teaching loads for inexperienced staff; focus on descriptive and positive feedback; continually emphasise the characteristics of high quality teaching which are part of your work unit's vision.

Work to remove barriers to good teaching

Resourceful leaders free up the people for whom they are responsible by striving to eliminate obstacles which stand in their way. There are assuredly plenty of obstructions in the path of academics who want to be excellent teachers. Irritating administrative difficulties, as well as burgeoning demands for reporting on processes and outcomes and a widespread belief that universities care less and less about staff who are committed to teaching, continue to form barriers to good teaching and stifle commitment to improving teaching in many universities and departments.

Carry out a review among your colleagues of the factors that hinder their teaching effectiveness: it is likely to include elements such as increased administrative loads and committee work; equipment and facilities (even simple apparatus such as overhead projectors) that are not present in classrooms or do not work; larger numbers of students; imposed (rather than negotiated) official deadlines; increased pressure to obtain external research funding and publish additional papers; lack of rewards for making an effort as a teacher and lack of interest from colleagues in innovative educational methods; support staff who see their function as applying rules rather than working beside academics to deliver the primary service of the organisation. Taken together, these 'little' things impose massive strain on the supply of high quality teaching.

Depending on the degree of control over budgets and staffing you may have, it is sometimes possible to address specific administrative problems such as access to facilities and support for producing materials at the level of the work unit. This may require tradeoffs with other functions, and must of course be discussed with colleagues and coherently linked to goals and management plans for the department. It is also beneficial to stress through your own statements and actions that serving academics in their teaching capacity is in no sense a humble or secondary role – helping staff to do their jobs effectively and maximise their potentiality is, after all, one of your own central duties as an academic leader. Authorise administrative staff to seek new and creative ways of supporting academic colleagues in discharging their teaching duties successfully. It will also be necessary to work strategically to influence the wider system, using the techniques discussed in chapter 7 to work through appropriate decision-making bodies and with key individuals.

Make it a priority to seek out and convey new ideas about teaching to your departmental colleagues, especially those which maintain or increase quality without compromising workloads. It is not possible to teach well and to derive enjoyment from teaching in today's university environment if we use the same methods of instruction and assessment as we did in a climate of smaller numbers of more able students. But there are many successful ways in which the quality of education can be maintained in this climate, ranging from increased use of peer and self-assessment to applications of information technology, and new ideas are being generated and published continually. Send out the good news about the ways in which staff in other departments or other universities have successfully addressed the challenges. Valuable sources include the four books on teaching more students produced by Gibbs and his colleagues for the former Polytechnics and Colleges Funding Council (see, for example, Gibbs, 1992).

Encourage staff to reconceptualise teaching for the twenty-first century

Inevitable features of teaching and learning in the higher education of the future include global competition for students, widespread use of information technology, larger numbers of students, transparent accountability processes, an increased client service orientation, and greater emphasis on facilitating learning rather than disseminating knowledge. In order to prepare staff for these and similar changes, and to encourage a spirit of being in control of change rather than merely responding to it, consider convening some meetings where staff explore appropriate courses of action and plan new strategies together. These meetings might start with a stimulating talk about what is happening in today's higher education system from an articulate and influential senior colleague, and how other departments in your field are dealing with the challenges.

In arts and social science subjects especially, invite colleagues to consider the place of these disciplines in a future rapidly changing society where the ability to deploy generic skills – communication, problem definition and solution, synthesis, analysis, information retrieval and generation, critical thinking, flexibility, independence, an orientation to lifelong learning – will be highly valued. In all fields, examine ways of providing undergraduate education and assessing learning outcomes that soften boundaries between disciplines and prepare students for employment.

A particularly effective way of reorientating undergraduate teaching is to forge strategic links with past graduates and local employers. What aspects of students' course experiences were most valuable? What do employers think are the strengths of your graduates? What improvements do both groups suggest?

Leadership for research and scholarship

I argued in chapter 4 that the 'enabling' properties of productive academic contexts, and their associated leadership characteristics, resemble those which enhance the effectiveness of academics as teachers of undergraduates. Scholarly activity and output is enlivened when staff perceive their departments to be places that provide a collaborative environment, clear goals, intellectual challenge, equitable workload distribution, and a large amount of dialogue and consultation. In contrast, creative work is hindered by, among other things, lack of choice, over-evaluation and emphasis on external rewards, time pressures, and a perception of a climate where risk-taking is frowned upon (see Sapienza, 1995, pp. 84–85).

The broad criteria of personal commitment, facilitating teamwork, appropriate recruitment, staff development, and removing barriers to fruitful work apply equally to improving the quality of scholarship, service, research, and postgraduate supervision as well as to improving the quality of undergraduate teaching.

However, the matter is complicated by differences between disciplinary cultures and types of university as well as by the changes in the wider environment which have led to a larger and more heterogeneous group of staff. It is impossible to provide specific advice which will meet the very different problems faced by, say, the head of a physics department in a prestigious older university and the head of a school of tourism at a new, small, regional institution. The effects of research assessment and quality-related research funding have been to strengthen the culture of what Anderson *et al.* (1996) called 'Big R' research: the kind of research work typified in the empirical natural sciences, requiring large amounts of external funding, demanding precise project management, employing teams of research students and assistants, and leading to large numbers of publications in refereed journals of high international repute. The reflective processes that may lead a lone arts scholar to produce a single book in a period of ten years seem very distant from this model.

At the same time, changes in higher education to produce a larger and more diverse system have meant that a smaller number of staff can realistically aspire to be 'Big R' researchers, even in empirical science subjects. We have not in the UK and Australia reached the clear division of institutions from top doctoral institutions through comprehensive universities to community colleges which characterises a true mass system such as that of the USA. But there are plenty of examples of staff who, appointed to teaching and service aligned departments and institutions in the days of the binary system, now find themselves under pressure to acquire research qualifications, chase external competitive grants, and publish more (I know one university which recently announced to its staff that *all* of them would be expected to produce a minimum of two refereed journal articles a year).

How can we temper the 'frenetic chasing of grants and publications', the emphasis on research quantity rather than quality (Anderson *et al.*, 1996, p. 63), and the depressingly one-dimensional view of academic status which many staff believe to have been encouraged by research performance measures?

I referred in chapter 2 to Ernest Boyer's reconceptualisation of academic work to allow greater recognition of diversity and to bring legitimacy to the entire compass of academic work. Sixty-eight per cent of respondents to his 1989 survey agreed that 'We need better ways, beside publications, to evaluate the scholarly performance of the faculty' (Boyer, 1990, p. 34). He argued for American institutions and individual staff to adopt varying combinations of the 'four scholarships': of discovery, of integration, of application, and of teaching. Boyer identified the dangers of the uni-dimensional view of quality in American higher education:

> Simply stated, what we have on many campuses today is a crisis of purpose. Far too many colleges and universities are being driven not by self-defined objectives but by the external imperatives of prestige. Even institutions that enroll primarily undergraduates – and have few if any resources for research – seek to imitate ranking research centers. In the process, their mission becomes blurred, standards of research are compromised, and the quality of teaching and learning is disturbingly diminished.
>
> (Boyer, 1990, p. 55)

I believe that Boyer's message is even more true today across the Atlantic and the Pacific. It is important to broaden the concept of scholarship and its enabling if academic leaders are to help all their colleagues realise their potential. A recognition of the advantages of flexibility in enabling academics to pursue different mixtures of these four scholarships is highly appropriate for academic leaders. It would in no way decrease the status of 'Big R' research, and it would surely not reduce the commitment of researchers to expand knowledge and publish their findings – but it would enable more staff to be recognised and rewarded for their contributions to the intellectual life of their university and their community.

Commitment and modelling

'There is nothing gaines a Prince such repute, as great exploits, and rare trialls of himself in Heroicke actions', said Machiavelli. Whatever form of scholarship we aspire to support in our colleagues, the academic leader's own reputation as a scholar has a profound effect on his or her credibility among them. Middlehurst (1993, p. 135–6), summarising several studies of staff expectations of heads of departments, says they show that heads are expected to play a major part in departmental productivity by being engaged in research of a high standard, and by obtaining research funds themselves. The importance of scholarly distinction and personal commitment to research was also apparent in the comments of staff which I reported in chapter 5. Leading through providing a scholarly example inspires and motivates colleagues to be more active themselves.

Not having the respect of your colleagues as a researcher is hardly conducive to their effective leadership and management. Whether it is essential to continue an active research career when in the service of one's colleagues as a leader is less clear. I am aware of no association between the effectiveness of academic leaders and their continuation, or slackening, or complete interruption of their research career.

I have suggested that your vision of research and scholarship should be flexible and capable of accommodating diversity. One of the harder lessons new academic leaders have to learn is that not everyone will fit into our pattern. A Procrustean bed which tries to force colleagues into a single mould of academic productivity is bad news. We must remember that we are in the business of working with our colleagues as partners rather than using them to realise our own objectives. Unhappiness and minimal compliance are certain results of a vision which is not shared but imposed. You may think you are within an ace of a Nobel Prize; your colleagues may aspire to a community project taking science into schools, or to writing a first year text, or to pursuing new applications of ideas with two local firms, or to producing scholarly articles describing innovative methods of teaching the subject. Naturally, everyone in a university must show that they are able to be intellectually creative, continue to be excited by manipulating ideas, and committed to continually learning. But they can do these things in diverse ways. Building on these interests, linking them to the work unit's goals, giving their agents equal status and recognition when they pursue their interests successfully – these are critical academic leadership tasks. One head of a successful engineering department put it this way:

> It's only a slight exaggeration to say that I don't mind what people do, whether it's original research, lots of publications, consultancy with regional industry, innovative first year teaching, international marketing of our courses, serving on national task forces – so long as they do it well, so long as it's excellent.

Teamwork, collaboration and support

We have seen how collaboration and a cooperative academic environment is associated with higher research productivity: but what can be done to help produce such an environment? Practical strategies that are known to work well include those listed below. Clearly, many of these ideas are applicable mainly to staff who are relatively inexperienced in research, although advantages accrue to both groups when structures linking experienced and inexperienced people together are in place.

Learn the skills of project management

Equally applicable to managing teaching teams, project management skills are factors in leading academic research and consultancy groups successfully. Sapienza (1995) distinguishes *informal* from *formal* collaboration among scientists. The former happens when people simply want to work together to address a problem. In this case, the academic leader's task is to remove barriers to collaboration, including minimising the impact of university procedures and norms that make collaboration difficult. Formal collaboration is needed when there is an assignment to be completed in the work unit (a consultancy contract to be filled, a sponsored research project involving research students, research assistants and lecturers to be undertaken, a new course unit to be planned and delivered).

Successful project management through formal collaboration requires careful planning to bring together small groups of people with complementary skills and needs. The project manager has overall responsibility for the project, but must be prepared to respect the capacity of team members to direct parts of the project process, depending on their special expertise (the 'first among equals' phenomenon again). He or she needs to adapt their leadership strategies to different stages in the project, focusing at the beginning and end of the project on people, and during the main stage on tasks. Sapienza (1995, p. 146) recommends strong emphasis on ensuring that a team is built from the beginning as a collaborative one by disseminating all information to everyone, not designating people for specific tasks ahead of time, emphasising consultation beyond the team, calling frequent short meetings, and modelling close communication and wide-ranging discussion.

Establish peer support networks

Talking to other people about research is, of course, a major way in which we learn to do it better. Peer support networks apply Senge's idea of enabling individual and team learning through stimulating dialogue and discussion (see p. 163). New researchers are especially wary of advancing creative ideas before their colleagues; negativity and pessimism soon grow from experiences of delicate, half-formed proposals being criticised by colleagues trained to be uncompromising about academic standards. Peer support networks emphasise the positive aspects of a new scholarly idea, stressing dialogue and constructive feedback (Lucas, 1995, p. 160). They may consist of informal groups in which advice and support from more senior staff can be obtained; they may be linked to a concrete goal such as an external grant application; they may be in the form of weekly seminars focused on free-ranging dialogue, literature study programmes, interdisciplinary seminars, or joint professional–academic meetings. As a general rule, network groups should be small and meet at least every two weeks. They should ensure that each member recognises the need to create a non-threatening, respectful, mutually stimulating environment and that each considers not only what she can gain from the group but also what she can put into it (Cundy, 1994).

Support networks may be specially valuable in helping less experienced and younger staff to manage conflicting demands on their time, and to achieve the transition from PhD to publication of articles and a subsequent independent research programme. Setting clear goals for scholarly activity through negotiating objectives with staff, especially inexperienced scholars and people making a shift from one research focus to another (jointly developing a 'performance plan' or 'creativity contract') is a topic covered in the next chapter.

Develop a scholarship management plan collaboratively with colleagues

A scholarship management plan can be used as an instrument to monitor progress against targets, argue for increased research support from the university, and act as a point of reference for all staff when they review their research and scholarly directions. It might identify special strengths of the work unit, proposals for using research infrastructure effectively, and strategies for increasing numbers of graduate students, external and internal consultancies, publications, performances, industry links, and community service activities (as appropriate to your work unit's field of study, strategic directions and university policies).

Use departmental research seminars and research visitor programmes

'Faculty perform better when they have the opportunity to observe others being productive' say Gmelch and Miskin (1995, p. 46).

187

Regular colloquia or seminars where staff, graduate students and external speakers present both work in progress and reflections on the process as well as the content of scholarly enterprise in their field are invaluable means of stimulating a productive research climate. Discussions with senior researchers on the research process enable more junior staff to appreciate the different trajectories that a research career may follow, and increase their confidence by demystifying research procedures. Lucas offers a helpful list of the kinds of process questions which expert presenters might be asked to consider:

> How did you become interested in this topic? What was the process you used to bring yourself from the germ of an idea to the steps you would take in doing the research? What kind of help did you get from other people in stimulating your thinking? . . . What do you do to be productive? Do you schedule a number of hours each day? How many days a week do you write? Do you ever feel stuck or feel that what you are doing is not worth anything?
>
> (Lucas, 1995, p. 159)

In many fields, it will be helpful to include in these seminar series some presentations by 'consumers' or potential consumers of a department's research and academic work and perhaps employers of its graduates – teachers, medical practitioners, media professionals, accountancy firms, consulting engineers, and so on. The presence of a successful researcher or consultant from another university, especially if that person is skilled in mentoring more junior colleagues, has often been found to stimulate interest and productivity in a department.

Experiment with publications syndicates and workshops on grant application writing

Most people find it difficult to write. A successful strategy for helping less experienced researchers to produce publishable articles is the 'publications syndicate' (Sadler, 1990; 1994). A syndicate consists of a group of academics who agree to act cooperatively to increase their publication levels. Consisting of four to six members, and led by a convenor, it meets regularly to help its members draft papers, obtain feedback, and handle issues of submission, referees' reports and rejection.

You may also find it useful to complement any institution-wide programmes for developing grant proposal writing skills with a local scheme of your own.

Help people to see how to tap existing resources and
support inexperienced researchers financially

Act strategically to bring research support into the work unit. Sometimes collaboration with other departments or faculties, or other local institutions, can lead to the equivalent of increased resources through making more efficient use of space and personnel. Encourage staff to consider the advantages of interdisciplinary research and scholarship directions; imagine new ways of doing research (in some fields, meta-analysis of existing empirical data is an alternative to original data collection). Existing experiences as a consultant to commercial and public sector organisations may provide data which, systematically analysed, could form a useful article; development of new learning materials, computer-based or otherwise, and research into new assessment and teaching processes in a particular field, can provide a substantial contribution to scholarship, and should be recognised as equal to other forms of research.

Relatively small amounts of money for data collection and research assistance can make a decisive difference to the success of precarious research projects.

Malcolm Calvert describes his approach to enhancing research output in an interdisciplinary department

'In the last analysis, you have to have people who are research minded if you want good research and lots of it. So recruitment is important and the continuing education of new staff as researchers is essential. But you can't rely on these things alone. You have to create an environment which actively influences existing staff. One of the first things I did here was to try and get new researchers to apply for grants. I used an incentive scheme to encourage them to apply for university small grants. The second thing was that I decided I would never stop trying with people who were not performing. I don't give up on anybody. I inherited a person who joined the department and in 1976 and had really just opted out. Of course some people will not want to get involved in research, but this one, I sensed, did want to get back into it. So we encouraged him to get involved in a research project with other staff last year, and then this year he was successful in getting a university seeding grant. A head must try and provide opportunities by setting up research projects, sharing students, and encouraging them to go for grants. That's a reality of academic leadership.

'We have a research allocation of up to $2,000 a year for each staff member in this department. They can apply for support on the basis of several criteria – not only their publication record, but whether they are new, or have applied for an external grant, not got it, but been highly rated, or they have taken on additional research students. We try to reward both success and effort. There's no one way of doing it; you have to find as many ways as possible. Once research is well established in a department, recognition and encouragement is still important in maintaining momentum. In fact most of the money we have put in has been a good investment in increasing the quantity and quality of publications. We will need perhaps to move more towards encouraging and rewarding teams in this broad field of study. Groups engender enthusiasm and the exchange of ideas in research, and bring PhD students into the mainstream'.

Enhancing postgraduate supervision and support

It is an academic leadership responsibility to ensure that support and supervision arrangements available to graduate students are clearly articulated, and to be certain that supervisors are fully competent to fulfil their duties. Some departments will contain many unskilled or inexperienced supervisors. Others may provide a climate that is not perceived by graduates to be supportive of their research. To identify possible sources of difficulty, you may like to invite your colleagues to conduct an audit of postgraduate experiences, using an instrument such as the postgraduate research experience questionnaire developed at Griffith University. This identifies possible areas for improvement in supervision, and also provides information about graduate students' perceptions of the resources and the climate for research in an academic work unit. It may be a useful basis for a meeting between graduate students and staff concerning ways in which the environment for postgraduate research can be improved.

190

The following guidelines for good practice at departmental level in supervising postgraduates are based on Elphinstone, Martin and Foster (1995). Depending on the university, some procedures will be laid down as institution-wide policy while others will be left to the department to decide.

- Ensure you have an agreed policy on the ideal size of the graduate programme and recruitment practices
- Agree procedures for assigning students to supervisors
- Provide workload guidance (number of students which a staff member may supervise)
- Ensure all supervisors have clearly stated procedures for monitoring student progress
- Provide development and training opportunities for inexperienced supervisors
- Provide students with clear statements about the department's research focus, achievement, vision, disciplinary culture, and specific expertise of members of staff
- Provide students with information about the level of support (access to equipment, space, computers, internet; administrative support; additional work and grants that may be available; financial support for making contacts with other researchers in the field; opportunities for talking to fellow students and academic staff informally; research seminars and meetings) they can expect
- Provide an orientation programme for graduate students in which they can clarify expectations, have an opportunity to meet other students and staff, be introduced to facilities and equipment, and discuss common problems associated with research in the field and how to surmount them
- Offer workshops on writing and analysis skills
- Enable students to set up mutual support networks

There are now several published manuals and other resources available to guide research supervisors; these may be used to establish agreed core postgraduate supervision skills and support responsibilities. You might use a guidebook such as Phillips and Pugh's *How to Get a PhD* (1987) or Zuber-Skerritt and Pinchen's *Third Manual for Conducting Workshops on Postgraduate Supervision* (1995) to form a basis for a series of department-based workshops on core supervision skills.

SUMMARY OF SOME SPECIFIC WAYS IN WHICH ACADEMIC
LEADERS CAN ENABLE GOOD RESEARCH AND
SCHOLARSHIP

Learn basic project management skills and help others to develop them

Set up publications and grant application writing syndicates and workshops

Support creativity and risk-taking by holding 'ideas and work in progress' seminars

Establish partnerships between experienced and inexperienced researchers

Enable colleagues to form interest groups in specific areas of research

Hold a meeting to discuss different conceptions of scholarship in your field (e.g. Boyer's discovery, integration, application, teaching) and how future developments in higher education may affect the appropriate balance in the department

Promote successes and milestones in publication and scholarship (hold small events such as afternoon teas to celebrate the appearance of articles, books, reviews, and so on)

Support a discussion on equitable distribution of service responsibilities and how these relate to the goals of the work unit

Encourage staff to research and publish on topics related to teaching and learning in their subject

Help staff develop their research careers through your own contacts with professional associations, journals, and local and national groups

Provide small incentive grants to inexperienced researchers related to outcomes such as an article in a refereed journal

Hold 'what's on top' lunchtime meetings where staff can safely explore problems in their research (Begin with a problem of your own)

Encourage visiting scholars who are known to be good mentors of academic staff

Reduce service and teaching loads for new staff

Provide travel funds for some conference attendance, on the condition that a recipient holds a seminar to discuss key outcomes from the conference on his/her return

Evaluate the quality of graduate research supervision and research students' perceptions of the climate for research in the department; apply the results to making improvements

9

RECOGNISING AND DEVELOPING PERFORMANCE

> Education makes a people easy to lead, but difficult to drive;
> easy to govern, but impossible to enslave.
>
> Brougham

I have argued that academic leadership means helping one's colleagues to enlarge their competence, improve their performance, and maximise their potential. In these senses, it is about helping people to learn. At the same time, the prosperity of any organisation and the fulfilment of every employee within it depends on a workable process of staff recognition and reward. This in turn requires fair and just processes for assessing achievements and for linking individual development to organisational objectives.

These imperatives would be just as important for morale and for the discharge of our departments' and our universities' goals even if there were no increased pressures for external accountability, and no need to adapt to a new environment outside higher education. This is because we have not addressed them convincingly in the past. Most universities have not handled staff development well; most have not provided good feedback to staff on their performance, and related individual performance to organisational goals; most have not rewarded and recognised achievement (especially in teaching) successfully; most have not dealt firmly with the wasteful inequities of the underachieving academic and the difficult colleague. The climate of change provides a stimulating opportunity for people in academic leadership positions to realise a more effective and enabling context of academic work.

Development and recognition of academics parallels the process of assessing students. Like assessing students, it needs to be understood as a process that combines, rather than separates, judgements about performance and feedback to enable more effective learning. The most profound effects on the quality of student learning arise from students' experiences of assessment processes. When students

194

perceive that assessment requires no more than the unreflective reproduction of ideas and facts, or the heedless application of algorithms, then their approach to studying alters to reflect their perception, resulting in poor quality of learning and recall. Quite predictably, precisely this process has been observed in academic staff in their reaction to inappropriate reward and appraisal systems (see Ramsden, 1992). Like students, lecturers respond to the assessment requirements. The 'wrong' kind of assessment – as perceived by staff and students – results in an attitude of compliance; and this path leads quickly to dissatisfaction and mediocre performance. This does not mean that the right kind of assessment will automatically lead to higher achievement. It does mean that it increases the chances of closer engagement with academic work and better outcomes.

The special challenge of recognising and developing academic staff performance is to work in ways that are consistent with the distinguishing characteristics of academic culture – without being dominated by its less adaptive features. Prominent in this culture, as we have seen, are norms of self-direction, loyalties beyond the organisation, peer review and collective decision-making, management as unessential or intrusive, and variety in outputs. Set against these distinctive – but by no means unique – features are the almost identical expectations of academic staff and workers in other types of organisation for credible and dynamic leaders who provide direction and who motivate, inspire, and educate their people so that they can perform to their best ability.

In chapters 5 and 6 I showed how effective academic leaders are admired for their integrity, competence, clearly-stated expectations, and capacity to be good mentors and developers of their colleagues. If as leaders we can get recognition and development right, we can enable staff to change and to be confident of their future. If we get it wrong, the quality of our relationship with colleagues is impaired; we construct an academic culture that does not 'work' (Sapienza, 1995, p. 79). We will reduce morale, leave people without a sense of purpose, block communication, hinder achievement, and quite possibly sabotage our work unit's survival.

Look at Table 9.1, which compares the characteristics of 'working' and 'non-working' professional environments. Your job is to use development and recognition to attenuate the aspects listed in column 2 and accentuate those in column 1.

To assess students well, lecturers need a clear understanding of how assessment drives learning and why it must be conceptualised as integral to learning, rather than additional to it. They need to know how it can serve the multiple functions of feedback, grading, judgement, and evaluation of teaching. They should appreciate that

Table 9.1 Working and non-working professional environments

'Working'	'Non-working'
Straight and open communication, including non-judgemental criticism	Faultfinding attitude prevails among colleagues and discourages openness
Focus on future successes and strengths	Focus on past errors and weaknesses
Creativity encouraged by rewarding receptiveness to new ideas	Creativity discouraged by punishing 'incorrect' procedures
Attempts to minimise distance between rhetoric and behaviour	People manipulated and made to feel incompetent by hidden deals and secret messages
Collaboration recognised and intellectual challenge encouraged through questioning	Questions inhibited; staff feel they must defend territory to compete successfully against each other
Leaders seek feedback including bad news as well as good	Leaders certain they are right; unwilling or frightened to listen to bad news
Leaders invite comment and consult on goals and plans	Leaders do not share goals and plans, only solutions and requirements
Atmosphere of joint problem-solving	Atmosphere of accusation and censure

good assessment implies learning from students about how effectively they, as their teachers, have helped them to learn the subject matter.

In evaluating and developing academic staff, leaders will need to acquire a similarly relativistic and complex understanding of delegation, recognition, and performance management. We need to 'align' the developmental and assessment aspects of academic leadership with our vision, goals, and enabling strategies (Biggs, 1996). Unless we do this we will find that insurmountable barriers stand in the way of creating an environment in which our colleagues can continually learn.

The three keys to effectively developing staff and aligning their goals with those of the work unit are delegation, recognising achievement, and performance management – including the management of underperformance and conflict.

The craft of delegation

> Not the least of the qualities that go into the making of a great ruler is the ability of letting others serve him.
>
> Richelieu

'It's impossible to do the job of head of school properly, even in 60 or 70 hours a week,' a newly-appointed head complained. 'University committees and selection panels, planning new courses, managing the finances, the constant flow of bureaucratic demands for more information, people wanting forms signed, putting out fires lit by staff conflict, fighting for resources, appraisals . . .

'The problem is that academics don't want to be assigned tasks, especially now that they're working harder and there are fewer support staff in the faculty. And in any case many of them don't have a view of the big picture – they're focused on their own welfare rather than the needs of the school, the faculty and the university. They're not trained to deal with political and academic management issues. You can't rely on them to argue for the interests of the school in university committees. They could be leading a coup against you, and you'd never know. I am never confident that they will pull together. As far as teaching, examining and getting new research proposals together is concerned, I'm sure none of them can do as good a job as I can, and anyway, I *am* supposed to be the academic leader here, I am supposed to be setting the example. Delegation? It's a good idea in theory and it works in other organisations. But it isn't applicable in universities, certainly not in the universities we have now'.

Most academic leaders complain of being overworked – of having too little time to carry out the multiple functions of planning, administration, sitting on committees, maintaining staff confidence, dealing with personnel issues, seeking resources, doing research and teaching. Balancing leadership duties with one's own academic work was one of the challenges identified in the international survey of department heads reported in chapter 1. Some heads try to continue all their research and teaching activities while trying to fulfil a leadership role; some ignore administrative functions unless a crisis occurs – resulting in an under-managed department which cannot deliver services on time; some see leadership and support of their colleagues as an unnecessary and even intrusive duty – producing discontent, confusion and even revolt.

Delegation means authorising someone to do a job. A delegate is an agent or representative. This implies entrusting the other person with responsibility for achieving the task itself and giving them the authority to do it. It is impossible to have enough time to be an effective academic leader unless you learn the art of delegation. But this is only one reason for knowing how to do it. The main reason is that it is central to a view of academic leadership as enabling, developing and recognising people. Effective delegation demonstrates that you value your colleagues. It helps people to learn, developing their skills and self-assurance. Moreover, it imbues the work unit with a spirit of continual learning. We have seen how the capacity to bring confidence and hope to bear on difficult conditions is a characteristic of academic leadership. There is no surer sign of your own confidence, your positive outlook, your flexibility, and your trust in your staff than the assignment of authority.

It is a cardinal error to believe that academic staff, as professionals, do not need help to define targets, monitor their progress towards them, and develop their careers. Professionals need these things as much as anyone, and good delegation helps achieve them. Delegation will not solve all the problems of academic leadership, but you cannot be a really capable academic leader unless you master its art.

Academics find it difficult to delegate. They are used to doing things for themselves. It may be some consolation that everyone, not just people in universities, finds it difficult. Many managers in every organisation cannot bring themselves to believe that anyone can 'really solve that problem' except them; many think that their responsibility implies that they should do everything. (This is a misunderstanding of leadership, of course; while leadership will almost certainly mean working harder, it emphatically does not mean doing all the jobs, any more than being the captain of a football team means playing every position on the field). When I asked academic leaders in a workshop to identify the things that hindered delegation, they produced the following list:

- No-one to delegate to
- It takes time and effort
- People don't want to be delegated to
- You can't trust people to do the job
- Too risky – delegates can lead coups against you
- It makes you feel guilty
- People aren't competent enough
- No-one can do it as well or as quickly as I can

Compare this with the list produced from research into why European chief executives do not delegate (Adair, 1988):

- It's risky
- We enjoy doing things
- We daren't sit and think
- It's a slow process
- We like to be on top of everything
- Will our staff outstrip us?
- Nobody can do it as well as I can

The problems (or excuses) overlap a good deal. Yet both academics and other managers are quite aware of the advantages of delegation. It can increase productivity, provide you with more time to lead and manage, and help develop other people's skills. It can give colleagues a sense of being in control, provide them with greater satisfaction, and make it easier for us to evaluate future staff potential. To move from the problems to the solution it is necessary to escape from the 'spiral of distrust' which discourages you from delegating and at once reinforces a culture where delegated tasks will be handled badly (Figure 9.1). We acquire trust by showing it ourselves.

Remembering the strong sense of autonomy, intrinsic motivation and the capacity to adapt to new challenges which distinguish academic people, one point of escape from the spiral is to give assignments which are likely to be ones that a person or team would choose to do and which you are confident can be handled capably by staff whom you trust. Getting to know your colleagues well, and spending time talking to them and seeing the results of their work, makes it easier to form a judgement on their capacity to take responsibility and the likely results. It is worth remembering that delegation is a continuum, rather than a dichotomy (Adair, 1988, p. 115). There are different levels of delegation, ranging from 'Here is a new course; plan and deliver it in the way you see fit, here are the resources, you have full authority to go ahead and are accountable for the outcomes; let me know how it goes' through to 'Please have a look at the three universities running similar courses to the one we're planning, and let me know what their characteristics are'. The competence and experience of your colleagues, the urgency of the task, and its significance for the work unit's future, and the need to develop and recognise people, are factors you should take account of in deciding what level of delegation – if any – to use in a particular circumstance.

Giving more power and responsibility to our colleagues requires tenacity and self-confidence. It will always be something a of gamble. Its risks should be carefully assessed, but in the end it is another of the uncertainties that academic leaders have to live with if they want to be effective. The more power is given, the greater

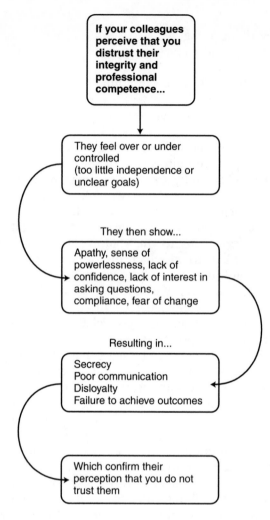

Figure 9.1 The downward spiral of distrust
Source: Derived from Marlow (1995)

the risk, but the greater the potential rewards in time saved and people developed. The time saved has to be used wisely. I suggest that prudent choices would include the leadership responsibilities of long-term future planning, creative synthesis of data, good judgement, and forging strong working relationships both internally and externally.

After having delegated a task, it is important to develop the art of judging when to intervene in its progress and when not to. Students want help in understanding the subject matter, but they don't want

200

to be tested every five minutes (and will never develop as independent learners if they have no choice over how and what they learn). Academic people want support, but they don't want us breathing down their necks. The seductiveness of prying into the progress of an assignment must be resisted. Poor delegators either find it hard to avoid the temptation to intrude, or don't offer help when it's needed. As in so many aspects of academic leadership – and in teaching – a useful technique is to imagine yourself in the place of your colleagues when you are considering whether to step in. A good team climate (see chapter 8) makes it easier to judge the moment, and of course provides team members with the confidence to ask for help when they need it.

These observations should remind us that delegation is not a surrender of responsibility. Another paradox of both leadership and of teaching in higher education is that control is needed to make autonomy effective. Just as student independence in learning is not achieved by leaving students to their own devices, so developing our staff through delegation is not achieved by abdicating control. In particular, we will never acquire trust by using delegation to avoid academic leadership. Leadership is a process that should be shared. But like your ultimate accountability, it cannot be delegated. If you find yourself wanting to delegate your primary leadership functions, such as scanning the environment, increasing confidence, and bringing in new ideas, it may be time to ask whether you are in the right position.

An important feature of effective academic leaders, from the lecturers' perspective, is that they act as mentors or teachers. One respondent in chapter 5 spoke of the way in which she was constantly pushed to enhance her academic capacity by being assigned challenging tasks. This is exactly how good leaders 'turn followers into leaders' – not through some arcane process known only to management gurus, but by skilful delegation. Skilful delegation for development implies authorising someone to undertake an assignment which is some slight distance beyond their capacity to achieve. People, especially university people with their capacity for lifelong learning, grow into responsibilities, as long as the space to fill is not too large. Many readers will remember the awesome sense of loneliness, tinged with excitement, upon first realising a substantial academic leadership position. How can I possibly do all this? What will happen if I fail? Why have they made me responsible for so much? These feelings, suitably attenuated depending on the size of the assignment delegated, encourage high standards and strengthen self-confidence. Progress in learning motivates more learning.

Failure to delegate means that people grow wary and insecure in their ability to take responsibility, resulting in poorly-developed staff who will be unwilling to take on leadership roles. We are not good in universities at 'succession planning' – developing new leaders – because we are not well adjusted to the sharing of work and the risk-taking that delegation implies. If we were better, we would not only foster people's capacity to take responsibility, but we would get a clearer idea of the potential of each member of a department to undertake a leadership role. If you can develop your own delegation skills, you will have a strong basis for influencing your university to improve its planning for educating its next generation of leaders, an issue which I shall return to in chapter 11.

Recognition of achievement

Recognition is the first cousin of delegation. In today's climate, promotion and increased earnings are rewards that fewer and fewer academic staff are likely to realise; other forms of recognition therefore take on added importance. For students, grades and marks are the 'currency of the campus'; for academics, the currency is *reputation* (Becker, Geer and Hughes, 1968; Becher, 1989). As we are well aware, academic reputation in all fields comes from recognition by one's peers, mainly through quality and quantity of publication, but also from the standing of the university where the person studied and where they are employed. The fact that academic status is related to recognition and reward from the national and international scholarly community implies limits to the influence that can be exerted at the local level by an academic leader such as a department head. However, the limits are not so narrow as people sometimes think. Grading, ranking and the search for reputation are congenital properties of academic life which can be wisely and fairly used to enhance leadership effectiveness.

We have not used these features of the academic culture very well to recognise achievement, encourage commitment and develop competence. I have referred several times to the results of studies of lecturers' attitudes to the recognition given by their universities to their most basic function of teaching students: many staff, especially more junior staff and women, believe that while their universities pay lip service to good teaching, they do not recognise and reward it in practice. It is vital, then, for a leader to use as many means as possible to show genuine appreciation of academics' commitment to helping students to learn, including the kinds of strategies described in chapter 8 to raise the status of teaching and to reward team as well as individual effort. The daily display of one's own commitment to excellence in teaching and learning is one aspect of recognising it. Since recognition from academic peers is so important, try to create an atmosphere in which members of course teams feel comfortable about complimenting each other on their achievements.

How should we recognise people's performance? To be effective in academic settings, the process of giving recognition should follow certain principles (based on Adair, 1996, chapter 17; Donaldson, 1991; and Kouzes and Posner, 1995, chapter 11):

- It should always be genuine and sincere – that is, you must believe it is worth giving. Above all, do not be perceived as arrogant and patronising when giving recognition.
- It should not be used in a manipulative or inequitable way.
- It should reward achievements which further the collective cause of the group, and are linked to its common academic vision, as well as individual success.
- Recognition should be linked to the leadership principles of having high expectations of others and having a credible record

---

Vicky,

Just a short note to say how much I have appreciated working with you over the last few months on the academic review and appraisal scheme. You've kept us all well organised in terms of venues, materials, invitations and confirmations for the meetings. I think I've mentioned before how important it is to me as head of department to know that all those details are well taken care of and that everything should happen as it should do 'on the day'. All this has been in addition to your other duties and I regard it as a significant achievement for you.

I'm looking forward to your continuing to provide the same support in 1998. Please keep on ensuring that everyone (particularly me) knows what to do and does it properly!

John

Figure 9.2 Public recognition of achievement: an email message to a junior general staff member copied to the dean and the departmental administrative officer (her immediate supervisor)

Source: I am grateful to John Swinton for allowing me to adapt his material

of achievement oneself; search out extraordinary accomplishments and ensure they are fully appreciated.

- Recognition of self-evaluation and of learning from mistakes is as important as recognition of achievement – but not more important. Match what is recognised to the individual's experience. (To recognise our staff appropriately, we have to know each of them well.)
- It should be an everyday, informal activity as well as a ceremonial one. Routine recognition is an important aspect of a departmental culture that 'works'. Show concern about colleagues' professional activities. Don't wait for them to come to you. If someone does a good job, tell them so. 'Catch someone doing something well', say the management manuals: how many times did you give words of praise to your colleagues last week? (An individual letter of congratulation, placed also on a colleague's personal file, and public appreciation in committees and before peers, are slightly more 'official' methods'; see Figure 9.2.)
- While it shouldn't be overdone ('Be sparing in praise, but liberal in thanks'), remember the fact that innovative organisations record higher levels of expressions of thanks than non-innovative ones (Kouzes and Posner, 1995, p. 279). Make it a rule to give some positive comments to staff daily.
- Design any formal system for recognising academic work collaboratively with your colleagues – performance management procedures that are not planned in a participative way stand little hope of success.
- Recognition should help people improve, as well as make them feel wanted – it is closely related to *feedback*.

We continue to be poor at giving regular feedback on performance to staff and students in higher education. Everyone knows that feedback tells you about your progress and that it is integral to effective learning. Most people would agree that assessment without feedback is of limited value. But we do not put the knowledge to work. High quality student learning is directly and strongly associated with perceptions of prompt and useful feedback; yet the most common criticisms of graduates about their courses concern the fact that they did not receive adequate feedback. As we have seen (p. 44), 33,600 Australian graduates complained in 1995 that feedback had been provided only in the form of marks or grades, while 31,200 said their lecturers had not put a lot of time into commenting on their work. In a series of interviews I held with deans and heads in 1995, nearly every one mentioned the fact that they sought more information about their progress and more judgements of their performance in their role than they had received from their supervisors.

The issue of providing feedback to your colleagues is closely bound up with two others: the process of performance management and the use of information from our staff to improve our own effectiveness. I shall deal with the latter in chapter 10.

Performance management

Evaluating, recognising and developing staff performance are the very essence of the academic leader's responsibilities. From the outlook on academic leadership I have adopted, the primary questions of performance management are: 'What do we want our colleagues to achieve?' 'How can we help them achieve it?' 'What conditions will enable them to do their best?' and 'How will we, and they, know when they have achieved their objectives?' The formal processes you use to assess performance are secondary to these questions (though this does not mean they are inconsequential). Performance management and staff assessment which will truly improve academic productivity and satisfaction should follow similar principles to assessment which helps students to learn. We need to try and develop in our colleagues a self-critical, independent attitude, an orientation towards change and development, and a commitment to constant improvement (Ramsden, 1992, p. 221).

Universities have used an assortment of methods for assessing academic staff performance in recent years. As a broad generalisation, it can be said that they have seldom been a success. Pressures to adopt staff appraisal systems in universities derive from 1980s reports, such as the Jarratt Report in the UK, which assumed that commercial organisations used appraisal effectively, that staff development without appraisal was of limited value, and that closer links between formal reward systems and achievement would motivate staff to enhance their performance. But staff appraisal has been seen by many academics as a prescription for mediocrity, a hindrance to creativity and innovation, an unwarranted intrusion on academic freedom, an attempt to impose inappropriate 'managerialist' techniques on universities, and a conspiracy to increase the power of personnel and human resource administrators over lecturers.

Whether these perceptions are objectively true is not as important as the fact that they are still widely shared and undoubtedly influence staff approaches to their work. Few lecturers, it seems, feel a sense of ownership and commitment to staff appraisal; even schemes which have focused entirely on development and improvement (as preferred by some academic staff associations) have been criticised by lecturers for being limited in value because they are unrelated to formal rewards.

As in so many other areas of management and leadership, the differences between universities and other organisations concerning appraisal are easily exaggerated. Egan (1995) argues that most appraisal systems are ineffective, do not enhance employee performance, are too rigid to meet different employee needs, are focused on procedural detail rather than principles, disempower both employees and managers because they are seen as a form of policing rather than a means to development, and waste firms' money. Sound familiar? It is not so much that universities have imported a model which is inappropriate to their particular circumstances, but that they have imported a model that does not accomplish what it was designed to accomplish in any organisation.

What can an academic leader do to improve this situation? It is highly unlikely that performance management will disappear from universities. In fact it offers great scope for the exercise of transformational leadership and especially for helping people through change. What we need to do is to adapt existing schemes to our own needs and influence our universities to use best practice. To do this it will be useful to be aware of the principles of successful performance management.

A good performance management system is analogous to a good student assessment regime. It is concerned first and foremost with enabling people to learn. It is about helping them to transform their understanding, helping them address change, and helping them to link their own development and performance to the work unit's and the university's goals. It should encourage reflection and collaborative problem-solving. Organisational objectives are the counterpart in performance management of the subject content and skills which we expect students to learn; individual students develop, but they should develop in relation to the subject matter they are studying; academics develop, but they should develop in relation to the broad aims and vision of their university. I believe that performance management should merge the management of people with the management of the university, in the same way that good courses bring knowledge and students together.

Since it is about learning, performance management should be forward-looking. It should not be focused on the review of past performance, as appraisal generally is, but on using the past to help structure future objectives. It should provide our colleagues with feedback on their progress towards achieving their objectives. While it is a system of control and discipline only in exceptional circumstances, it will, like a good student assessment process, relate the 'formative' and the 'summative': it will not only provide feedback, but will enable people to gain credit and recognition for their achievements. It is a process that operates at different levels of formality; it cannot be successfully carried out by a once-yearly meeting, but must be integrated with the day-to-day work of a department. Many small meetings will be needed to monitor progress and renegotiate objectives. Paperwork should be minimal, and evidence should preferably relate to two or three key objectives (CVs, 'activity logs', results of student evaluations, lists of publications, and so on do not belong to this process). The more seamlessly performance management links with normal academic work, the more effective it is likely to be. An effective scheme is embedded in an organisational culture that encourages staff to ask questions (see Table 9.2).

A performance management system that is not 'owned' by academic staff – believed in as a beneficial rather than a time-wasting device, and accounted to be fairly constructed and operated – *cannot work* (Bright and Williamson, 1995). It will generate at best compliance and defensiveness, and at worst non-compliance and rebellion; it cannot in any circumstances produce commitment. We have all seen the process of compliance in operation in relation to quality assessment procedures; we are getting rather good at it in universities. It resembles a 'surface

Table 9.2 Performance management: what an organisational culture should encourage staff to ask

Objectives	'What key things will I achieve this year in my academic career?'
Delegation	'What authority do I have to make them happen?'
Work plans	'What are the best routes to my destination?'
Initial training	'What new skills do I need to achieve these things?'
Facilitation	'What will my head of department do to help me achieve them?'
Feedback	'What feedback can I expect from the head of department?'
Tracking	'What is the best way of tracking my progress?'
Recognition and reward	'What recognition will I get for my accomplishments?'
Development	'How can I prepare myself to do bigger things?'

Source: Based on Egan (1995).

approach' to quality enhancement designed to minimise effort and avoid significant change, while at the same time delivering acceptable, though ultimately dissatisfying and soon forgotten outcomes. It is the antithesis of the engagement and passion that is needed to propel a successful academic work unit and ensure that its people are constantly learning.

Ideally, all academic colleagues should be involved in designing a practicable system; it is probably the only way that they will truly own it. Given a brief to design an effective scheme which will work for them, lecturers are more than capable of reaching a solution. A performance management system's effectiveness depends equally on the active involvement of the 'managers' who will be responsible for making it work. It is therefore unfortunate that some universities have constructed performance management schemes which have not been designed by those who will operate them, but instead by working parties of senior staff, personnel officers, and staff association representatives. Supervisors then find themselves in the unenviable position of having to administer a refractory system which imposes an additional burden on everyone. These are themselves symptoms of an academic culture that is not 'working'. Tinkering with appraisal structures and industrial agreements will not make it work. The result is a foregone conclusion, and the failure reinforces the downward spiral of distrust (Figure 9.1) in an academic organisation. In contrast, an effective system shifts the emphasis from a focus on controlling staff to one of *creating the conditions in which they can be successful.*

Figure 9.3 summarises the direction in which an effective performance management scheme should be heading – from the conception implied by the upper left hand quadrant to the one implied by the lower right hand one.

From these principles you will see that performance management reaffirms the similarity between good teaching in higher education and competent academic leadership. Performance management should provide people with a clear view of what they are expected to do, give them constructive feedback, invite discussion of how the goals can be achieved (and what support is needed to achieve them) and encourage a degree of risk taking. It should help each individual to feel that they matter to the department and to the university. The people involved in it should believe that the process is useful to them and not think if it as a 'managerial' imposition. Otherwise, like students faced with an irrelevant curriculum whose assessment does not test their understanding, they will find ways of engaging with it minimally.

We can now also discern that performance management presents

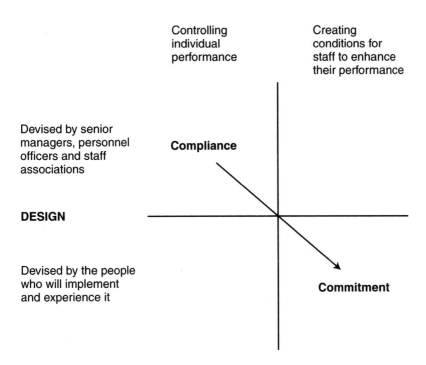

Figure 9.3 Types of performance management

an interesting duality. While it is primarily a means of enabling and recognising people, and thus assists us in becoming more satisfactory academic leaders, at the same time its effectiveness rests on the leadership and management skills of the people who operate it.

Developing people through feedback on performance

A key skill in performance management is the capacity to provide useful feedback. Without it, people in academic organisations are less likely to learn from their mistakes and to have a sense of whether they are making progress towards their objectives. High quality feedback encourages persistence and reflection on how to improve.

How can we get better at providing feedback to our colleagues? First by thinking about why we do not give it, or give it grudgingly, rarely, and imprecisely:

'Academics here are self-motivated and self-evaluating. They don't need to know whether they're being effective or not. They wouldn't want me to butt in anyway'

'There isn't time in the day for a head of department to be going around stroking people'

'Too many lecturers in this department already think they're brilliant when they only produce one paper a year. If I give them positive feedback they'll rest on their laurels. If I tell them to pull their socks up they'll bring a union complaint against me'

'The university has an appraisal system where all staff meet me once every two years to report the courses they teach, the research they're doing, and the graduate students they have supervised. I can tell them then if they're keeping on track'

Similar excuses are made for not giving students high quality, regular feedback. Lecturers and leaders who make them need to consider the findings of research on student learning and academic leadership: undoubtedly both staff and students not only benefit from routine, prompt feedback, but most need it in order to excel. Do not, in any circumstances, restrict the giving of feedback to formal appraisal interviews.

Feedback is a very important component of the academic leader's communication repertoire. Think of it as a two-way transmission, for strange through it may seem, feedback is best conceptualised as a conversation that involves listening as well as telling. It is part of the leadership dialogue we should establish with our colleagues. We need to put ourselves in the shoes of the other person. Listen. Find out what they think. Invite reflection. (How did they feel the class went? How far did they think they achieved their objectives for increasing their research productivity this year? Why do they think that? What helped and hindered them in reaching their targets?) From that information, you can invite further comments on the reasons for successes and weaknesses and then start to suggest your options for change. Don't impose your own solutions.

Notice how practising this approach to feedback renders extra value. It establishes closer relationships, it encourages self-reflection, and it also supplies us with feedback on *our* performance. The data provided by the listening aspect of a feedback interchange gives us feedback as academic leaders on the quality of the working environment which we have constructed. In particular, it may give clues about the effectiveness of reward processes, insight into barriers to communication, and useful details about how to streamline administrative processes.

CHECKLIST FOR DEVELOPING PEOPLE THROUGH FEEDBACK

- Listen actively
- Find out how the other person sees the situation
- Establish a genuine dialogue
- Pay attention to 'signals', especially non-verbal signs of unease
- Be comfortable with emotional aspects (allow/accept anger; understand feelings of vulnerability)
- Avoid producing a defensive climate that deters people from finding creative solutions
- Show respect and concern about the other person's needs and hopes
- Offer options not solutions
- Encourage and support rather than criticise and confront
- Be open and positive
- Acknowledge and recognise the person's contribution and successes
- Give clear direction without being over-dominant
- Give bad news honestly and quickly
- Look at causes of problems as well as symptoms
- Provide constructive advice
- Suggest avenues for professional development

CHECKLIST FOR PERFORMANCE MANAGEMENT INTERVIEWS

- Ensure you are both well-prepared
- Agree a joint agenda
- Set the interview in its context
- Focus on behaviour, not on personality
- Listen actively and ask questions
- Focus on improvement
- Look to the future, using the past to provide a framework

- Invite disagreement and comment on the work environment
- Summarise and paraphrase as appropriate
- Ask questions and clarify issues to check understanding
- Pay attention to signs of discomfort
- Do not be hurtful
- Balance criticism with encouragement
- Learn to express personal trust and professional dissatisfaction concurrently
- Explore solutions
- Ask what's needed to help the person achieve their goals
- Work towards agreement, not just acceptance
- Jointly set objectives and discuss ways of achieving them
- Agree objectives that are specific, challenging, realistic, and measurable

---

Information given by leaders through feedback should stress the positive and the hopeful. Find small successes among the work of individuals and teams and praise them sincerely. Positive feedback is especially critical in the area of undergraduate teaching, where lecturers too rarely feel that their efforts are recognised. When providing constructive feedback to encourage development, it is good practice to emphasise first descriptions of observable behaviours and results, rather than evaluative comments. Separate the evaluation of the behaviour from the person; don't comment on personality issues, and restrict critical comments to only one or two aspects of someone's work. Suggest specific actions that will improve performance. To give feedback that leads to improvement in academic colleagues, you must, as Donaldson puts it, 'be able to project personal trust and professional dissatisfaction simultaneously' (Donaldson, 1991).

In chapter 10, I suggest ways in which we can become more comfortable with and positive about receiving and interpreting feedback on our own performance. We need to be receivers as well as givers of feedback.

Feedback can be provided by peers as well as by leaders; the arrangements suggested in chapter 8 provide some guidelines for establishing a context in which people feel free to criticise colleagues' work constructively. Help turn followers into leaders by developing everyone's skills in giving useful feedback.

212

Patricia Thompson's approach to performance management

'My previous university used an appraisal system which was mandated by an industrial agreement. It concentrated on – from the staff association's point of view – avoiding anyone getting sacked for unsatisfactory performance and – from the university's point of view – filtering the residue of dead wood out of the system. As you can imagine, it was a near-total disaster. People saw it as yet another unjustifiable demand on their time.

'Here, I had an opportunity to work with the staff to devise a system that fulfilled the university's requirements in a more flexible way. I felt that the detail ought to be decided after we determined what we wanted to achieve as a group of fairly committed academic staff in a large and reasonably successful department. We talked about the conditions for academic productivity and came up with a pretty ordinary list: self-determination of how to achieve academic goals; challenging problems and a belief in solving them better; rewards for good performance; openness in communication; willingness to take a chance; collaboration between colleagues; a feeling that your special contribution is valued; support for junior people from their seniors in both research and teaching.

'The interesting thing about the list was that it included no features that the conventional appraisal systems in higher education we had all experienced contained. These traditional schemes actually promote second-rate performance. They reward only individual achievement, whereas we know that collaboration in academic departments and science R&D leads to higher performance. They encourage people to play it safe, avoid risky alternatives, and look to past achievements rather than the future – all of which stifle creativity. They make academic staff feel that they are being pushed around by 'the management' and seem hell-bent on denying academic autonomy. They put lecturers on the defensive and inhibit open communication about problems with supervisors. They push everyone into the same mould; they're not equitable and especially they aren't fair to women and to staff whose main commitment is to teaching. And they don't recognise and reward mentoring and helping others!

213

'The scheme we have trialed is now working pretty well. It contains elements of group and project assessment, so it actually rewards communication and collaboration. It asks everyone to use past achievements to plan future goals. Achievement of goals is linked to committing resources and support, as well as longer-term aims like promotion and career advancement. We aim for flexible, negotiated goals – not everyone is expected to do the same mixture of research, scholarship, teaching and service every year – you can plan your own 'performance contract' with me. It has to fit the department's strategic plan, of course. That's a requirement of the university for all performance management. Fair enough. Academic autonomy doesn't mean you just do your own thing, as far as I'm concerned. Here, every senior colleague is expected to include in their contract the service she or he gives to his or her colleagues in helping them to develop and improve – that was a departmental majority decision. The system does not deal with unsatisfactory performance. That is a separate university process which our system theoretically feeds into, if necessary, though so far it hasn't been necessary.

'I've had to be prepared to listen more carefully to criticisms of the department and to accept that people who take risks and fail must be supp orted not punished. Not so easy for an academic head. I've also had to spend more time talking to staff individually. You can't have one appraisal meeting a year if you really want to help people be effective. The reason why the system works is not that it is based on management theory; it isn't, just on common sense. I think the reason it works is because we made it ourselves, and we believe in it.'

Difficult people, conflict and underperformance

'Not counting me, there are three staff here who do 75 per cent of the work of the department', said the head. 'Six others are more or less coasting but not disruptive. But two are actively malicious, devoting the energy they should be putting into research and teaching to ridiculing students and fighting running battles with me, with each other, and with the rest of their colleagues. Abusiveness in staff meetings is

214

the name of the game here. What I need is a way to sort these people out. They don't respond to suggestions and they know they can't be got rid of. The university isn't interested in helping me'.

'What's the point? I've lost interest in this place', his colleague replied. 'They're all against me. No-one appreciates the work I've done over the years. Teaching seems to count for less and less in this department, even though the students are lazier and the classes are bigger. I get sick and tired of trying to bring them into line. Last year I was turned down for promotion yet again because I don't turn out nice little papers to order every three months. Ms Fancy Pants down the corridor who spends all her time on research got promoted, needless to say. Then she had the cheek to go running to the head with a complaint after I commented on it at a staff meeting in a frank and open, normal academic way. The head tries to muzzle discussion and won't reply to my complaints about *his* behaviour. He says we're all about communication and visions but he acts unethically. I've got a permanent job here and that offers some protection from people like him'.

Well, there are always two sides to every story, but this is small comfort when a head has to face colleagues who are difficult.

We know that academics are sometimes eccentric, and that eccentricity shares a narrow border with stubborn perversity. The myth of the difficult academic colleague is that intractable people are to be indulged in higher education since they are geniuses at heart. Denied their academic freedom they would not achieve. Few difficult colleagues are in fact geniuses; most are probably closer to incompetence. Even the exceptions are less exceptional than you might think. The archetypal difficult colleague was J.B.S. Haldane, who became Professor of Genetics at University College London in 1933. He was famous as the person who showed mathematically how Darwin's theory fitted into the Mendelian genetic system. 'Cantankerous to a degree, he became a legend for mismanaging business, terrorising secretaries and abusing administrators' (Harte and North, 1991). But even Haldane, who probably was a genius and certainly was difficult, did not quite live up to the myth. His achievement as a professor at UCL was 'limited by his own perversity' (Harte and North, 1991). Difficult colleagues hinder their own performance as well as sometimes making life a misery for those around them.

These days, most difficult academic people are not near-geniuses at all; they are distinct underperformers. Underperformance is another leadership challenge about which I shall have something to say in a moment. In chapter 2 I referred to the phenomenon of academic bitterness and the increasing sense of anguish, bewilderment and estrangement from their environment which many academic staff feel. Although both positive and negative features of academic life have always been with us, changes in higher education mean that the problem of difficult and possibly resentful colleagues has grown larger.

It is no longer practicable for academic leaders to ignore staff who behave in inadmissible ways. Interestingly enough, difficult colleagues in some ways resemble bad managers (see Drucker, 1955, p. 193). Like weak managers, they can cripple the spirit of an academic work unit. They may destroy the most valuable resource in any enterprise – its people. They breed contempt for the academic profession. They make communication difficult and contribute to decreased productivity. They waste their own talent and damage their own careers. They consume disproportionate amounts of our time. What can we do about it?

The basic principles of effective leadership and management for academic work apply to dealing with difficult staff. First we need to understand the symptoms outlined in the list on pp. 218–19. Firmness, fairness, integrity, a capacity to overcome the fear of confronting forceful colleagues, open communication, knowledge of local procedures, and timely action are vital. Like a teacher, you need to establish your authority through your credibility and use that authority wisely. It is crucial not to delay action, but it needs to be the correct action. This judgement can only be learned through experience. The attitude of mind that makes it possible to handle difficult people is more important. 'The foremost art of kings is the power to endure hatred' said Seneca. If we are afraid of tackling difficult people, feel unable to live with the fact that we will not invariably be able to solve their problems, reproach ourselves for the faults of staff who may disrupt the work of others and harass their colleagues, and cannot accept that there will be people who dislike us, we should consider whether a formal academic leadership position is the right job for us.

It is important to understand how the problem of troublesome academic people arises, and to describe how it varies, if we are to attack it resolutely and effectively. At some time, most difficult colleagues were not difficult. The difficult colleague syndrome is clearly a result of an interaction between staff and their working environment. Latent individual factors in previous experience and personality connect with present experiences to produce the symptoms. It is therefore a shared liability. It is true that it is our responsibility to manage difficult people well. But in the last analysis it is in the hands of each difficult member of staff to stop being difficult. All difficult staff will ascribe their behaviour on their environment, just as failing students blame their teachers. The other side of this coin is that ineffectual academic leaders will attribute all *their* problems with difficult people to their staff and none to themselves. We need to chart a course between these two extremes. Attributing blame is definitely not a helpful starting point.

Obviously, the display of one or two of the less serious of the characteristic behaviours of the difficult colleague syndrome, especially for a short period, does not constitute 'being difficult'. In fact, most of us will have shown some of these symptoms ourselves, quite possibly deliberately as a protest against ineffective academic leadership! (I am one of them). However, their occurrence should signal to the manager a need to monitor the person's activities carefully, and to sketch out solutions before the situation deteriorates. Over-reaction must be avoided, but early intervention is essential. It is extremely hard to tackle chronic cases which have been allowed to continue untreated for several years. Prevention is always preferable, and it should be seen as an important leadership skill.

Prevention strategies

When Ann Lucas interviewed 25 academic staff who had been identified as 'difficult individuals' by their heads of department, she found that they most often ascribed their feelings and behaviours to having been treated unjustly by senior colleagues. They believed they had been unfairly passed over for promotion, or had been given more teaching and less support for research than their colleagues. Other reasons given were that they had never been recognised or thanked for their work; that they had lost power and influence, and been pushed into an adversarial attitude, when the department made a decision opposite to their preference; that their colleagues had been insensitive when they had undergone a personal tragedy such as family illness or substance abuse (Lucas, 1995, pp. 90–2).

These accounts, taken together with the comments about lack of recognition, conflicting messages about the value of teaching and research, and lack of support from senior colleagues which we have already noted in academics' experiences of unsatisfactory academic leadership (chapter 5), provide a strong foundation for prevention and early intervention procedures. In a word, show you appreciate your colleagues and treat them benevolently. Transparent fairness in processes for allocating teaching and research support; discussion and dialogue about the work unit's goals and strategies; feedback, praise and support as part of a regular conversation with each staff member; visiting each colleague's office to show you are available to explore their needs and current worries, if they like; private and public recognition of the particular combination of academic scholarship that the individual provides to the group: these actions help to thwart feelings of isolation, alienation, and injustice, and may enable us to identify early signs of problems.

THE DIFFICULT COLLEAGUE SYNDROME

- Haunted by suspicion; believe that conspiracies abound against them
- Attribute their poor performance to an unsatisfactory departmental environment
- Work alone, stay in their offices, and communicate little with colleagues
- Stand on their 'academic freedom' when criticised or disciplined by the head; may complain to more senior staff about the head's perceived unfairness or ineptitude
- Sense of being persecuted and 'wanting to get even' with imagined tormentors
- Reluctant to accept departmental service and administrative responsibilities
- Disloyal and untrustworthy: do not stand up for the department; make comments critical of its environment or leadership in university meetings or to the press
- Perform to minimum standards (or below) in research and teaching
- Exceptionally critical of changes towards greater external accountability and corporate norms in universities; frequently and articulately regret loss of academic autonomy; appeal to tradition to justify behaviour more often than other staff
- Make sarcastic and insulting comments in meetings

- Harass and criticise administrative staff, especially junior staff
- Send spiteful memos and emails complaining of colleagues' behaviour, usually copied to other staff (but do not regard these actions as in any way unreasonable)
- Feel alienated and unwanted

Management strategies

Unfortunately, it is not realistic to think that all the problems of difficult colleagues can be prevented. Management strategies vary from active intervention to disciplinary procedures to finding personal support from colleagues. The following general suggestions may be useful; for more detailed advice you should refer to the sources indicated:

- First explore the history of the case with any former head or senior manager and with your colleagues. Try to identify the main reasons for the person's behaviour, as seen by others. Plan your campaign based on as full a picture of the past as you can acquire.
- Simply go and talk to the person; appeal to their humanity and sense of fairness. Tell them you wish they could be more actively involved in the department's work. Be prepared for a harangue about your faults and the general unfairness shown in the department. Listen. Expect that the person will subsequently come to see you to discuss how they could contribute; if they do not, suggest something they might do that would involve communication with colleagues. This strategy, described in more detail by Lucas (1995, pp. 92–5), is reported to have a success rate as high as 92 per cent.
- Confront the person with the problem as you see it and request changes in their behaviour. Explicitly separate your evaluation of their behaviour from their personality ('I am asking you not to do X; I am not asking you to be a different person or saying that I'm against you'). Practising confrontation techniques for handling problems with professional employees, such as those described by Sapienza (1995), is valuable training.
- Speak to your senior colleague (supervisor) about the problem. Ask their advice. Help them to understand your problem, and why it is important to you and your colleagues to be supported.

Tell them what you have done and propose to do. Keep them informed of progress.

- Convene a group of other heads to share experiences and solutions.
- Don't lose hope.

Managing conflict between staff

No work unit, academic or otherwise, can avoid conflict between its staff. I do not think that conflict is intrinsically more likely in an academic department than in any other kind of work unit. The essential difference is that values and norms of academic individuality and autonomy often permit conflict to degenerate into chronic unpleasantness, personal intimidation, and erosion of trust. In these circumstances the entire work unit's efficiency can be injured as people take sides, avoid communication, work for themselves alone and not for the good of the team, and suffer stress-related absences.

While mediation of conflict and negotiation between academics to achieve harmony are important aspects of most academic leaders' roles, there is nothing unique about academic environments which makes conflict more or less acceptable than in other organisations. Conflict between colleagues may arise over teaching allocations, access to resources, ideas about pedagogy and assessment, interpretations of disciplinary boundaries, research methodology, views of academic democracy and management, and numerous other factors. Whether the parties are academics, academic and administrative staff, or academics and students, departmental conflicts resolve into two types: the constructive and the destructive. The former, properly handled, enhance productivity by encouraging debate and spurring staff to achieve higher standards. People treat each other as team members and respect the value of dialogue as well as discussion (see pp. 163). They can limit their disagreement to a focus on issues, not on personalities. They recognise the creativity inherent in constructive conflict and genuinely believe that through cooperation they can arrive at better solutions than they would alone.

Destructive conflict, however, must be either prevented or challenged. It may be due to differences in ideologies, sheer old-fashioned jealousy, or the academic bitterness highlighted in chapter 2. On occasion, if you are unlucky, undiagnosed and untreated personality disorders on the part of one adversary may make things worse. The golden rule for managing destructive academic conflict is the same, uncontroversial principle that applies to managing difficult people (who are often, sadly, among the main protagonists in intra-department conflict). Prevention is very much easier than cure. A common vision and a clearly-understood role for everyone in achieving that vision, good communication of expectations, plenty to do, recognition of performance, a sense of fairness as the norm in the work unit, integrity and decisiveness on the part of the leader, successful performance and reputation of the department in the university – in fact all the qualities of a 'working' and comfortable academic environment that are linked to high morale and output – are the principal strategies for preventing destructive conflict.

In these circumstances, internal strife seems to most people so to distract from the common design that they have neither time nor energy to become bogged down in it. There will always be some minor antagonism in every workplace, but in these conditions its noise will be muted and it will never grow to ruinous proportions. When linked to explicit ground rules of behaviour for academic staff, an enabling environment can vitiate many budding conflicts.

The ground rules, which you should establish jointly with your colleagues as fair and just ways that everyone should work in the department, might include:

- Don't attack people behind their backs (talk to the individual whom you perceive to be the source of the problem before talking to someone else about it)
- Listen actively to your colleagues' points of view
- Don't criticise a colleague's work unless you can make practical suggestions for how they might improve it
- Act on how people actually feel, not on your assumptions about how they feel
- When there is a problem, look for sources to blame for it other than immediate colleagues
- Criticise ideas, not personalities
- Don't back people into corners from which they can't escape without humiliating themselves or intensifying the conflict
- Never demand public apologies for real or assumed transgressions

(see Lucas, 1995, pp. 205–6; Rowntree, 1989).

For your own part, make it a rule to pinch out any attempts to form hostile cliques or factions: an academic department where sides are taken by opposing groups cannot be as productive and serene as one where people are aligned only to their own goals and their work team's contribution to the strategic vision of the whole group. Remind your colleagues that, more than ever before in today's higher education environment, survival and success depends on people working as a team and presenting a common front to the university. Reward people for cooperating with each other. Search out in the performance management process early signs of destructive conflict: ask how you can help to thwart it. Establish an understanding that the persons involved will regard it as part of their performance goals to prevent its escalation.

Failing prevention or very early intervention – and many heads will inherit existing conflicts – management rather than cure is often the only option. Great firmness of purpose and the spirit to confront unpleasantness rather than avoid facing the opposing parties is required. Sometimes the conflict between two staff will be transformed by your intervention into a conflict between one of them and you; and that is a burden an academic leader must learn to bear. Perhaps the most serious fault is to hope that conflict will subside or disappear if nothing is done about it.

Techniques for managing conflict between staff such as mediation and negotiation processes require a separate treatment which is beyond the scope of this book (see Lucas, 1995, for an introduction). Other techniques include effective but fundamentally coercive management tactics building on the principle of rewarding cooperation and punishing continuing disharmony. You may be able to convince the antagonists that they are more likely to succeed in achieving their individual goals if they cooperate with each other than if they continue fighting (Rowntree, 1989, p. 216).You may find it necessary to direct them to solve the problem with the sanction that duties related to the conflict will be re-allocated if they fail to do so. A valuable exercise is to explore your own preferences for dealing with conflict (typically classified as competing, collaborating, compromising, avoiding and accommodating; see Thomas and Kilmann, 1974) and to develop a sense of the different approaches that can be applied to suit different situations. A useful discussion of different kinds of academic conflict, and ways of dealing with it, using examples from heads of departments filtered through the wisdom of the book's authors, is contained in Moses and Roe (1990).

Underperformance and unsatisfactory performance

It is essential to distinguish between difficult people, underperformance and unsatisfactory performance. Difficult academic staff are often underperforming, and sometimes unsatisfactory, but all three conditions may appear separately. Underperformance means that a staff member is working at a lower level than they are capable of, while unsatisfactory performance means they are functioning at a level below that stipulated in their employment contract. This may include unacceptable behaviour such as sexual harassment and physical violence. In such cases, immediate action must be taken and it must be carried out precisely according to the university's procedures. Get advice from your human resource or personnel office and consult your own supervisor without delay. Never act alone. Expect and require support from your senior colleagues: you will need it. Do not regard your actions as a punishment, but try to see them as steps taken to improve performance. Similar considerations apply to cases of presumed unsatisfactory performance which does not cross the boundaries of behaviour for which immediate suspension would be a normal procedure.

Underperformance is a very different matter. The person may be working in a way that produces a lower performance than that of his or her colleagues, or may simply be capable of a more energetic contribution. It is important not to label people as underperformers. The process of performance management should enable underachievement to be tackled as an issue that stresses underperformance rather than 'an underperformer'. Remember the principles of setting objectives, alignment of personal objectives and work unit goals, the need for recognition of achievement in order to motivate academics, and the need to establish a dialogue with your colleagues, in order to tackle underperformance. Spend time with your underperforming colleague. Find out what they need to help them be more effective. What motivated them to become an academic? What are their unique hopes and special proficiencies? What do they enjoy most? What new skills do they want to acquire? What do they think you could do to help them? A well-tried method of dealing with academic underperformance is to invite the person to suggest ways in which he or she might become more involved in the work of the department, and in particular to ask the person to advise on how a particular problem or assignment which you are facing – such as increased student numbers, changes in accountability processes, an application of information technology, or new staff orientation – can be addressed (Bright and Williamson, 1995; Lucas, 1995).

Underperformance provides an opportunity for academic leaders to demonstrate their creativity and humanity, and to renew people's vitality through inspiration and support. As academic managers, we should demand of underperforming colleagues what we demand of all our colleagues: agreement to setting challenging objectives, rigorous standards of achievement, and the exercise of autonomy in deciding how to meet these standards. Underperformance tests a manager's capacity to deploy the key academic leadership abilities of guidance, encouragement, and teaching. You may not succeed in eliminating the problem. But from the attempt you should expect to learn to improve your own performance – which leads us to the theme of the next chapter.

Part III

CHANGING UNIVERSITIES AND IMPROVING LEADERSHIP

10

LEARNING TO LEAD: PERSONAL DEVELOPMENT AS AN ACADEMIC LEADER

Paul Ramsden and Alf Lizzio

> A Prince therefore ought alwayes to take counsell, but at his
> own pleasure, and not at other mens; or rather should take
> away any mans courage to advise him of any thing, but what
> he askes: but hee oughte well to ask at large and then
> touching the things inquird of, be a patient hearer of the
> truth . . .. For this is a general rule and never failes, that a
> Prince who of himselfe is not wise, cannot bee well advisd.
> Machiavelli, *The Prince*, Chapter XXIII.

A.N. Whitehead said that knowledge kept no better than fish; it must 'either be new in itself or it must be invested with some novelty of application' (Whitehead, 1932, p. 147). As with knowledge, so with leadership skills. To advance our leadership capacity, we must be constantly renewing it by learning from experience. This implies *evaluation*. I don't mean establishing ideal standards and deciding whether someone has enough 'leadership knowledge' to be an academic head of department. I mean an analytic and synthetic process designed to understand the effectiveness of the processes we use to help transform presage factors into academic outcomes.

Conceptualised in this way as a form of learning, evaluation is at the heart of the business of academic leadership. It is not for nothing that the centre of the academic leadership matrix (Figure 6.3) is made up of the task of *learning to lead*. No training programme or book can *teach* us to lead; no advice from followers will make up for insufficiency of wisdom. Nor will we ever learn enough to avoid mistakes as academic leaders; but we may hope to use these experiences to our advantage through systematic reflection on what we might have done better. There is no choice in the matter: learning to lead is a lifetime responsibility.

In the first part of the book I argued that we could grasp the qualities of effective university leadership by studying the experiences of academic staff, and by analysing the relations between different types of academic contexts and how academics go about their work. Lecturers' own perceptions serve to underline the properties of effective academic leadership and highlight the substantial overlap between management and leadership in universities and in other kinds of organisation. They constitute a most important source of learning material for academic leaders. Through examining these experiences, we actively enquire into how we can intervene in the relationship between presage and product, and thus we enhance our capacity to lead. Good leadership represents a commitment both to today and to tomorrow. Joined with efficient management, it helps produce high quality academic work in the present and it implies confidence in the future. It entails creating the conditions that enable staff to welcome change and to delight in finding new ways of addressing it. These are abiding goals which have gained fresh meaning in today's arduous environment.

The second part of the book tried to show how we could apply ideas of different ways of leading and managing to improving the context of academic work – through attention to vision, planning, inspiring and enabling academic people, and developing staff performance. Political aptitude, communication skills, optimism, a sense of direction, a view of the big picture, imagination, good judgement, concern for staff development, ability to live with the consequences of decisions – all these can be seen as aspects of the fundamental responsibilities of academic leadership. They are deployed through such practical strategies as performance management, recognition of achievement, strategic thinking, resource management, project planning, and close support for teaching and research.

Now, in the last two chapters, I want to extend these propositions to enhancing our own performance as academic leaders and to improving the university environment in which we operate. I hope to show that the same principles that should inform our practice as academic leaders can be applied to organising our own development and to managing the universities of tomorrow. Like Machiavelli's Prince, universities and their leaders alike need the wisdom to learn from asking at large and being patient hearers of the truth.

Capacities and qualities for leadership

Put simply, one cannot be taught to educate or to lead; one certainly cannot be taught to lead educators. Instead, leaders

228

and educators must develop themselves, but not by themselves.

G.A. Donaldson (1991)

What are we trying to achieve through personal development as academic leaders? Essentially, we are trying to learn skills, sharpen them through practice, and integrate them within a conception of academic leadership; at the same time, we are hoping to adapt our individual proclivities to approximate some of the consistent characteristics that good leaders display. The leadership matrix and the four responsibilities of academic leadership (Figure 6.3 and Table 7.1) provide a general outline of these competencies and personal qualities. As we have seen, the tasks of leadership present a series of dilemmas and paradoxes, including looking after people versus getting tasks done, organised and sequential management versus visionary and situational leadership, direction versus participation, and assessment of performance versus developing staff. That these paradoxes are integral to academic leadership is confirmed by personal accounts of educational management such as Gordon Donaldson's exceptional history of his own experience as an American high school principal (Donaldson, 1991).

In a book that is an epitome of reflective practice, Donaldson catalogues capacities and qualities which reflect our 'four responsibilities'. His list provides a useful framework for a learning to lead programme. The unpredictable nature of academic leadership requires this framework to be equipped with material from the analysis of our own experiences.

Capacity 1 To understand the special goals of the department or institution and to articulate its purposes in such a way that the daily weight of routine tasks, administrative pressures and short-term activities does not submerge its vision. (This is easier said than done, as every academic leader will know. Clark Kerr once remarked of the University of California that 'I find the three major administrative problems on campus are sex for the students, athletics for the alumni, and parking for the faculty'. The measure of his success as a president was that he retained and verbalised his greater vision for it).

Capacity 2 To translate high purposes into daily work: to be realistic about what goes on and what should go on, to enable staff to adapt to change by negotiating progress through simultaneous consultation and assertion, and to provide a clear organisational structure that promotes learning and social responsibility.

Capacity 3 To communicate with, direct and motivate staff: to combine speaking and listening, direction and development, trust and professional dissatisfaction; and to read interpersonal signals, understand diverse motives, and understand how his or her own behaviour will influence others.

To these capacities, Donaldson adds three personal qualities which we should bear particularly in mind in our development programme. *Self-confidence* (not arrogance or self-promotion) provides a basis for successful consultation and the courage to make firm decisions (about which someone will always complain). This confidence is built through experience, reflection and professional knowledge. An *appreciation of diversity* permits the leader to respect different goals, agendas, needs and strengths in staff, and to avoid the view that there is a single 'right system' for the work unit while at the same time not compromising on values or vision, or avoiding action. *Enjoyment of personal contacts* with staff and students is the third quality. It is very hard to be either a successful teacher or a successful leader of academic staff unless we can learn to show genuine interest in and warmth towards people. Each of these three qualities reinforces the other two and supports the three capacities.

From our previous discussion, we might append to Donaldson's list:

- a desire to help others learn, and to become leaders; and the teaching skills to make these intentions happen
- an understanding of complexity and ability to bring disparate ideas together
- powerful sympathy with the nature and purposes of the academic enterprise
- a capacity to coordinate internal changes with external demands
- long-term thinking and political awareness

All these are specially important in periods of exceptional change in higher education. Together, these qualities and capacities supply the bedrock on which we can face the dilemmas of academic leadership with assurance.

The qualities of leader as learner

It is probably of little help to list a series of wishful statements about the generic qualities of the academic leader as an effective learner. It may be worth reminding ourselves, however, that the list would certainly include the kinds of competencies we seek to develop in university students – independence, communication, problem-solving, analytic skills, critical thinking, specialist competence, teamwork, self-motivation, and commitment to continuous learning itself.

There is no place in today's university where we can sit and watch the unruly world go by. Since leadership is about change, academic leaders must themselves be constantly changing. If they cease to take pleasure from addressing change, from desiring to learn, they cannot be effective university leaders any longer. They cannot hope to convince their followers to look outwards and to learn as well. The essence of 'lifelong learning' about leadership can perhaps best be captured in the idea that leadership is a *process of work in progress* (Lizzio, 1996). I suggest that academic leaders may improve their effectiveness if they:

- Regularly review essential values related to academic work and leadership of others.
- Try to clarify what difference they want to make to their work unit and the people in it.
- Have a sense of the underlying tensions in academic systems and critically evaluate their choices within them.
- Methodically assess how they achieved results, how well they motivated staff, how effectively they enabled them to achieve, and whether they adequately recognised their attainment.
- Work to maintain their self-possession and enjoyment in their work through careful management of their workload and commitments.
- Seek information from their departmental colleagues and senior managers about their perceived leadership strengths and weaknesses.
- Establish dialogue and discussion with a colleague in a similar role about their performance and their changing needs. They should, as Donaldson (1991) observed above, 'develop themselves, but not by themselves'. Having a learning partner provides support and maintains motivation.
- Set objectives for themselves and their continuing development.

In short, they need to apply the four responsibilities of academic leadership – vision, enabling, assessment of performance, and learning to lead – to their own development.

The remainder of this chapter examines practical ways of addressing these central developmental processes through making use of reflective templates, learning to manage time and tasks, learning from our colleagues using a feedback instrument, and creating a leadership portfolio.

Templates for learning through reflection[1]

Professional development requires us to reflect on our successes and failures and the ways in which we can learn from them. Nothing stays still. One certainty is that the hazards we face next year will be different ones. It is important to take time occasionally to reflect on what you stand for, where your leadership agenda is taking you, what you need to know in order to realise that agenda, what the results of previous attempts to intervene in change were, and how you would proceed differently next time. These activities help keep us energetic and motivated, and rightly focus attention on the future as well as the present.

One of the difficulties in all academic staff development programmes is making the leap from a focus on skills and techniques to a consideration of the underlying 'working theory' which informs those techniques. It is important to understand how working theories and practice form part of a unified system. We now know that, in the area of improving teaching skills, certain theories or conceptions of teaching and learning limit the capacity of lecturers to deploy techniques effectively; or more precisely, prevent them from seeing the possibilities inherent in those teaching techniques (Trigwell and Prosser, 1996). For example, a science lecturer who sees first year student learning as involving chiefly the acquisition of information, and her own role as transmitting that information, has a *limiting conception of student learning*. As a result, she will not 'see' the possibility of helping the students to learn through asking them questions, and there is no point in training her to use this technique unless she is also encouraged to change her conception.

The following templates assume, in uniformity with the rest of this book, that our academic leadership practice is similarly informed by our underlying theories of leadership. Therefore, reflective activities should aim to elucidate the links between practice and theory, and address both theory and practice concurrently. Skills and capacities derive their power from the conceptions that frame them.

Figure 10.1 illustrates the idea that academic leadership in practice and conceptions of leadership are joined through the concept of a leadership agenda representing the intentions and strategies which you deploy as an academic leader. It also shows how the

---

1 These templates are adapted from Alf Lizzio's *Academic Leadership Portfolio: Guidelines and Reflective Processes for Clarifying Your Frames of Reference as an Academic Leader* (Lizzio, 1996). This document was developed as part of the academic leadership materials produced by a team from the Griffith Institute for Higher Education for use in local and national programmes for academic leaders.

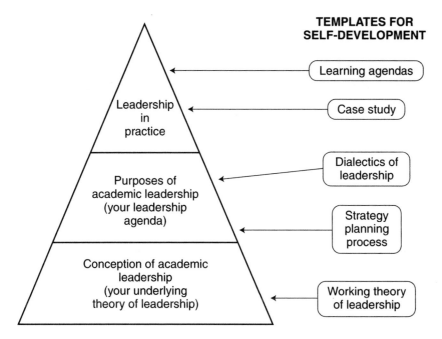

Figure 10.1 Using self-development templates to link theory and practice

following templates for self-development apply to the three different levels. The templates may be helpful in providing practical tools for developing your ability to learn through reflection.

Template 1: Identifying (and testing) your working theory of leadership

The purpose of this exercise is to help you articulate your own conception of academic leadership and the associated values and principles which direct your leadership behaviour.

Recall the stories of academics' experiences of effective and ineffective academic leadership presented in chapter 5. Consider again your own experiences of people whom you would regard as exemplary academic leaders – people who you felt were obviously competent.

- What was it about their approach that had a positive impact on you?

Now consider people you have worked with whom you would regard as poor academic leaders.

- What was it about their approach that had a negative impact on you?

Compare your own experiences with those described in chapter 5. Select an example of your own leadership behaviour in the light of your experiences of exemplary and poor academic leadership in others.

- In what ways was your leadership successful and unsuccessful?

Now review the material on leadership and management in chapter 6.

- Which of these models, ideas or theories appeals to you or helps to make sense of your leadership behaviour?

Take a moment to synthesise the main themes from your positive and negative models, your personal experiences as a leader, and the material on leadership and management.

- What are the key beliefs, principles or values that you hold about the appropriate leadership of academic people? If these people could say only one good thing about you, what do you hope it would be? At the end of the day, how do you hope that your success as a leader should be judged?

Test your working theory by comparing it with a real leadership task which is ahead of you. For example, you may have to convene a course team, plan a seminar on improving postgraduate supervision, try to discourage the university from reducing your budget, chair an academic staff meeting, interview a colleague about his negative student evaluations, or delegate an administrative responsibility to your secretary.

- How will you approach this task?
- In what ways will your approach agree or disagree with the theory you have articulated?
- What are the challenges you face in acting consistently with your theory?
- What is the match between what you intend as a leader and the actual impact you have?
- Is your theory actually applied in practice? If not, what is your real working theory?

Template 2: Strategic planning process

A useful way of identifying your current leadership agenda is to undertake a simple, personal, strategic planning process.

1 *Situation analysis* Identify within your current work unit trends related to changes in your university and to wider changes in the higher education environment; your colleagues' perceptions, values and competencies; and your own approach to leadership. The contextual changes described in chapter 2 and the developments in 'university cultures' shown in Figures 2.1 to 2.4 may be useful starting points. What is the culture or climate of your work unit? What are the key issues it will have to face? What is your preferred role and approach as an academic leader? What do you intend to do?

2 *Outcome analysis* Recalling the discussion in chapter 7, consider your vision of possibilities for your work unit – your picture of what you want it to achieve and how you would like the people in it to behave. Also consider what you think others might want you to achieve: what outcomes are expected of or prescribed for your work unit? Identify your key objectives and the approach to leadership that you think would best accomplish this vision and realise these outcomes.

3 *Leadership agenda* Compare the results of steps 1 and 2. What is the gap between the current situation (including your own skills and motives) and the outcomes you and others want to achieve? From this comparison, distinguish your leadership agenda, in terms of priorities, intentions, strategies, possible conflicts, and needs for new skills and ways of maintaining your commitment and your confidence.

- What are your short term goals? Your long term goals? What are your top priorities? What is the best way to listen and learn from your colleagues about how to attain these objectives? How will you sustain your energy when times get hard? What do you particularly need to know to become a better academic manager and leader? How will you gain this knowledge?

Template 3: Case study

This method involves reflecting on your leadership in action by analysing one or more actual instances of trying to implement change. For example, you may have tried to introduce a different approach to decision-making, a policy on workload allocation, a series of 'work in progress' seminars to encourage younger researchers, a new income-generation scheme to support research and consultancy, a teaching observation and peer review process, a simplified procedure for administrative support for academic staff, a flexible learning (resource-based teaching) subject, a different approach to allocating travel funds – or one of many other changes including the suggestions for supporting teaching and research made in chapter 8. You might use the following questions to organise your thinking:

Context	What were the circumstances in which you were trying to make a difference?
	Who were the people involved; what were their expectations and needs?
Intentions	What outcomes were you trying to achieve?
	What difference did you want to make?
Strategy	What approach did you use to address the outcomes?
	Why?
Implementation	What did you do to make it happen?
	What did you try to do, but gave up on?
	What compromises did you have to make?
Impact	What happened?
	Did you achieve your desired outcomes?
	Were there any unintended consequences?
Learning	What did you learn as a result – about yourself; about others; about how you might tackle a similar issue next time?
	If you had to do it again, what would you do differently?

Template 4: Dialectics of leadership

Prominent in any reflective process about academic leadership will be the dilemmas and tensions facing us. A difficult lesson that leaders and teachers all learn is that most problems are recurrent, that few have right answers, and that compromise and competing priorities seem to rule everyday choices and decisions. Judgment and firm decision-making in situations of imperfect information is a key leadership skill. The aspects of academic light and shadow described in chapter 6. guarantee that organisational positions such as head of a department will be subject to congenital tensions.

As I have indicated several times, it is possible to conceptualise effective academic leadership as a process of finding ways to be effective within a context of conflicting loyalties, differing agendas, and contrasting options and positions. It may be useful to make these dialectics explicit as part of the activity of developing our leadership capacity.

The exercise involves looking at the paired choices or dilemmas presented in Table 10.1. They have been classified under each of the four main leadership responsibility headings; ignore irrelevant pairs of choices, and add others to the list if you think they do not cover the challenges you personally face.

For each dilemma, consider:

- What is a concrete example of this choice in my own experience of being an academic leader?
- Is this really a choice between two alternatives, or can both aspects be addressed together?
- How did I (or would I) engage with, resolve, or manage this dilemma?
- What factors would lead me to favour one option over the other?

What do you conclude from your answers, and from the material presented in chapters 7, 8, and 9, are the most significant choices facing you as an academic leader? What do colleagues in similar positions think?

Template 5: Learning agendas

This simple exercise explores the way in which different sources of evaluative information – including data which emerges from applying the templates previously described – can be used to establish learning priorities related to your leadership practice. This template may be a helpful way of producing results that can be incorporated in a *leadership portfolio*, which I will discus later in this chapter.

Over time we accumulate various kinds of information about our effectiveness as students, researchers, teachers, and leaders. In the area of academic leadership, the sources may include:

- Informal feedback from colleagues and supervisors
- More formal evaluation through appraisal or a '360 degree' feedback instrument (discussed in a later section)
- Our own experiences of success and failure

Table 10.1 Dilemmas of the four responsibilities of academic leadership

Vision, strategic action, planning, resource management

Advocate your work unit's interests in the university and beyond	v.	Look after internal processes and people
Clarity of direction	v.	Consultative decision-making
Need to enhance teaching and research outputs continually	v.	Need to manage constant reduction in resource inputs
Academic and personal values	v.	Realities of political power and influence
Academic culture and tradition	v.	Turbulent environment and orientation towards change and innovation
Risk taking, bold moves, and entrepreneurial activity	v.	Resource and financial prudence
Comply minimally with external quality processes	v.	Eagerly embrace external quality processes
Focus on teamwork and collective goals	v.	Allow people to pursue individual agendas
Plan carefully for the long term	v.	Go with the short-term flow
Follow the university line	v.	Work to your department's advantage
Academic excellence	v.	Pressures of mass higher education
Disciplinary allegiance	v.	Corporate culture

Enabling, inspiring, motivating, direction

Meet staff needs and priorities (expert focus)	v.	Meet student needs and priorities (customer focus)
Efficient and effective management	v.	Inspirational and collaborative leadership
Focus on results and outcomes	v.	Focus on motivation and staff morale
Show you care	v.	Show you won't be deceived
Model academic excellence yourself	v.	Sacrifice your own academic career to help others
Follow the administrative rules	v.	Test, bend, or break the rules
When to tell and direct	v.	When to listen and consult
Work transparently and openly	v.	Work judiciously behind the scenes
Treat academic staff as a privileged group	v.	Remove status barriers between academics and administrative staff
Admit mistakes	v.	Cover your tracks
Control interruptions	v.	Pursue an open door policy

Table 10.1 continued

Encourage disagreement and discussion	v.	Avoid conflict and push issues through
Emphasise outcomes in research	v.	Emphasise quality in teaching and service

Recognition, development, assessment of performance

Delegation of tasks	v.	Control over quality of outcomes
Help others to learn how to lead	v.	Maintain your power and authority
See mistakes as learning opportunities	v.	Don't let people get away with bad work
Select the best staff	v.	Make do with what you have got
Support those with potential	v.	Treat everyone equally
Use regulation student rating forms	v.	Encourage staff to devise own feedback methods
Treat equity groups as a special case	v.	Same standards apply to everyone
Rewards, incentives, discipline	v.	Recognition, support and concern
Make staff accountable	v.	Let professionals set own standards
Development and feedback	v.	Assessment of performance outcomes
Reward achievement	v.	Reward effort
Goals of the institution	v.	Career of the individual
Confront underperformance and 'difficult' colleagues	v.	Avoid hostility and give people space to work it out

Reflection, evaluation, personal learning and development

Being a manager and supervisor	v.	Being first among equals
Regarding academic leadership as a career	v.	Seeing it as a temporary job
Being a likeable person	v.	Commanding respect
Help others to achieve	v.	Concentrate on what you want to achieve
Showing intellectual brilliance	v.	Displaying humility and avoiding arrogance
Leadership of the work unit	v.	Your own academic career
Manage your image	v.	Do what you feel
Time to reflect, plan, learn new skills	v.	Pressure of immediate demands

Table 10.1 continued

Personal survival, health and well-being	v.	Achieving more and more
Focus on the important issues	v.	Focus on the urgent issues
Focus on the present	v.	Focus on the future

- The current demands of our role, and how we manage its tensions
- The results of a personal strategic planning process, as outlined above
- Our own motivations for being an academic leader, and the costs we are willing to bear in doing the job
- Our future plans and intentions in our careers and personal lives

Consider what each of these sources can tell you about how to lead and manage people, resources, and systems.

From this analysis, what are the two or three most important learning priorities for you in becoming a more effective academic leader?

Learning to manage time and tasks

Time is the most precious of all resources. Many academic leaders mismanage it. Personal leadership development involves learning how to use it wisely.

'Give us some practical tips for handling the workload' is a favourite request at workshops on academic leadership. Most academics new to leadership positions find the sheer weight and diversity of tasks simply overwhelming. The pressure results in different kinds of adaptive response. There is no point in prevaricating, however; many successful new heads will train themselves to carry two or three times the workload that they had as regular academics, and the work will be very different (see Table 10.2). It is surprising how quickly the mind adapts through exercise to handling a 200 per cent increase in workload. However, it is still important to manage time well; there is a limit to our adaptability beyond which stress leads to diminished performance and illness.

Understanding the differences in the role is one of the keys to effective management of time and tasks. In my view it is impossible for most of us to be fully effective as academic leaders unless we capitalise on the differences rather than try to minimise them. I find it best to think of time management as *freeing up time to lead*. Some

Table 10.2 Transitions: academic to head of academic department

Academic		Head of Academic Department
Autonomy	➧	Accountability
Focused tasks	➧	Fragmented, short, variable tasks
Solitary or small team work	➧	Social and large team work
Explaining and professing	➧	Persuading and influencing
Private	➧	Public
Freedom	➧	Restriction
Little control over resources	➧	Considerable control over resources
Little administrative support	➧	More administrative support
Working without a secretary	➧	Working with a secretary
Being supervised/self-supervised	➧	Supervising others
Thinking	➧	Doing
Writing papers	➧	Writing memos
Little internal power	➧	More internal power
Considerable control over time	➧	Very limited control over time
Looking out for yourself	➧	Responsible for others
Specialist academic	➧	Generalist manager and leader

Source: Based on Gmelch and Miskin, 1993, p. 16

years ago, handbooks for heads of departments advised on ways in which they could continue their academic careers while being heads; typical advice was to spend a day a week at home, have a fixed time for research, confine teaching to certain days in the week, put a 'do-not-disturb: involved in research' notice on the door (see, for example, Lucas, 1995; Moses and Roe, 1989). But we can no longer take it for granted that an academic leadership position is a temporary role which distracts people from their 'real' work; increasingly it is becoming a career in itself, and an enjoyable career which does not have to be seen as a second best. As part of a business-like time and stress management strategy, it is important to decide to what extent you wish to embrace the transformation. It is not an either–or decision; it is possible for people to maintain an interest in research and to model good scholarly practice without being heavily involved in such activities. Partly it will depend on our previous achievements and reputation as academics. The priorities established in the previous reflective exercises may help to frame the choices you make.

Among the plethora of advice on time management techniques, there are three very practical strategies which are worth special attention. The first is to sit down and decide what you are being paid to do as an academic leader (Drucker, n.d., quoted in Adair, 1988, p. 55). What are the two or three things that, if you do them well, will really make a difference? Again, the priorities you have decided upon for yourself and your work group should help to provide the answers. These answers provide a framework to support your directions and purposes and the values which underlie them. This high-level framework should direct the more detailed tactical planning you do, by the year, month, and day. It can always be referred back to when you are in doubt. It can always be amended in the light of experience.

The second technique is carried out in association with the first. Carry out an audit of how you use your time now. Another self-development exercise that needs more effort for little reward, perhaps? If you ask a group of heads of departments about the demands on their time, some will certainly report that their work-load has increased, that they have more administrative tasks (such as those associated with quality assessment processes) to carry out, that the paperwork is overwhelming, that there are too many meetings, that they can't concentrate on one job without being inter-rupted, that they are not meeting deadlines, that their weekends have disappeared, and that 24 hours isn't adequate for doing the day's work. An audit can show where the time goes. It requires considerable self-possession to start the exercise, but once begun it takes little extra time – maybe half an hour of your week.

Over a seven-day week, record how you spend each hour of your time, classifying the results into convenient personal categories such as those shown on pp. 243–4. You may find that there is a big discrepancy between 'what would really make a difference' and how you actually spent your time. Almost certainly you will see oppor-tunities for change and identify areas for attention. What would happen if you went to fewer university meetings? Could you dele-gate more detailed and recurrent tasks to an administrative assis-tant? Could another academic take on some of your postgraduate teaching? Do you really need to see individual students every week? How much time each day do have to yourself, when you can plan and reflect? Would the world stop revolving if you didn't do as much writing and didn't visit the laboratory every afternoon?

The third strategy is actively learning from other leaders. Like the other two, it requires an investment of time and effort itself. Observe how more senior staff manage their time. They probably work long hours, but they typically will not be hurried. The more important the assignment or decision, the more they seem to slow themselves down. They find time to break from their work, walking around the campus or socialising to recharge their energy. They delegate a lot (see chapter 9). They use their administrative staff wisely, filtering phone calls and other types of interruptions through a secretary. They plan their days with their secretaries, and ensure that there is a strong bond of understanding between them.

If you talk to other academic leaders, you will find that they can collectively catalogue, from their own experience, virtually every tactic recommended in books on improving time management. You do not have to invent your own ideas or read all the books (although I would recommend Adair's *Effective Time Management* (Adair, 1988) as one of the most readable compilations). It is very well worthwhile to ask for their suggestions on techniques that work for them. One or more of them may work for you.

Some of the suggestions made by staff with whom I have worked are listed on pp. 244–5. Not all of them are necessarily feasible or effective, but they may give you some fresh ideas.

COMPARING 'WHAT WOULD MAKE A DIFFERENCE' WITH ACTUAL TIME SPENT

What would really make a difference? (WWRMD)

1 getting staff to be committed to quality in teaching
2 good forward planning and management of 'projects'
3 better grasp of how information technology can be used to free up staff resources and time

How did I actually spend my time? (percentages of 70 hour week)

- university meetings not related to WWRMD (25)
- self development and learning as leader (e.g. learning about uses of IT and project planning) (5)
- departmental interviews and meetings not related to WWRMD (10)
- departmental interviews and meetings related to WWRMD (5)
- own teaching and research including student contact, assessment, preparation (15)

- administrivia, paperwork, telephone, writing references and handling correspondence (15)
- travel between campuses (5)
- preparing for quality assessment (5)
- social events related to work (5)
- networking with colleagues in other departments (5)
- appraisals (5)

SOME PRACTICAL TIME AND TASK MANAGEMENT
TECHNIQUES SUGGESTED BY ACADEMIC LEADERS

- Plan the year and the term or semester before it begins.
- Take breaks to replenish your energy; don't stay cooped up in your room.
- Cancel meetings which have no substantial business (make sure colleagues understand that scheduled meetings may be cancelled).
- Ensure all meetings have a finishing as well as a starting time and stick to it.
- Never use departmental meetings to make management decisions. (Use meetings for policy advice. Individuals should make management decisions).
- Appoint a deputy – to develop their leadership skills, carry some of the load, and to provide a successor.
- Make to-do lists at the end of the previous day, not at the start of the next day, if you want to ensure you get important as well as urgent tasks done.
- 'Never be too proud to be present': be seen personally at university meetings that are vital for advocating your department's position.
- Arrange for other members of staff to attend other meetings which are important but not vital.
- Don't work in crisis mode all the time.
- Don't see colleagues who are angry about something straight away. (Make an appointment to allow them to cool off).
- Have your secretary provide you with a day sheet showing appointments and reminders for the next day as the last thing he/she does before leaving.

244

- Schedule a 15-minute meeting with your secretary at the start of every day to review your diary and reduce the chance of miscommunication. Once a week, review the whole next week ahead.
- Don't open your own post. Get someone else to filter the junk from what needs action and to place different categories of mail in different clearly-marked folders, including an 'important' folder.
- When in your office, only read material marked as important.
- Use travel time or time at the end of the day to read less important material.
- Use standard templates for references and reports.
- Delegate, delegate, delegate – have faith in your staff.
- Give yourself a present when you complete your day's tasks in the day.
- Have the courage to accept that you can't influence everything. Some things can't be changed.
- Don't take work home every night. Turn the mobile phone off sometimes. Life is too short.
- Talk to others about how they manage their time. Steal their ideas about time management shamelessly.
- Don't expect to carry on a full research agenda *and* be a head of department *and* have a personal life. Three into two won't go.
- Never procrastinate; make it a habit to do something every day that you really don't want to do.
- Don't spend time worrying over what might have been.

Learning from our colleagues

The significance of listening to colleagues about leadership has been a conspicuous theme of the preceding chapters. It brings together the literature and ideas on management and leadership in non-educational organisations with the concept of academic leadership as a process analogous to university teaching. The critical importance of attending to followers' perceptions of leaders, the staff with whom a supervisor or manager works with every day, is well-documented in the management literature, as we saw in chapter 6. Similarly, through evaluation, an effective teacher uses information from her students about the effects of her teaching in order to improve it, and thus enhances the quality of students' learning.

The most compelling reason for collecting evidence from our colleagues about our performance is that it models the qualities needed to make performance management successful; and as I have indicated, performance management is a first step on the path to creating an improved academic environment. For performance management – together with its attendant qualities of open feedback, focus on the future, and linking individual and work unit goals – to be effective, leaders must go first. We cannot expect to be followed if we do not take the same risks. Everyone fears being judged. No-one anticipates with joy that uncomfortable shiver when you realise you are being criticised for bad work. What will my colleagues say about my personal skills? Am I as good at inspiring people to teach well as I think I am? Will they use the opportunity just to moan again about decreased autonomy and decline in reputation? Will the Dean say I'm not up to the job? Yet without this evidence our progress towards both self-development and improving our colleagues' working conditions will be impeded. Feedback *should* be unsettling if it is to help polish our skills and think about new directions for development. We must show that we are prepared to accept feedback, reflect on it, and set goals for change as a result of integrating that feedback with other sources of evidence.

Feedback of this kind tells you how you are perceived by others. It is not an objective assessment of your performance; it is a source of subjective data to work on. Think less about whether it is valid, and more about whether it is useful. You will receive confirmation of your leadership abilities as well as opinions about areas for development. You should make a habit of inviting feedback from your colleagues, both senior and junior, to help create an atmosphere in the department where open and constructive communication is the norm. Regularly asking for comments about your performance and areas for improvement, formally as well as informally, and reporting back on what you have done with the information to those who provided it, gradually develops a recognition that evaluation is an ordinary part of the work unit's activity.

There is no excuse for hiding from feedback on ourselves. It reminds us that our unique function as academic leaders is an educational one. What excellent teachers do is to help their students go beyond their current understanding. What effective academic leaders do is to provide their colleagues with the means to perform beyond their expectations.

Actions you might take to obtain useful feedback and act upon it

Feedback from colleagues is not an end in itself but a point of departure. Its purpose is to provide useful information that can be incorporated into a considered plan of development, and perhaps into one or more of the reflective exercises described earlier in this chapter.

- Take the initiative in asking for evaluative comments from your boss. Arrange a meeting with your immediate academic supervisor, explaining that you would like to get some comments on your performance and the performance of your work unit. Agree an agenda at the beginning: expect to discuss about what they hope you and the unit will achieve in the next 12 months; how this will harmonise with the department's or faculty's or university's strategic goals; what two or three objectives are critical indicators of your performance in that time; how the achievement of these will be measured; what feedback you will get at the end of the period about your achievements.

- Give yourself some honest feedback. Carry out a self-evaluation of your effectiveness in discharging your leadership responsibilities (use the 'quick self evaluation exercise' below). Fit the results into a leadership portfolio, as outlined later in the chapter.

- Arrange to use the formal 360-degree feedback instrument described below.

- Prepare your colleagues to give you useful feedback. They should become aware that providing comments about observed behaviours is more beneficial than giving global judgements about your merit as a leader. You can more readily use specific information, both positive and negative, to develop practical solutions and assess their effects.

- Ask individuals regularly about specific actions you have taken and the results they perceived. For example: 'I felt I could have managed that meeting about preparation for research quality assessment better. What do you think I could have done?'

- Carry out a follow-up exercise based on reporting the results of your evaluation (including the goals you have set yourself for improvement) to the department (see Lucas, 1995, pp. 233–4).

Using the Leadership for Academic Work 360-degree feedback instrument

The *Leadership for Academic Work* questionnaire, first introduced in chapter 5, focuses on behaviours and competencies that are seen by academic staff and academic leaders to be important in helping them to pursue their academic work effectively. The 50-odd questions are grouped into seven areas. To use this form of feedback, you need to arrange for your supervisor, yourself, and about ten colleagues to complete the appropriate version of the forms, shown in Appendix 1. The data from the closed questions and the open comments from your colleagues should be analysed and compiled by someone else; you should stress to your colleagues that you will not have access to the individual forms. The open questions are analysed by separately compiling the comments about strengths and areas for development.

The Griffith Institute for Higher Education offers a confidential service of printing and analysing your feedback forms, and producing an extensive report, for a moderate cost. Data may be entered directly by respondents through the World Wide Web. Details of this service can be obtained by email to P.Ramsden@gu.edu.au or by writing to GIHE at Griffith University, Nathan 4111, Australia.

Quick self-evaluation exercise

Step 1: Imaginary advice Imagine you are going to run a one hour session for heads of departments on the topics discussed in chapters 7 - 8. What five main ideas would you want them to take away from the session?

Using these main ideas as a background, construct a model of the different aspects of academic leadership with which *you* feel comfortable as a starting point. This could be the four responsibilities model (Table 7.1), the two-by-two matrix of leadership, management, tasks and people (Figure 6.3), the lists of staff expectations of leaders (pp. 87–8), the ten dimensions of the *Leadership for Academic Work* questionnaire (Table 5.1) – or your own compilation of areas of effective academic leadership which are important to you.

Whichever model you use, review the items in the *Leadership for Academic Work* questionnaire and the examples on pp. 87–8. In the light of what you have read, evaluate your own performance on each aspect (such as recognising and rewarding staff, inspiring and motivating, being an effective resource manager) of your model.

Step 2: List strengths Mention only strengths which you can substantiate with evidence, such as informal or formal feedback from colleagues and supervisors.

Step 3: Identify needs for development List up to three aspects of leadership within each of the broad areas of your model which you wish to improve.

Step 4: List activities leading towards development List specific actions you will take to address each of the aspects you have identified as developmental needs in step 3. What actions might you take to consolidate the strengths listed in step 2?

Quick self-evaluation exercise 2 – specifically for heads of departments

Complete the following questionnaire to obtain an idea of your academic leadership strengths and weaknesses.

Listed below are 16 statements which describe aspects of effective academic leadership behaviour. Rate your own effectiveness on each statement. Add your scores in each section (one total score for each of leader, manager, political animal, and staff developer). Compare them with the averages shown in Table 10.3 and draw your own conclusions.

Leader

	Ineffective					Highly effective
Bringing new ideas about teaching into the department/school/faculty	1 2 3 4 5 6 7					
Getting people to move collaboratively towards a common purpose	1 2 3 4 5 6 7					
Bringing new ideas about research into the department/school/faculty	1 2 3 4 5 6 7					
Motivating people to do more than they ever thought they could	1 2 3 4 5 6 7					

Manager

	Ineffective						Highly effective
Maintaining simple and effective administrative procedures	1	2	3	4	5	6	7
Delegating responsibility fairly and consistently	1	2	3	4	5	6	7
Managing the work unit's resources effectively	1	2	3	4	5	6	7
Always making my expectations of staff clear	1	2	3	4	5	6	7

Political Animal

	Ineffective						Highly effective
Working to build the reputation of my department/school/faculty	1	2	3	4	5	6	7
Advocating the interests of my work unit to the senior management of the university	1	2	3	4	5	6	7
Considering problems from a university perspective as well as a local one	1	2	3	4	5	6	7
Working to bring more resources into my school/faculty/department	1	2	3	4	5	6	7

Staff Developer

	Ineffective						Highly effective
Readily acknowledging my colleagues' contributions	1	2	3	4	5	6	7
Encouraging people to share ideas and learn from each other	1	2	3	4	5	6	7
Actively working to develop others as leaders	1	2	3	4	5	6	7
Not being abrasive when under pressure	1	2	3	4	5	6	7

Table 10.3 Comparative scores for quick self-evaluation – exercise 2

	Bottom group	*Middle group*	*Top group*	*Averages for 60 leaders*
Leader	Less than 18	18 to 23	More than 23	20
Manager	Less than 17	17 to 22	More than 22	19
Political animal	Less than 21	21 to 31	More than 31	23
Staff developer	Less than 18	18 to 23	More than 23	21

Putting the results of our learning to good use: a leadership portfolio

Over a period of time, carrying out the various exercises and feedback processes outlined in this chapter will gradually lead you to accumulate an archive of material about your academic leadership activities, your successes and mistakes as an academic leader, the results of your leadership, and the changes you have experienced through your leadership career.

This material offers an excellent opportunity to put together a leadership portfolio which can be used to document achievements and which could form a basis for goal-setting and career development planning with your supervisor or dean. It might also be useful as a means of communicating more explicitly with your departmental colleagues about how you do business as an academic manager and leader, and for modelling the processes of self-evaluation and transparent exchange that help distinguish a 'working' academic culture from a 'non-working' one (see Table 9.1).

By a 'leadership portfolio', I mean a short, coherent account of your academic leadership – a document of three to four pages only. It will show clearly:

- What your goals are
- What results you have achieved
- How these goals and results relate to the expectations of your department and university
- What your central values and beliefs are as an academic leader
- How these relate to characteristics of effective leadership
- How you have learned from your experiences
- How you managed the tensions and dilemmas of academic leadership
- What evidence there is to support your claims

A leadership portfolio would include an account of aspects of your work such as the kind of climate you have tried to create in your work unit; your vision, planning, and strategy; your management processes; your approach to enabling and motivating academic people; your approach to assessing their performance and recognising what they have accomplished; how you have helped develop your staff; and how you have monitored and improved your own effectiveness. There is no one right model for organising a leadership portfolio. It could be constituted around the 'four responsibilities'; around case studies of good leadership; around a list of outcomes; or around some combination of these models. Whichever approach is used, a leadership portfolio should reflect good practice in academic leadership. It should indicate how your leadership has constructed an environment in which colleagues can perform excellently as researchers and teachers. It should show how you have learned from others to enhance the quality of your leadership through systematic and scholarly reflection and action.

11

IMPROVING UNIVERSITY LEADERSHIP

Advice is what we ask for when we already know the answer
but wish we didn't.

Erica Jong

Developing tomorrow's academic leaders

'The prosperity if not the survival of any business depends on the
performance of its managers of tomorrow' said Drucker in 1955.
We have seen in previous chapters how the productivity of higher
education, especially in teaching, might be substantially improved.
We have also seen how effective leadership can produce improvement. Academic leaders' performance will in its turn depend more
and more on support for their learning at the highest levels.

The process of learning to lead applies equally to universities and
to the academic leaders within them. Both can learn to build an
environment in which leadership capacities can grow. Both can learn
to create the conditions for staff to embrace change. If they were to
follow the principles of effective academic leadership I have tried to
describe in the preceding chapters, what would universities do to
ensure they had the leaders – especially the heads of department –
they will need in the future?

Universities know the answer, but perhaps they wish they didn't.
'The art of leadership is to transform the ordinary into the extraordinary': the proof that a university as an organisation is concerned
about leadership is that it can help its 'middle managers' perform
better than they think they are capable of, that it can make up for
their weaknesses and bring out their strengths, that it can recognise
and reward their commitment. This is what Drucker calls 'the spirit
of the organisation' (Drucker, 1955, p. 178). It must be created
from the top with courage and vitality. A university can expect its
heads of department regularly to exercise the qualities of academic
leadership only when it excites them with that same spirit.

Leadership responsibilities and leadership learning

Reduced to its essentials, the measure of an effective academic leader which I have argued for has two elements. Can he or she enable average people to do excellent things? Can he or she help these people address change enthusiastically and energetically? Achieving these broad outcomes depends on the wise exercise of the responsibilities described in previous chapters.

We delude ourselves, though, if we think we can specify precise competencies and then train academic leaders in the practice of these competencies, perhaps in a short orientation or in-service course. Leadership is a balancing act. We might wish it were systematic and predictable; in reality, it is disordered and episodic; and each leader's history is scattered with omissions, confusion and failures. Academic leaders must learn in their departments to apply principles and interpret leadership needs. Once more the common sense of Gordon Donaldson is helpful here: the leader's 'dominant task is to learn what questions to ask [of their departments], what resources to seek in order to answer those questions, and what personal talents are called forth from them and others if [the department] is to act productively' (Donaldson, 1991, p. 203). This task cannot be taught. It can only be learned by doing the job, seeking feedback and instruction from colleagues, actively interpreting that information, and doing the job again. 'The only real training for leadership is leadership' (Jay, 1970, p. 171).

The steps of preparing heads for the beginning of the continuous process of leadership learning might well be like Donaldson's preferred model of educating principals: an orientation to the job involving access to formal knowledge and information (generally lacking in most universities, in my experience); immersion in the role through shadowing an actual head, a career decision to become a head, or not; and mature professional development through evaluation involving feedback and its interpretation, communication with colleagues in similar positions, and self-development activities of the kind outlined in chapter 10. As far as I am aware, no university follows a sequence of this type in preparing its academic leaders.

It is hard to overestimate the importance of leadership and management development for heads in contemporary UK and Australian universities. Yet it remains an area in which efforts have been faltering and largely incoherent. It is perhaps another paradox of academic leadership: much is known about what makes for its effective practice, but little is systematically applied. Academic leadership, like much university teaching, continues to be an amateur performance whose consistency is unpredictable.

The development of academic leaders, like the development of academics as teachers, is too vital to be seen as a distinct activity delivered by a central unit to a small proportion of heads, separate from the university's everyday work, and with an emphasis on local procedural knowledge. Since it needs to be focused on tomorrow's needs, academic leadership development for heads should be a normal expectation for all headship posts. It should address questions of the future of the university, its distinctive place in the prospective higher education scene, and the skills and knowledge that tomorrow's academic staff will need to meet these new requirements. It must ultimately become a responsibility of today's leaders to educate those of tomorrow, thus realising the fundamental principle of academic leadership as a process of developing others, and through this process consolidating learning for oneself.

To stimulate leadership learning and ensure that tomorrow's academic leaders can manage the sort of challenges they have themselves identified (see chapter 1), it is not sufficient to provide vague performance objectives and assume that heads will relinquish the job after a relatively short period. On the contrary, our universities need to elevate the status of headship and provide those who fulfil the function with proper authority and rewards. Management and administration are not lesser academic functions. But they will continue to be seen thus, and lack of professionalism will continue to impede university performance, until those who fill the part are properly educated and satisfactorily recognised.

Creating a fertile environment for leadership to grow

The development of leaders in formal positions can only be effective if the university provides the organisational conditions in which leadership can be effectively exercised at the level of head of department. Leaders may be predisposed to work in capable ways, and they may experience opportunities to learn. But whether their preferences are realised, their learning is applied, and they become committed to, rather than compliant with, their university's corporate direction, depends ultimately on the organisation, spirit and culture of the institution.

This means that career structures in higher education institutions should enable academic leaders to face new challenges and to develop through these experiences. We need to ensure that actual performance in the job of leader and manager is the criterion for further progression. We need competitive selection and better tangible rewards for heads. This is not the whole story, however. As academic roles become more fragmented, accountable, public, uncertain and diverse, so the need for leadership proficiency at all levels becomes more pressing. Far from changes to higher education such as the growing use of information technology, stronger external accountabilities, and international competition implying a de-skilling of academics, they indicate a need for all university staff to exercise leadership responsibility and develop the ability to do it well. A task for universities in the next century is to create the conditions in which the dormant potential for leadership is nurtured – among every member of the academic and administrative staff.

The need for dispersed leadership

It is a truism that universities have shown themselves to be highly adaptable institutions. One secret of their persistence has been their aptitude for combining two apparent opposites. Van Vught (1995) has called these the 'intrinsic' qualities – such as the values of fundamental search for truth and disinterested pursuit of knowledge – together with an 'extrinsic' capacity to respond to changing economic needs. Recent adaptations to reductions in the unit of resource, increased student numbers, global competition, flexible delivery, and the demands of a broader array of constituents have been achieved through higher efficiency, restructuring of courses, inventive planning, and strategic alliances. As we know, the adaptation has had its costs: a severely negative impact on staff career prospects and morale and a growing anxiety about the future linked to a sense of betrayal. To continue to adapt successfully, universities cannot ignore this discontent; they will need to do more than they have done. Specifically, they will need to be more active in influencing the system in which they work, and more concerned to make their internal processes function better.

Both these requirements demand effective leadership at multiple levels. The second calls for a stronger focus on the 'softer', human side of leadership as enabling and supporting people, and in aligning their goals to the future of the institution in an innovative way. The first requires a different view of university planning as a shared process which assumes that the environment can be controlled, and does not simply have to be responded to. The two requirements are related; 'contextual planning' (Peterson, 1995) actively creates contexts that are favourable to institutional success by changing both

256

internal structures and influencing external markets; it pre-empts new demands by stakeholders by addressing them before they arise.

The dispersal of leadership across the organisation is a key constituent of these active strategies. The basic academic values and norms of self-direction, creative knowledge production, diffused decision-making, professional autonomy, peer review, individualism, and separation of knowledge into separate areas build pressure towards fragmentation and incoherence of products and internal processes. Typical symptoms of this pressure are persistent inter-faculty rivalry for resources, grudging compliance with internal quality processes, lack of confidence among middle academic managers in the senior management of the university, the withdrawal of staff into specialist individual academic concerns, and conflict between administrative and academic staff. These indications are ill-matched to proactive adaptation, organised ability to change, client-centredness, and a common vision. As essentially federal organisations in a turbulent external context, universities increasingly need strong and responsive leadership at local level exercised by people who fully understand the corporate direction of the institution. Paradoxically, the more leadership is distributed, the more necessary it is to have clear objectives and high level vision at the centre to which local leaders are committed. At the same time, these local leaders must never forget the limiting characteristics of academic leadership as the leadership of professionals – people who set their own standards, have a vision and commitment beyond the organisation, who can be guided but not controlled, who seek a collective vision but who believe in independence. These stable features of academic life underline the continuing need in universities to disperse leadership, use it to encourage the positive features of academic culture, and conceptualise it as a process of guidance and development as well as direction.

Creating the conditions for effective distributed leadership requires universities to sidestep a series of errors associated with single models of academic excellence, teaching and research, human resource management, and structure and process.

Fallacies of uniformity and the supremacy of research

The culture of UK and Australian universities has not yet accommodated the plural vision of a mass higher education system. Sometimes it seems that we still seek a single model of academic excellence that is a slightly revised version of the expert-dominated, research-orientated and exclusive vision that informed the then 'new universities' of the 1960s. It is as if we aspire to discover a general factor of university intelligence, whose geniuses comprise the top performers in research assessment exercises and whose morons include the also-ran regional colleges fit only to teach undergraduates.

People have constructed a historical mythology of research and scholarship to legitimate this very recent model of quality. It sits awkwardly with increased student numbers, greater diversity in ability and cultures among the student body, accountability to clients, and the need to provide for lifelong learning through individually-negotiated modes of education and flexible modes of delivery. The educational or teaching function of universities dominates these imperatives. It is hard to see how they can be met without a re-conceptualisation of the teaching and learning responsibilities of universities, which in turn cannot happen without both central and local leadership to drive the change to an essentially more client- or student-centred view of university teaching.

It is evident that this requires more attention to recognising the contributions of those academics who are strongly committed to helping students to learn. Performance management and incentive systems provide the means to make this happen. Serious damage has been done to the potential of universities to respond to change by failing to provide sufficient incentives to focus on the quality of teaching. Although universities have many customers, there can be no universities as such without students; developing their knowledge and modifying their understanding is fundamental to universities' existence, and always has been. The use of performance-based funding of research in the absence of any real equivalent for teaching has effectively reduced still further the borderline status of teaching. It acts as a disincentive to investing resources to improve it. To maximise their future chances in the market, and to ensure effective distributed leadership in teaching, many universities will need to take more initiatives to recognise and reward it.

Closely associated with the need to move from a single, research-dominated view of academic excellence is the establishment of more focused, distinctive features for individual universities (Clark, 1995). Many universities still aspire to the arduous objective of becoming comprehensive containers of all fields of study, all professional training, and all forms of research. Hopes run high in some former colleges and polytechnics that they will eventually become 'real' research universities. Many strive to represent in their plans and mission some general qualities of higher education rather than to define a special role for themselves. This is not the stuff of which marketable visions are made. Limitation of fields and developing a small suite of characteristic features would provide a focus for an organisational spirit to grow and enlarge national and international perceptions that *this* institution is a special place. If there is an essence of a university, it is not that it teaches all disciplines, attains international standards in research, and is free of government intervention. It is simply that it combines people who are seeking to continually to learn. There are as many imaginative ways of realising this essential truth as there are universities.

The fallacy of employment inflexibility

Systems of promotion, grading and reward for academic staff in universities remain tied to a time when higher education was more stable than it is now. A senior lecturer was a senior lecturer was a senior lecturer. A lecturer might hope for between one and two promotions in his or her entire working life. A job's importance was enduring.

Times have all too obviously changed. We are meant to be competitive and adaptable, and able to address new demands rapidly and innovatively. But inflexible employment arrangements encourage a mentality of dependence and apprehension of new challenges. It is no use upbraiding academics for being intractable when their working environment rewards indifference. In non-static organisations such as today's higher education institutions, jobs vary in importance and value depending on who does them, not on which grade someone is in. Jill Smith as lecturer and coordinator of first year physics may expand the role into a vitally important activity which might save the department's bacon through increased student numbers and a high quality assessment; she is also helping two of her colleagues to take over her leadership role in the future, through effective delegation. John Jones in the same position for the second year of the course ambles along, works adequately, focuses his sights on a nice long vacation, and does not regard the development of his colleagues as future leaders as part of a lecturer's job. Jill believes she is worth a lot more than John; John, of course, thinks he is relatively poorly paid, and hopes for an increase for all lecturers.

When we find that people, including creative leaders, see others around them who have worked less hard in the same grade, and possibly on a higher salary, there is something wrong with the system. It is not Jill's fault that she feels unrewarded and bitter. She has every right to be; but which university can afford to be without Jill? Promotions and grading are a visible and real sign of the importance a university attaches to its people and the jobs they do. Nothing is more damaging to morale, more encouraging of complacency, and less likely to ignite the spark of leadership, than to see others in your department or faculty working less diligently and not only getting away with it, but taking more money home.

Here is another unhappy instance of the 'poor leadership' characteristic of lack of integrity, or doing one thing and saying another: saying (as all universities do) that they value their people, but in reality misusing their goodwill and not rewarding their effort; saying that they value enterprise, but showing by their actions that they do not reward it. Universities are too often guilty of 'offering a secure future disguised as an exciting challenge' (Jay, 1970, p. 172). The fallacy of inflexibility of employment and rigid grading is self-perpetuating because it breeds fear of change. It can only be addressed by explicit action to break the mould and allow for actual work performed to be properly rewarded. I have described in chapter 9 the kind of performance management system which could make this idea into reality.

Fallacies of structure and process

We have seen that leadership in business organisations and academic leadership are very similar phenomena. Still, people often say that universities cannot be managed like businesses. Their heterogenous products of knowledge production and education, their staff who espouse professional authority, their decentralisation of working units consequent upon the differentiation of knowledge into disciplines, their diffused decision-making, and so on – these things are held to be features which, if compromised, would lead to a disappearance of the values which are fundamental to universities, and thus to the destruction of universities themselves.

It would be far more accurate to say that universities cannot be successfully managed using a certain model of business management: one which ignores the special needs of professional staff, which treats employees as mere cogs in a production process, and which focuses on profit, new markets, technological innovation and efficiency to the exclusion of social and moral responsibility both for employees and for society at large. Substantial movement towards this model would certainly ensure the downfall of many businesses in today's conditions. The need for lateral structures and federal governance in businesses employing professionals has long been recognised and universities are not unique in this respect. Universities need to be managed similarly to cognate organisations if they are to enhance their performance. That good leadership of professionals is a reliable attribute across universities and different organisations is clear from van Vught's recommendations for management for quality in universities (van Vught, 1995, p. 208). His suggestions for recognising their distinctive nature by stimulating coherence in teaching and learning through cooperative processes, analysing the needs of different clients, and providing a framework in which academics are encouraged and enabled to improve their professional effectiveness, reflect generally applicable principles of skilful leadership in educational and scientific institutions.

It is a delusion to think that universities are not becoming 'like businesses'. They are more and more susceptible to the vagaries of markets and need increasingly to address these markets innovatively to maintain their position – precisely the two distinguishing characteristics of business organisations (Drucker, 1955). There is a difference, nevertheless; not in leadership, but in the focus of the organisation's goals. The agenda for tomorrow's universities of a stronger customer focus, more market responsiveness, more international competition, more innovation, and greater accountability to an array of stakeholders can be met through a determined emphasis on very traditional university goals: their wider obligation to act as a source of public intellectual comment and criticism, and to produce responsible citizens. These are important markets in which universities have undisputed supremacy.

'Crisis management mode'

One response by universities to environmental fluidity has been to adopt a 'management by drives' approach to maximising performance. At times of uncertainty and external pressure – to get a higher research ranking, to attract more overseas students, to introduce different policies for managing staff performance, to cope with yet another resource reduction – universities have often given in to the temptation of working in crisis management mode (CMM). Symptoms include statements such as 'The only way we'll get these people to move is by wielding a stick', 'The directors need a target of 5 per cent savings by yesterday', 'We don't have time to consult – we will tell them what they've got to do', 'The quality assessment report is to be completed next week, or heads will roll' and haphazard agendas with timescales that don't allow adequate time to conceptualise the problem. CMM is underpinned by a belief that jumping is the only way to make progress, even though there may be a perfectly good car parked around the corner which would take us to the destination more easily. It is a short-term management strategy that makes people feel they are not trusted; it breeds cynicism and doubt about senior management's integrity. When a real crisis comes, people treat it as another case of management-generated hysteria (Drucker, 1955, p. 158).

Continually focusing on immediate demands distracts people from discovering longer term strategic solutions. Change generated by crisis management generates more crises. CMM rarely achieves long term solutions, and it usually results in staff neglecting things they should be doing, so that they have to catch up later and any temporary advantage is lost. CMM inhibits leaders from practising effective leadership by causing the very things that good leadership tries to overcome. It pushes them into hasty decisions; it discourages their motivation to innovate; and it penalises an orientation to the future. It is a signal to academic leaders that the university itself does not know how to exercise leadership. CMM is a sure sign that leaders are confused and lacking fortitude.

Culture and structure

Decentralisation in the leadership of the university can work either to unite staff and increase market responsiveness or to produce incoherence, unwillingness to change and internal warfare. The basic error which many universities have made is to believe that structures are superordinate to cultures. But no structure can be effective unless the culture also 'works' (see Table 9.1). Putting this another way, if there is a problem with the culture in an organisation employing large numbers of professionals, then it is a waste of time to tinker with the structure (Sapienza, 1995). After the culture is right, then the structure can be improved. The structure is very important. But it is secondary.

This conclusion is identical to an essential concept of effective leadership: if people are motivated and committed to a vision, they will achieve great things despite the functional structure. It is another measure of leadership inadequacy that addressing the question of whether the culture is working – whether processes that lead to desired outcomes are operative – is an assignment which, unlike many other businesses, universities have been reluctant to take on. I have mentioned the *Leadership for Academic Work* survey questionnaire several times; one way of measuring the university's culture and of identifying areas for improvement is to employ a similar instrument which allows staff to comment on discrepancies between ideal and actual patterns of work, communication, and strategic directions.

As I argued in chapters 1 and 2, many universities have responded to unprecedented external pressures, especially reduced public funding, by recognising the need to manage efficiently and seek new markets. These things are fundamental to their survival. But as we have also seen, university leadership is about learning and about listening, as well as about being entrepreneurial and managing resources competently. This aspect of leadership is especially but not uniquely relevant to the management of professional employees. It is right that academic staff should have the standards of their work resolved outside the individual academic institution as well as within it, and that they should have a large measure of control over how they pursue academic objectives. It is not right simply because academics have a natural claim to liberty or intrinsic immunity from the discipline consequent upon working in an enterprise. It is right because in the last analysis it is these things, rather than external forces or institutional supervision, that guarantee quality and continual improvement in standards. Academics can be guided and helped to learn; they can be recognised and rewarded and encouraged; but they cannot be effectively commanded and overseen.

That this commonplace conclusion has to be drawn at all may be significant of the crisis facing leadership in universities. Academic leadership at all levels is about understanding academic staff and being courageous enough to know that responding sympathetically does not mean weakening your power, but strengthening it. The university that develops leadership in its people will model the leadership qualities it desires by listening to their hopes. It will have sufficient confidence to monitor its own performance by comparing its objectives with their perceptions of what it has achieved for them.

Changing university cultures and changes in conceptions of academic leadership

If you can accept the general arguments I have made for more effective academic leadership, you will concede that a modification is needed in traditional conceptions of academic management and leadership to accommodate the needs and hopes of university staff. It must at once become more like helping students to learn and more like best practice in the leadership of other types of organisation. It must tread the narrow line between inevitable change and persistent values. It must move at the same time further away from outdated conceptions of academic organisation and governance, and from simple crisis management. It must recognise achievement and require commitment, while maintaining conditions of professional employment that assure high standards.

No one would presume to have a single blueprint for university organisation that can accomplish these goals. There will be many different ways of approaching them. Universities will address them in varied ways, depending on their own missions. The 'enterprise culture', identified by heads of departments in several universities as an increasingly important quality of university organisation in the future (see chapter 2 and McNay, 1995), provides one possible model for developing university leadership which is consistent both with enduring academic values and with the fresh hazards facing universities (Figure 11.1). It provides a way of reconciling central authority for institutional objectives with distributed power over local methods of realising collective goals, thus realising an important aim of a working culture in an organisation dominated by professionals. It accommodates the dilemma of balancing intrinsic qualities with extrinsic demands (van Vught, 1995), avoiding the shadowy consequences of academic isolationism and excessive specialisation which have unquestionably contributed to public perceptions of the declining worth of higher education. It offers an escape route from the excessive bureaucratic control characteristic of newer universities in their earlier incarnations as colleges and polytechnics, and from the crisis management and egotistical approach of the corporate university. And it is, of course, consistent with the perspective on leadership adopted in this book as a process of encouraging excellent academic work while simultaneously orientating people towards change.

An intensifying movement towards more coherent policy objectives at university level, balanced by decreased direction from the centre about means by which these objectives are to be achieved, provides a framework for more entrepreneurial leadership at local levels. The conception of academic leadership that is compatible with this culture is of the leader as strategist, representative, guide, educator, and articulator of shared vision. These heads of departments and their colleagues will need to be innovators, team builders, and decision-makers with strong personal skills. They will focus on outcomes and comprehend the wider agendas of the university in relation to the environment in which it functions. In this model of university culture, academic leadership and management are understood to be professional skills, learned through education and reflection, and best assessed by evidence of their successful performance in real academic settings.

The model of leadership in the 'enterprising university' summarised in the lower left hand sector of Figure 11.1 is of particular interest in the light of an investigation by Burton Clark. He studied the ways in which higher education institutions might transform themselves to increase their level of entrepreneurial energy and

Policy control & definition (ends)

	Weak/loose	Strong/tight
Control of implementation (means) **Weak/loose**	*Collegial* Servant leadership. Leadership as a consensual background activity. Control through consultation, persuasion, consent, permission. Authority derives from professional status. Leaders represent the academic group. Management and leadership, like teaching, is for gifted amateurs and does not require formal preparation.	*Bureaucratic* Managerial leadership. Leadership as formal rule-governed behaviour. Control through systems, administration, transactions, rationality. Authority derives from position. Leaders represent managers more senior in the hierarchy. Management skills are learned through induction and experience.
Strong/tight	*Enterprise* Entrepreneurial and adaptive leadership. Leadership as guidance, enabling, articulation of vision, support for task achievement. Authority and control derive from successful performance. Leaders represent clients/customers/ staff. Leadership and management are professional skills learned through education and reflection on experience	*Corporate* Planning and crisis-handling leadership. Leadership as command, charisma, transformation, power, strategic positioning. Authority and control derive from mission-congruence and political connections. Leaders represent the CEO. Leadership and management are learned through training.

Figure 11.1 Changing university cultures and changes in academic leadership
Source: Derived from McNay (1995)

compete effectively in national and international markets (Clark, 1996). Clark asked: What are the features of the universities that are able successfully to change their way of doing business? How do they become truly innovative and learning organisations? What are the keys to tackling the problem we have met so many times in this book – the problem of linking traditional academic procedures to new ways of doing things?

The common features of successful adaptation among Clark's sample of institutions were an ambitious vision; an integrated administrative core that connected component work units to the whole university's objectives; new sources of funding; flexible developmental units to reach out to external markets and create goodwill; and a 'possible essential element yet to be explored'. This is the means of activating traditional basic units to seek new sources of support and become more outward-looking. In our model, this might well be seen as leadership at head of department level, which is the critical coupling between conventional academic culture and the needs of the innovative university. It will not be satisfactory for these leaders to focus on their own disciplines or their own staff; they will need to integrate their work units' goals with the wider vision of the institution and link their local decisions to the environment beyond it.

Without this form of leadership, and the support it requires to be exercised effectively, it is hard to see how a university can ensure the commitment of its staff to pursue radical programmes of change.

Conclusions

In 1846 Robert Liston, Professor of Clinical Surgery at University College London, performed the first operation under anaesthetic conducted in Europe, 'an event which marked one of the most striking advances in the history of surgery' (Harte and North, 1991, p. 64). Liston's application of ether was an imaginative and enterprising act: he had learned of its first use in America two months previously. Beside him as a student that day was Joseph Lister, the man who was later to transform surgery by his work on infection and antisepsis; the two developments together perhaps did more than anything else in the nineteenth century to alleviate suffering.

When people ask whether universities are accountable and value for money; when they say they are full of cloistered grumblers who pontificate about research and teaching and workloads; when they say academics need some tougher management tactics to bring them into line, I think about Liston and Lister. The severest assignment for leaders in universities is to create a climate which ensures that innovations like these can happen, while at the same time recognising that they will not happen very often. The obligation is equally large to reach the great majority of staff and students who will never change the world in so radical a way, but without whom universities and the communities which they serve would be impoverished. Academic leadership is about providing an environment for enterprise, bold moves, and imagination – in teaching, research and professional practice – for everyone.

There can, of course, be no tidy conclusion to a book whose main argument has been the need to recognise constant change and to combine insight and practical application in order to make academic work possible. We have seen how the great similarity between lecturers' expectations for effective academic leadership and those of other employees, together with revolutionary changes in higher education, require an approach to leadership and management that helps people seize the future and draws on good practice in other organisations. But this does not mean to say that the approach should be exactly the same as in other organisations. In the last analysis, the most fundamental difference lies not in academic values and culture, or in whether universities are businesses or not, but in the main product of higher education. The product of universities is change. The business of a university is learning. The job of academic leaders is to help people learn.

No-one can take us back to a mythical golden age of collegiality and unrestrained academic freedom. It is futile to deny the imperative for universities to earn their keep in a competitive international market. And we certainly need firmer and fairer management of people and resources in higher education. I hope, however, that I have been able to demonstrate that attempts to impose solutions to today's problems of managing lecturers which ignore the characteristic outcomes of academic work, and the need to regulate it from within as well as without to attain these outcomes, cannot be effective. Productive learning requires an acceptance that freedom and discipline are partners rather than adversaries.

Enhancing leadership ability among staff in higher education requires universities to practise, at all levels, the multiple leadership responsibilities of vision, enabling, developing, and learning. In short, leadership is developed when the organisation enacts what it says it values: in its broad vision, in its strategic activity, in its inspirational qualities, in its commitment to helping people believe in its goals. The university that develops leadership in its staff will model the leadership qualities it desires through arranging contextual conditions that sanction people to be independent. It will focus on products as well as processes. It will address the imprecise realities of 'culture' as well as the solid certainties of structures. It will hand the responsibility for most short-term decision making to accountable individuals. It will strive to remove inequities caused by inflexible employment arrangements suited to an older, more stable time. It will link planning at the level of the institution to departmental and individual goals, applying the principles of effective assessment in order to encourage and reward achievement. And above all, it will listen to and learn from its people.

The authentic task of academic leadership at the turn of the century is to amalgamate innovation and tradition, excellence and access, independence and discipline, business enterprise and professional autonomy, management and leadership, commerce and imagination, people and tasks, technology and human interaction. In leadership, as in higher learning, 'either–or' solutions are illusory. When students develop facility in a field of study, they move from a search for right answers to recognising complexity and the provisional nature of knowledge. In developing our leadership skills, as individuals and as organisations, we change from being reactive or bureaucratic to being cooperative, from domineering to firm and supportive, from dichotomies to creative symmetry. Leadership and learning are inseparable in universities. Genuine learning requires an atmosphere of trust and an absence of fear; in these circumstances academics, like their students, take risks, improve, and do remarkable things. There is nothing utopian or unrealistic about the conditions for future success, and in some cases survival, in the world that tomorrow's universities will inhabit. Both will depend on leadership which recognises that transformation through learning is no more and no less than the entire business of higher education.

APPENDIX:
LEADERSHIP FOR ACADEMIC
WORK – COLLEAGUE
FEEDBACK

Paul Ramsden and Alf Lizzio[1]

In your experience, how characteristic of this person are the following behaviours? Circle the number on each line which indicates your response.

		Very characteristic			*Moderately characteristic*			*Not at all characteristic*
1	Works to build the reputation of the work unit	7	6	5	4	3	2	1
2	Delegates responsibility fairly and consistently	7	6	5	4	3	2	1
3	Motivates people to do more than they ever thought they could	7	6	5	4	3	2	1
4	Provides guidance in the development of scholarly habits and practices	7	6	5	4	3	2	1
5	Has an inflated sense of her/his own importance	7	6	5	4	3	2	1
6	Readily acknowledges colleagues' contributions	7	6	5	4	3	2	1

1 This instrument was developed with the assistance of John Swinton as part of academic leadership programmes organised by the Griffith Institute for Higher Education, Griffith University.

		Very characteristic			Moderately characteristic			Not at all characteristic
7	Brings new ideas about research into the work unit	7	6	5	4	3	2	1
8	Encourages participation in decision-making	7	6	5	4	3	2	1
9	Brings a good understanding of the 'big picture' of higher education to the work unit	7	6	5	4	3	2	1
10	Actively works to develop others as leaders	7	6	5	4	3	2	1
11	Wants things her/his own way	7	6	5	4	3	2	1
12	Conveys a sense of excitement about teaching to colleagues	7	6	5	4	3	2	1
13	Welcomes questioning of his/her ideas	7	6	5	4	3	2	1
14	Inspires respect for her/his own ability as a researcher	7	6	5	4	3	2	1
15	Inspires respect for her/his own ability as a teacher	7	6	5	4	3	2	1
16	Seems to be more at home with things than with people	7	6	5	4	3	2	1
17	Sets a challenging climate for academic work	7	6	5	4	3	2	1
18	Manages the work unit's resources effectively	7	6	5	4	3	2	1
19	Facilitates collaboration between academic and administrative staff	7	6	5	4	3	2	1

		Very characteristic			Moderately characteristic			Not at all characteristic
20	Raises and faces difficult issues or touchy subjects	7	6	5	4	3	2	1
21	Works to create a shared vision of the future direction of the work unit	7	6	5	4	3	2	1
22	Advocates the interests of the work unit to the senior management of the university	7	6	5	4	3	2	1
23	Rewards people who show initiative	7	6	5	4	3	2	1
24	Helps good people develop their skills	7	6	5	4	3	2	1
25	Can be overly critical of others' mistakes	7	6	5	4	3	2	1
26	Rewards academic excellence	7	6	5	4	3	2	1
27	Works to bring more resources into the school/faculty/centre	7	6	5	4	3	2	1
28	Brings new ideas about teaching into the school/faculty/centre	7	6	5	4	3	2	1
29	Maintains simple and effective administrative procedures	7	6	5	4	3	2	1
30	Talks about change in a positive way	7	6	5	4	3	2	1
31	Doesn't show a lot of concern for the people with whom he/she works	7	6	5	4	3	2	1
32	Works to build understanding between different groups/points of view in the work unit	7	6	5	4	3	2	1

		Very characteristic			*Moderately characteristic*		*Not at all characteristic*	
33	Helps colleagues seek resources to support research	7	6	5	4	3	2	1
34	Champions other people's ideas as well as her/his own	7	6	5	4	3	2	1
35	Manages the work unit so that decision-making is transparent and open	7	6	5	4	3	2	1
36	Helps staff by providing opportunities for professional development	7	6	5	4	3	2	1
37	Gets people moving collaboratively towards a common purpose	7	6	5	4	3	2	1
38	Isolates herself/himself from colleagues	7	6	5	4	3	2	1
39	Conducts the business of the work unit in an organised and efficient manner	7	6	5	4	3	2	1
40	Works for the school/centre/faculty as much as for him/herself	7	6	5	4	3	2	1
41	Encourages people to share ideas and learn from each other	7	6	5	4	3	2	1
42	Establishes a climate where staff are accountable for their performance	7	6	5	4	3	2	1
43	Stimulates the lively exchange of ideas and theories between colleagues	7	6	5	4	3	2	1
44	Doesn't make his/her expectations clear	7	6	5	4	3	2	1

		Very characteristic		Moderately characteristic			Not at all characteristic	
45	Shows an interest in talking about ways of improving teaching	7	6	5	4	3	2	1
46	Enables you to think about old problems in new ways	7	6	5	4	3	2	1
47	Addresses problems quickly and doesn't allow them to get out of hand	7	6	5	4	3	2	1
48	Ensures an equitable distribution of workloads	7	6	5	4	3	2	1
49	Shows concern for students and their needs	7	6	5	4	3	2	1
50	Considers problems from a university perspective as well as a local one	7	6	5	4	3	2	1
51	Encourages people to regard mistakes as opportunities for learning	7	6	5	4	3	2	1
52	Works to create an environment that supports quality research and scholarship	7	6	5	4	3	2	1
53	Can be abrasive under pressure	7	6	5	4	3	2	1
54	Doesn't 'follow through' on issues	7	6	5	4	3	2	1
55	Praises and supports colleagues' successes	7	6	5	4	3	2	1
56	Ensures that colleagues take account of student expectations and satisfaction	7	6	5	4	3	2	1
57	Gets things done	7	6	5	4	3	2	1

	Not very satisfied			Satisfied			Extremely satisfied
Overall, how satisfied are you with the academic leadership that this person is currently providing?	7	6	5	4	3	2	1

Specific feedback

In this section we ask you to take a little time to consider specific comments you would like to make or specific feedback you would like to provide to this person. People typically report this 'customised feedback' as being particularly valuable in stimulating specific personal changes or confirming current approaches. Remember that this person is seeking your honest and frank perceptions of their behaviour. All comments will be typed and provided in a collated form.

What do you appreciate most about this person's leadership and wish them to continue doing?

-
-
-

What would you like this person to do *more of* as an academic leader?

-
-
-

What would you like this person to do *less of* as an academic leader?

-
-
-

What are the particular issues, problems or challenges for this person's work unit that you would like them to address?

-
-
-

REFERENCES

Adair, J. (1988) *Effective Time Management*, London: Pan Books.

—— (1996) *Effective Motivation*, London: Pan Books.

Ainley, J. and Long, M. (1995) *The 1994 Course Experience Questionnaire*, Melbourne: Graduate Careers Council of Australia.

Anderson, D., Johnson, R. and Milligan, B. (1996) *Performance-based Funding of Universities*, Higher Education Council Commissioned Report No. 51, Canberra: Australian Government Publishing Service.

Baldwin, G. (1996) 'First among peers: An essay on academic leadership', *HERDSA News* 18: 6–9.

Bass, B.M. (1985) *Leadership and Performance Beyond Expectations*, New York: Free Press.

Beare, H., Caldwell, B.J. and Millikan, R.H. (1989) *Creating an Excellent School*, London: Routledge.

Becher, T. (1989) *Academic Tribes and Territories: Intellectual Enquiry and the Cultures of Disciplines*, Buckingham: Open University Press.

Becker, H.S., Geer, B. and Hughes, E.C. (1968) *Making the Grade: The Academic Side of College Life*, New York: Wiley.

Bennett, J.B. (1988) 'Department chairs: Leadership in the trenches', in M.F. Green (ed.) *Leaders for a New Era: Strategies for Higher Education*, New York: Macmillan.

Biggs, J.B. (1996) 'Enhancing teaching through constructive alignment', *Higher Education* 32: 347–64.

Blackburn, R.T., Behymer, C.E. and Hall, D.E. (1978) 'Research note: Correlates of faculty publications', *Sociology of Education* 51: 132–41.

Bland, C.J. and Ruffin, M.T. (1992) 'Characteristics of a productive research environment: Literature review', *Academic Medicine* 67: 385–97.

Boice, R. (1992) *The New Faculty Member. Supporting and Fostering Professional Development*, San Francisco: Jossey-Bass.

Boyer, E.L., (1990) *Scholarship Reconsidered: Priorities of the Professoriate*, Princeton: Carnegie Foundation for the Advancement of Teaching.

—— Altbach, P.G. and Whitelaw, M.J. (1994) *The Academic Profession: An International Perspective*, Princeton, NJ: Carnegie Foundation for the Advancement of Teaching.

Bright, D. and Williamson, B. (1995) 'Managing and rewarding performance', in

D. Warner and E. Crosthwaite (eds) *Human Resource Management in Higher and Further Education*, Buckingham: SRHE and Open University Press.

Burns, J.M. (1978) *Leadership*, New York: Harper & Row.

Candy, P., Crebert, G., and O'Leary, J. (1994) *Developing Lifelong Learners Through Undergraduate Education*, National Board of Employment, Education and Training Commissioned Report No. 28, Canberra: Australian Government Publishing Service.

Clark, B.R. (1995) 'Complexity and differentiation: The growing problem of university integration', in D.D. Dill and B. Sporn (eds) *Emerging Patterns of Social Demand and University Reform: Through a Glass Darkly*, Paris: IAU Press/Pergamon.

—— (1996) 'Substantive knowledge growth and innovative organization: New categories for higher education research', *Higher Education* 31: 417–30.

Coaldrake, P. (1996) 'University management a "on the run": Corporate management in higher education – a global perspective', Address to the AVCC Forum, 'Managing for Performance', Adelaide, September.

Coorey, M. (1996) '"Administrivia" overload stresses academics', *The Australian*, 3 July.

Cundy, L. (1994) 'Using peer group support to increase research productivity', in L. Conrad, (ed.) *Developing as Researchers*, Brisbane: Griffith Institute for Higher Education, Griffith University.

Deetz, S.A. (1992) 'Departmental leadership and departmental culture', in M. Hickson and D.W. Stacks (eds) *Effective Communication for Academic Chairs*, Albany: State University of New York Press.

Department of Employment, Education and Training (1989) *Discipline Review of Teacher Education in Mathematics and Science*, Canberra: Australian Government Publishing Service.

Department of Employment, Education and Training (1996) *Diversity in Australian Higher Education Institutions, 1994*, Higher Education Series Report No. 26.

Donaldson, G.A. (1991) *Learning to Lead: The Dynamics of the High School Principalship*, New York: Greenwood Press.

Drucker, P.F. (1955) *The Practice of Management*, London: Heinemann.

Egan, G. (1995) 'A clear path to peak performance', *People Management*, 18 May: 34–7.

Elphinstone, L., Martin, E. and Foster, E. (1995) *Manual for Supervisors of Postgraduate Students*, Melbourne: Royal Melbourne Institute of Technology.

Entwistle, N.J. (1995) 'The use of research on student learning in quality assessment', in G. Gibbs (ed.) *Improving Student Learning through Assessment and Evaluation*, Oxford: Oxford Centre for Staff Development.

—— and Percy, K.A. (1974) 'Critical thinking or conformity? An investigation into the aims and outcomes of higher education', in *Research into Higher Education 1973*, London: SRHE.

Falk, G. (1979) 'The academic department: chairmanship and role conflict', *Improving College and University Teaching* 27: 79–86.

Fox, M.F. (1983) 'Publication productivity among scientists: A critical review', *Social Studies of Science* 13: 285–305.

—— (1992) 'Research productivity and environmental context,' in T.G Whiston and R.L. Geiger (eds) *Research and Higher Education*, Buckingham: Open University Press.

Gibbs, G. (1992) *Assessing More Students*, London: Polytechnics and Colleges Funding Council.

—— (1995a) 'How can promoting excellent teachers promote excellent teaching?' *Innovations in Education and Training International* 32: 74–84.

—— (1995b) 'Can academics change?' *People Management*, April.

——, Habeshaw, S. and Habeshaw, T. (1987) *53 Interesting Things to do in Your Lectures*, Bristol: Technical and Educational Services Ltd.

Gmelch, W.H. and Miskin, V.D. (1993) *Leadership Skills for Department Chairs*, Bolton, MA: Anker.

—— and —— (1995) *Chairing an Academic Department*, Thousand Oaks, CA: Sage Publications.

Gray, P.J., Froh, R.C. and Diamond, R.M. (1992) *A National Study of Research Universities: On the Balance Between Research and Undergraduate Teaching*, Syracuse, NY: Center for Instructional Development, Syracuse University.

Green, M.F. (1990) 'Why good teaching needs active leadership', in P. Seldin and Associates (eds) *How Administrators Can Improve Teaching: Moving from Talk to Action in Higher Education*, San Francisco: Jossey-Bass.

Halsey, A.H. (1992) *Decline of Donnish Dominion*, Oxford: Clarendon Press.

Hammons, J. (1984) 'The department/division chairperson: Educational leader?', *Community and Junior College Journal*, March: 14–19.

Harris, A., Jamieson I. and Russ, J. (1996) *School Effectiveness and School Improvement: A Practical Guide*, London: Pitman.

Harris, G.T. (1990) 'Research output in Australian university economics departments: An update for 1984–88', *Australian Economic Papers* 29: 249–59.

Harte, N. and North, J. (1991) *The World of UCL 1828–1990*, London: University College London.

Harvey, L. (1993) 'Employer satisfaction: Interim report', Keynote presentation, Quality in Higher Education Seminar, University of Warwick, December 1993.

—— (1995a) Editorial, *Quality in Higher Education* 1: 5–12.

—— (1995b) 'Beyond TQM', *Quality in Higher Education* 1: 123–46.

Her Majesty's Inspectors' Report (1977) *Ten Good Schools*, London: HMSO.

Hoare, D. (1995) *Higher Education Management Review*, Canberra: Australian Government Publishing Service.

Hollander, E.P. and Offerman, L.R. (1993) 'Power and leadership in organizations', in W.E. Rosenbach and R.L. Taylor (eds), *Contemporary Issues in Leadership*, Boulder, CO: Westview Press.

Ince, M. (1997) 'Survey reveals crisis fears', *Times Higher Education Supplement*, 10 January.

Jay, A. (1970) *Management and Machiavelli*, Harmondsworth: Penguin.

Jensen, E.J. (1995) 'The bitter groves of academe', *Change* 27, January/February: 8–11.

Knapper, C. (1990) 'Lifelong learning and university teaching', in I. Moses (ed.) *Higher Education in the Late Twentieth Century: Reflections on a Changing System*, University of Queensland: Higher Education Research and Development Society of Australasia.

Kogan, M. (1985) 'The "Expectations of Higher Education" project', in D. Jaques and J.T.T. Richardson (eds) *The Future for Higher Education*, Guildford: SRHE & NFER-Nelson.

Kotter, J.P. (1990) *A Force for Change: How Leadership Differs from Management*, New York: Free Press.

—— (1993) 'What leaders really do', in W.E. Rosenbach and R.L. Taylor (eds) *Contemporary Issues in Leadership*, Boulder, CO: Westview Press.

Kouzes, J.M. and Posner, B.Z. (1993) *Credibility*, San Francisco: Jossey-Bass.

—— and —— (1995) *The Leadership Challenge*, San Francisco: Jossey-Bass.

Leithwood, K.A. (1992) 'The move toward transformational leadership', *Educational Leadership* 49: 8–12.

Lizzio, A. (1996) *Academic Leadership Portfolio: Guidelines and Reflective Processes for Clarifying Your Frames of Reference as an Academic Leader*, Brisbane: Griffith Institute for Higher Education, Griffith University.

Louis, K.S. (1993) 'Beyond bureaucracy: Rethinking how schools change', Invited address, International Congress for School Effectiveness and Improvement, Norrköping, January 1993.

Long, J.S. and McGinnis, R. (1981) 'Organizational context and scientific productivity', *American Sociological Review* 46: 422–42.

Lowe, I. (1994) *Our Universities are Turning us into the 'Ignorant Country'*, Sydney: University of New South Wales Press.

Lucas, A.F. (1995) *Strengthening Departmental Leadership*, San Francisco: Jossey-Bass.

Machiavelli, N. (1944) *The Prince: An Elizabethan Translation* (ed. H. Craig), Chapel Hill: University of North Carolina Press.

Marlow, L. (1995) *'Leaders and Managers' Workshop Materials*, Brisbane: Griffith Institute for Higher Education, Griffith University.

Martin, E. and Ramsden, P. (1994) *Effectiveness and Efficiency of Courses in Teaching Methods for Recently Appointed Academic Staff*, Canberra: Australian Government Publishing Service.

Martin, E., Prosser, M., Benjamin, J., Trigwell, K. and Ramsden, P. (1997) 'Heads of academic departments' conceptions of leadership of teaching,' in G. Gibbs (ed.) *Improving Student Learning through Course Design*, Oxford: Oxford Centre for Staff Development.

Massy, W.F. and Wilger, A.K. (1995) 'Improving productivity', *Change* 27: 10–20.

——, —— and Colbeck, C. (1994) 'Overcoming "hollowed" collegiality', *Change* 26: 10–20.

McInnis, C. (1992) 'Changes in the nature of academic work', *Australian Universities' Review* 35: 9–12.

—— (1996) 'Change and diversity in the work patterns of Australian academics', *Higher Education Management* 8: 105–17.

—— and James, R. (1995) *First Year on Campus*, Canberra: Australian Government Publishing Service.

——, Powles, M. and Anwyl, J. (1994) 'Australian academics' perspectives on quality and accountability', CSHE Research Working Papers 94.2, Centre for the Study of Higher Education, University of Melbourne.

McNay, I. (1995) 'From the collegial academy to the corporate enterprise: The changing cultures of universities', in T. Schuller (ed.) *The Changing University?* Buckingham: SRHE & Open University Press.

279

Middlehurst, R. (1993) *Leading Academics*, Buckingham: SRHE & Open University Press.

Mortimore, P., Sammons, P., Stoll, L., Lewis, D. and Ecob, R. (1988) *School Matters: The Junior Years*, Salisbury: Open Books.

Moses, I. (1995) 'Tensions and tendencies in the management of quality and autonomy in Australian higher education', *Australian Universities Review* 1/1995: 11–15.

—— and Roe, E. (1989) *Heading a Department*, Kensington, NSW: HERDSA.

—— and —— (1990) *Heads and Chairs: Managing Academic Departments*, Brisbane: University of Queensland Press.

O'Neil, J. (1995) 'On schools as learning organizations: A conversation with Peter Senge', *Educational Leadership* 52: 20–3.

Peterson, M.W. (1995) 'Images of university structure, governance, and leadership: Adaptive strategies for the new environment', in D.D. Dill and B. Sporn (eds) *Emerging Patterns of Social Demand and University Reform: Through a Glass Darkly*, Paris: IAU Press/Pergamon.

Phillips, E.M. and Pugh, D.S. (1987) *How to Get a PhD*, Milton Keynes: Open University Press.

Prosser, M. and Trigwell, K. (1997) 'Perceptions of the teaching environment and its relationship to approaches to teaching', *British Journal of Educational Psychology* 67: 25–35.

Raelin, J.A. (1991) *The Clash of Cultures: Managers Managing Professionals*, Boston: Harvard Business School Press.

Ramsden, P. (1988) 'Studying learning: improving teaching', in P. Ramsden (ed.) *Improving Learning: New Perspectives*, London: Kogan Page.

—— (1991) 'Study processes in grade 12 environments', in B.J. Fraser and H.J. Walberg (eds) *Classroom and School Learning Environments*, Oxford: Pergamon.

—— (1992) *Learning to Teach in Higher Education*, London and New York: Routledge.

—— (1994) 'Describing and explaining research productivity,' *Higher Education* 27: 207–26.

——, Margetson, D., Martin, E. and Clarke, S. (1995) *Recognising and Rewarding Good Teaching in Australian Higher Education*, Canberra: Australian Government Publishing Service.

—— and Martin, E. (1996) 'Recognition of good university teaching: Policies from an Australian study', *Studies in Higher Education* 21: 299–315.

——, —— and Bowden, J.A.(1989) 'School environment and sixth form pupils' approaches to learning', *British Journal of Educational Psychology* 59: 129–42.

—— and Moses, I. (1992) 'Associations between research and teaching in Australian higher education', *Higher Education* 23: 273–95.

Reeders, E., Engelhard, M., Horvat, L. and Hough, G. (1996) 'An embarrassment of meanings: A case study of the introduction of a quality assurance scheme', Paper presented at the Annual Conference of the Higher Education Research and Development Society of Australasia, July 1996.

Reynolds, D., Sammons, P., Stoll, L., Barber, M. and Hillman, J. (1996) 'School effectiveness and school improvement in the United Kingdom', *School Effectiveness and School Improvement* 7: 133–58.

Roche, V. (1996) 'The academic's progress: Changes and stages in the journey',

Paper presented at the Annual Conference of the Higher Education Research and Development Society of Australasia, July 1996.

Rowntree, D. (1989) *The Manager's Book of Checklists*, Aldershot: Gower.

Sadler, R. (1990) *Up the Publication Road*, Kensington, NSW: HERDSA.

—— (1994) 'Publications syndicates', in L. Conrad (ed.) *Developing as Researchers*, Brisbane: Griffith Institute for Higher Education, Griffith University.

Sapienza, A.M. (1995) *Managing Scientists: Leadership Strategies in Research and Development*, New York: Wiley-Liss.

Sarros, J.C., Gmelch, W.H. and Tanewski, G.A. (1997) 'The role of the department head in Australian universities: Changes and challenges', *Higher Education Research and Development* 16: 3–27.

Sashkin, M. and Rosenbach, W.E. (1993) 'A new leadership paradigm', in W.E. Rosenbach and R.L. Taylor (eds) *Contemporary Issues in Leadership*, Boulder, CO: Westview Press.

Sawyer, W.W. (1943) *Mathematician's Delight*, Harmondsworth: Penguin.

Scott, P. (1995) *The Meanings of Mass Higher Education*, Buckingham: SRHE & Open University Press.

Senge, P. (1990) *The Fifth Discipline: The Art and Practice of the Learning Organization*, New York: Doubleday.

Sheehan. B.A. and Welch, A.R. (1996) *The Academic Profession in Australia*, Canberra: Australian Government Publishing Service.

Smyth, J. (1989) 'Collegiality as counter discourse to the intrusion of corporate management into higher education', *Journal of Tertiary Education Administration* 11: 143–55.

Snow, C.P. (1956) *The Masters*, Harmondsworth: Penguin.

Startup, R. (1976) 'The role of the departmental head', *Studies in Higher Education* 1: 233–43.

Thomas, K.W. and Killman, R.H. (1974) *Thomas-Killman Conflict Mode Instrument*, Sterling Forest, NY: XICOM.

Times Higher Education Supplement (1996) 'Research assessments 1996', *Times Higher Education Supplement*, 20 December.

Tobin, A. (1996) 'Couldn't teach a dog to sit', *Times Higher Education Supplement*, 26 July.

Trigwell, K. (1995a) 'Increasing faculty understanding of teaching', in W.A. Wright (ed.) *Teaching Improvement Practices: Successful Strategies for Higher Education*, Bolton, MA: Anker.

—— (1995b) 'Conceptions of teaching: the key quality determinant', in J. Sachs, P. Ramsden and L. Phillips (eds) *The Experience of Quality in Higher Education*, Brisbane: Griffith Institute for Higher Education, Griffith University.

—— and Prosser, M. (1995) 'Relations between teaching approaches and conceptions of teaching and learning', *Research and Development in Higher Education* 17: 7387–94.

—— and —— (1996) 'Changing approaches to teaching: A relational perspective', *Studies in Higher Education* 21: 275–84.

Tucker, A. (1984) *Chairing the Academic Department: Leadership Among Peers*, New York: Macmillan.

van Vught, F.A. (1995) 'The new context for academic quality', in D.D. Dill and

REFERENCES

B. Sporn (eds) *Emerging Patterns of Social Demand and University Reform: Through a Glass Darkly*, Paris: IAU Press/Pergamon.

Veblen, T. (1957) (First published 1918) *The Higher Learning in America*, New York: Hill & Wang.

Wagner, L. (1995) 'A thirty-year perspective: From the sixties to the nineties', in T. Schuller (ed.) *The Changing University?* Buckingham: SRHE & Open University Press.

Weber, M. (1946) 'The sociology of charismatic authority', in H.H. Gerth and C. Wright Mills (trans.) *From Max Weber: Essays in Sociology*, New York: Oxford University Press.

Whitehead, A.N. (1950) *The Aims of Education and Other Essays*, London: Ernest Benn (first published by Williams & Northgate, 1932).

Williams, G. and Loader, C. (1993) 'Identifying priorities', Newsletter 3 of the project *Identifying and Developing a Quality Ethos for Teaching in Higher Education*, London: Institute of Education, Centre for Higher Education Studies.

Wilson, K., Lizzio, A. and Ramsden, P. (1997) 'The development, validation and application of the Course Experience Questionnaire', *Studies in Higher Education* 22: 3–25.

Woodhouse, D. (1994) 'TQM in HE: A sceptical view', in *Quality Assurance in Education and Training: Conference Papers*, Wellington: New Zealand Qualifications Authority.

Wright, W.A. and O'Neil, M.C. (1995) 'Teaching improvement practices: International perspectives', in W.A. Wright (ed.) *Teaching Improvement Practices: Successful Strategies for Higher Education*, Bolton, MA: Anker.

Zuber-Skerritt. O. and Pinchen, S. (1995) *Third Manaual for Conducting Workshops on Postgraduate Supervision*, Brisbane: Griffith Institute for Higher Education, Griffith University.

INDEX